Fundraising FOR DUMMIES

3RD EDITION

by John Mutz
and Katherine Murray

WILEY

Wiley Publishing, Inc.

Fundraising For Dummies®, 3rd Edition

Published by
Wiley Publishing, Inc.
111 River St.
Hoboken, NJ 07030-5774
www.wiley.com

WILEY

About the Authors

For more than two decades, **Katherine Murray** has specialized in writing how-to books for general audiences on a variety of topics, ranging from business to technology to parenting. A number of years ago, Katherine's writing led her into the nonprofit world, when she volunteered her research and writing skills to help selected nonprofit organizations with missions close to her heart. Since that time, Katherine has completed a certification in Fundraising Management from the IU Center on Philanthropy and become a kind of "fundraising coach" for small and struggling nonprofits. Katherine's recent books include *Green Home Computing For Dummies* with coauthor Woody Leonhard (Wiley) and *First Look Microsoft Office 2010* (Microsoft Press). As a member of the Society for Environmental Journalists, she writes articles and blogs about earth-care issues. You can follow Katherine's Twitter feed at http://twitter.com/kmurray230.

John Mutz is a fundraising expert and speaker who has an extensive array of fundraising credits. He was named 1997 Volunteer Fundraiser of the Year by the Indiana Chapter of National Association of Fundraising Professionals. In 1999, John served as Chairman of the United Way of Central Indiana, which raised more than $36.5 million. From 1996 to 1998, John served as Chairman of the Indianapolis Zoo, where he chaired a $14.5 million fundraising campaign for White River State Park Gardens. From 1989 through 1994, John was the president of the Lilly Endowment, one of the nation's five largest private foundations, which supports the causes of religion, education, and community development. The Endowment included in its grant-making activity special grants intended to improve the financial viability of nonprofit organizations. During his time there, the Lilly Endowment made the grant that brought the Fundraising School to the Center on Philanthropy at Indiana University Purdue University Indianapolis (IUPUI). In addition, the Endowment initiated the GIFT program, which utilized matching and challenge grants to create a network of community foundations that now covers all 92 of Indiana's counties.

In 1988, John was the Republican Candidate for Governor of Indiana, during which time he raised $4 million for the campaign. He is also co-founder of the Indiana Donor's Alliance, a statewide organization of community foundations. In addition to his board positions, John serves as a regular speaker for the Executive Leadership Institute (National Association of Fundraising Professionals), the National Council of Foundations, and the Center on Philanthropy. He has also been a speaker for the Rocky Mountain Council of Foundations and Hillsdale College and has given dozens of speeches to community foundations. John served as Indiana's Lieutenant Governor from 1980 to 1988 and in 1999 retired as president of the state's largest electric utility. He currently serves as Board Chairman of Lumina Foundation for Education, a billion-dollar private foundation which supports access and success in post-high school education.

Dedication

To the tens of thousands of caring volunteers, staff, and development professionals who do all they can to give of their time, effort, and wealth in supporting the causes close to their hearts. Because of you, the world keeps turning.

Authors' Acknowledgments

We would like to thank a number of people who have helped us by volunteering their anecdotes, fundraising tips, editorial prowess, and technical expertise during the writing of this book. First thanks go to Burton Weisbrod, Dan Yates, Marc Owens, Robert Payton, Ken Gladish, Peter Goldberg, Jeff Bonner, and Ken Bode, for their professional expertise and insights. Thanks also to the folks at Wiley, in particular Erin Calligan Mooney, Vicki Adang, and Amanda Langferman for their great, timely, and insightful help as we prepared this third edition. We are appreciative of Tammy Zonker, who reviewed the manuscript. A big thank you to our families for encouraging and supporting us in the midst of late nights, long hours, and looming deadlines. Special thanks go to Carolyn Mutz for getting us together to write this book and for creating the opportunity for a great collaboration.

Lastly, heartfelt thanks go to all the volunteers, staff members, and leaders in the many nonprofit organizations we have served throughout the years. We've been touched and inspired by your dedication and persistent work to make this world a better place, and we hope that this book makes your goals seem more reachable than ever.

Publisher's Acknowledgments

We're proud of this book; please send us your comments at http://dummies.custhelp.com. For other comments, please contact our Customer Care Department within the U.S. at 877-762-2974, outside the U.S. at 317-572-3993, or fax 317-572-4002.

Some of the people who helped bring this book to market include the following:

Acquisitions, Editorial, and Media Development

Project Editor: Victoria M. Adang
(Previous edition: Jennifer Connolly, Kristin DeMint)

Acquisitions Editor: Tracy Boggier

Copy Editors: Caitlin Copple, Amanda M. Langferman
(Previous edition: Jennifer Connolly, Carrie A. Burchfield)

Assistant Editor: Erin Calligan Mooney

Editorial Program Coordinator: Joe Niesen

Technical Editor: Tammy Zonker

Editorial Manager: Michelle Hacker

Editorial Assistant: Jennette ElNaggar

Cover Photo: iStock

Cartoons: Rich Tennant
(www.the5thwave.com)

Composition Services

Project Coordinator: Katherine Crocker

Layout and Graphics: Ashley Chamberlain, Samantha K. Cherolis, Nikki Gately

Proofreader: Laura L. Bowman

Indexer: Glassman Indexing Services

Publishing and Editorial for Consumer Dummies

    Diane Graves Steele, Vice President and Publisher, Consumer Dummies

    Kristin Ferguson-Wagstaffe, Product Development Director, Consumer Dummies

    Ensley Eikenburg, Associate Publisher, Travel

    Kelly Regan, Editorial Director, Travel

Publishing for Technology Dummies

    Andy Cummings, Vice President and Publisher, Dummies Technology/General User

Composition Services

    Debbie Stailey, Director of Composition Services

Contents at a Glance

Table of Contents

Introduction

Chances are you were initially drawn to nonprofit work because of a cause you cared about — whether that cause was homeless families, environmental concerns, cutbacks in the arts, or public policy issues. You heard or saw something that touched your heart, and your mind opened up to the possibilities of doing something to help. Maybe your checkbook opened up, too.

Whether you wound up helping as a volunteer, joining a staff, or serving on a board, you most likely connected with the agency because, first and foremost, you believed in the work it was doing. At some point, you realized that the role of the fundraiser is right at the heart of the organization. After all, without funding, the agency wouldn't be able to do any of the good work that got you hooked in the first place.

As you certainly know, fundraising in any economic climate is a challenge, but raising funds in a time of financial upheaval is a challenge of new proportion. Not only is your organization vying with other groups for donors' attention, compassion, and financial gifts, but now you must swim against the tide of economic uncertainty, reduced assets, and general insecurity in the market. How do you encourage donors to give when they're fearful about their finances? How can you demonstrate the good stewardship of your group and share your success stories — all while reducing costs and furthering your reach? Is it possible to connect with your donors in new ways during economic hardship, honoring their contributions and inviting their engagement no matter how big the check they write today is?

Fundraising For Dummies, 3rd Edition, answers these questions and many more, offering practical, tried-and-true ways to raise the funds you need in any financial landscape. Whether you run a one-person development office or chair a 20-member board of directors, this book walks you through the process of assessing your fundraising climate, getting ready to raise funds, preparing a far-reaching fundraising plan, gathering your resources, and putting your plan in place. Additionally, this book shows you how to find and work with donors, set up a variety of fundraising campaigns, and explore effective, low-cost ways — such as reducing your four-color print budget and beginning to use social marketing techniques — to get the word out about the good your organization is doing in your community and around the world.

About This Book

No matter where you are on your fundraising journey, this book is here to help you find just what you need. You don't have to read it cover to cover to find value, but we do suggest that you start by taking a look at Chapter 1, which gives you a sense of the factors that influence raising funds in a shifting economic landscape. Then feel free to wander where your interests and most urgent needs lead you. When we cover a particular topic in more detail elsewhere in the book, we include a cross-reference so you can easily jump from chapter to chapter to read up on the areas that interest you most.

Throughout the book, we strive to make ideas and phrases easy to understand, putting things in simple terms with advice straight from the school of practical experience. The idea is to give you effective fundraising techniques fast — ideas you can put in place right away — without requiring you to spend a lot of time with complicated concepts that will rarely, if ever, affect what you do in real-world fundraising for your organization.

Conventions Used in This Book

We use the following conventions consistently throughout the book:

- New terms appear in *italics* and are closely followed by an easy-to-understand definition.
- **Boldface** text either indicates keywords in bulleted lists or highlights action parts of numbered steps.
- All Web and e-mail addresses appear in `monofont`.

When this book was printed, some Web addresses may have needed to break across two lines of text. If you come across a two-line Web address, rest assured that we haven't put in any extra characters (such as hyphens) to indicate the break. So when you're using one of these Web addresses, just type in exactly what you see in this book, pretending that the line break doesn't exist.

What You're Not to Read

Sidebars — the gray boxes set apart from the regular text — are side topics that may be interesting but aren't exactly essential to the fundraising topics at hand. Sidebars may point out the background of a term or practice, for example, or give you additional details on a topic mentioned in the text. If you want to speed through the book and skip the sidebars, go ahead; no need to feel guilty.

Foolish Assumptions

We made some assumptions about you as we wrote this book. Basically, we think the following:

- ✔ You're a current or aspiring fundraiser.

- ✔ You're feeling the impact of the shifting economy and want practical ideas for effective fundraising.

- ✔ Whether you have 20 years of experience or are just starting out, you'd like some fresh ideas and advice that will help you use the best approaches and technologies available today.

- ✔ You may be anyone from a full-time staff member to a volunteer charged with fundraising tasks.

- ✔ You don't have a huge staff or open-ended budget.

- ✔ You care about the mission you're raising funds to support and want to make a positive difference.

- ✔ You don't have time to waste; you need to get to work right away with ideas and tools that can help you succeed.

How This Book Is Organized

Fundraising For Dummies, 3rd Edition, is organized into five different parts, with chapters arranged to walk you (more or less) through the process of preparing for, creating, implementing, and evaluating a cohesive fundraising system.

Part 1: Putting Your Fundraising Ducks in a Row

Part I is all about your readiness — as an agency — to set up a fundraising system. Long before you start taking those checks to the bank, you need to make sure your organization is ready to raise funds. Getting ready involves gaining a sense of the climate in which you're planning to raise funds and identifying the factors that may impact your efforts. It also means getting a clear sense of the organization. What's your organization's mission? Why do you do what you do? Whom does your agency help? What does your board do? This part of the book helps you evaluate and answer these questions — and many more — to make sure that you are, in fact, ready to roll out your own fundraising plan.

Part II: Finding — and Winning Over — Donors

Part II introduces the all-important donor and helps you understand what role he or she plays in the effectiveness of your overall fundraising plan. Who are your donors and where can you find them? What motivates a donor to give? How can you lessen your chances of hearing "No!" on your donor calls? How equitable is the agency-donor relationship? How can you write a winning grant proposal that speaks directly to the grantor about the good your organization does (and how a grant would help you do even more)? This part introduces you to these donor-related aspects of any fundraising system and helps you prepare for your eventual dialog with your donors.

Part III: Telling Your Story and Building Your Brand

Much of your work as a fundraiser involves telling the story of your organization in a compelling and engaging way. Whether you're sending mail pieces, working with the media, writing grant proposals, using social media and e-mail approaches, or updating your Web site, understanding what your donors see, hear, and think about your organization is key to ensuring that you're building the brand value you hope to create. When your name and work are synonymous with compassion, quality, service, and good work, your donors will be glad to be part of your organization and will undoubtedly want to get closer. This part helps you use all these means — and more — to engage your donors in a way that enables them to give gladly.

Part IV: Engaging Your Givers with the Right Campaigns

As a fundraiser, you find out quickly that different campaigns enable you to connect with different types of donors in different ways. You fund your year-in, year-out operations with your annual fund. You purchase new playground equipment with the help of a special event. You build the new library building thanks to the dollars raised for the capital campaign. You can go after major gifts from corporations and foundations, or you can decide to build an endowment for longer-term financial security. This part explores these different campaigns and provides advice about when you should use each campaign, what to expect from them, and how to evaluate the campaigns so you can do more of what works next time.

Part V: The Part of Tens

In typical *For Dummies* fashion, this part of the book lists a few collections of ten items, grouped around a particular subject. Chapter 24 offers ten interesting ideas about changes on the fundraising horizon that may impact your work in the years to come. Chapter 25 offers great opening lines that you can use to engage your donors right off the bat. You never know when one may come in handy.

Icons Used in This Book

If you've ever used a *For Dummies* book before, you know that each book has a lot of little pictures on the pages, showing you what's special and important about a particular paragraph. Here are the icons we use throughout this book:

Anything having to do with money, people, and time lends itself to analysis. This icon draws attention to quantifiable ways that the fundraising landscape has changed over time.

This icon highlights useful concepts and practical information.

Basic "how-to-do-it-better" ideas appear with this icon so you can do things correctly from the start.

Pay close attention to the information listed with this icon, or your fundraising campaign could be a bomb.

Where to Go from Here

Well, you could take the afternoon off and go watch the Cubs play . . . but more than likely you're now fired up and ready to tackle some of the fundraising issues you face. Before you begin, however, review the following fundraising truths:

- ✔ Fundraising starts with passion.
- ✔ People want to give — even in tough economic times.
- ✔ You help donors achieve their goals. (Giving truly is good for both the donor and the organization.)
- ✔ Fundraising is a noble endeavor.

Don't believe these truths? By the time you're done reading this book, you will. In the meantime, sit back, feel confident that you're not alone out there in the big world of fundraising, and enjoy your trip through *Fundraising For Dummies,* 3rd Edition. Feel free to start at the beginning, or move to the topics that interest you most. Go wherever your fundraising heart takes you!

Part I
Putting Your Fundraising Ducks in a Row

The 5th Wave

By Rich Tennant

"If we eliminate the tchotchkes, suck up to the media, and time travel to the 13th century, we should be able to last another year."

In this part . . .

Before you can start bringing in the big bucks to fund your organization, you need to begin at the beginning — by figuring out the lay of the land and getting a sense of what's possible in your fundraising environment. Anytime you start something new, you have to take some time to get your feet under you and become familiar with the basics of your task. And in times of economic upheaval, being able to assess your starting point — and envision your end goal — is more important than ever.

This part of the book introduces you to the foundation of your fundraising efforts: your passion, your mission, your board, and your message. Use this part to put the cornerstones in place as you begin building your fundraising approach.

Chapter 1

Fundraising in a Changing Economy

Chances are you love a challenge. You probably also enjoy people, have a passion for your cause, have skills that help you communicate easily, are personable, and know how to focus on details while keeping in mind the big picture. In your heart of hearts, you also may have a never-say-die belief that good causes need good people to raise the funds that keep them going.

Congratulations! You're in the right line of work.

Fundraising may not be the easiest job you ever do in your life, but, as you gain understanding and experience, you discover that it offers great intrinsic and lasting rewards: relationships with passionate and dedicated people; the achievement of goals for a cause you believe in; the excitement of knowing your efforts are contributing to the common good — by way of putting food on the table for those who are hungry, opening doors for those who need them, or cleaning up the environment for the next generation. All along the way, you have the chance to be a matchmaker of good works and good people — bringing together people who have a desire to help with an organization that needs them.

Even with all these inherent benefits, however, now isn't an easy time to be a fundraiser. If you've been in the role for any length of time, you've probably spent a lot of time watching with a wary eye as the economy pitches and sways. You wonder whether donors will have anything left to give; you watch your endowment drop; you cringe at the economic forecasts. After all, in almost every industry today — education, healthcare, social services, environmental protection, public service, and so on — you find giving numbers down, corporations tightening their purse strings, foundations offering fewer grants, and government dollars slowing to a trickle.

Although it's important to have your eyes open, to know what's happening in the world, and to discern how the current economic situation is impacting your organization, not everything is doom and gloom. As you see in the world around you, times of disequilibrium find their way back to balance. As the economy shifts and topples, you get the opportunity to look more closely at your foundation, your approach, your programs, your messaging, and your people. You now have the time to give a closer look to the areas you took for granted when times were good. How has your organization changed? What are your opportunities today? How can you work together with your staff and board more effectively — while improving your efficiency and cutting costs at the same time — so that when the numbers begin to rise again (and they will), you're ready to move even more effectively into a time of abundance?

This chapter offers practical in-the-trenches ideas for navigating through tough times, capitalizing on your successes, and planting seeds now for some major blossoming in the months and years ahead.

Looking at the Stark Realities

Just how bad is it? According to the Center on Philanthropy at Indiana University, the Philanthropic Giving Index (PGI), which evaluates confidence in charitable giving, reached an all-time low in 2009, dropping almost 49 percent since December 2007. When the PGI was calculated in the depths of the U.S. recession, more than 93 percent of fundraisers said the economy had a negative or very negative effect on their ability to raise funds.

Even though the numbers show that donors who traditionally have given less than $1,000 are giving roughly the same amount they gave in previous years, donors who traditionally have given more than $1,000 are being impacted in a big way, and the size and number of gifts they are giving have been significantly reduced. Uncertainty is in the air, and even your more affluent donors may be experiencing difficult personal economic circumstances.

Giving USA 2009, a report showing the results of philanthropic giving in 2008, illustrates just how bleak the numbers really are. Compared to the philanthropic giving total for 2007 (just over $314 billion), total giving in 2008 was just over $307 billion, a drop of 5.7 percent (adjusted for inflation). Individual giving — which represents a full 75 percent of all philanthropic gifts — dropped 6.3 percent.

In most industry areas, fundraisers aren't surprised that giving is down — in some cases, with dramatic drops. Here's a quick tally of the drops in giving from 2008 to 2009 in a selection of industry areas:

- **Arts, culture, and humanities:** Down 9.9 percent
- **Education:** Down 9 percent
- **Environment/animals:** Down 9 percent
- **Human services:** Down 15.9 percent
- **Health services:** Down 10 percent
- **International affairs:** Down 3.1 percent

For religious organizations and those categorized as public-society benefit groups (for example, civil rights' organizations, community-improvement groups, and disaster-relief organizations), the numbers were slightly better:

- **Religious organizations:** Up 1.6 percent
- **Public-society benefit groups:** Up 1.5 percent

This means that unless you work in one of the few groups with an increase in giving, you are likely feeling the pinch in tough economic times, no matter where you're fundraising, how well-known your organization may be, or how many successful campaigns you've run. Yet, even though the funds available for your services seem to be stretching thin at times, the need for services isn't lacking in the slightest — in fact, the needs are undoubtedly increasing faster than you can supply them.

It's important to balance the dismal facts and figures that accompany economic downturns with a larger sense of the ebb and flow of philanthropic work. Money may be tight right now, but the number of people who care about your cause isn't in short supply. Being able to tell your story in a positive way that clearly shows others how they can help is an important first step toward fulfilling your mission in any economy. With a little creativity, vision, collaboration, and passion, you may find that you can easily do more with less — while serving a greater number of people than you'd previously thought possible.

In the following sections, we outline some of the difficulties your organization may be facing and point you in the right direction for coping with them.

Identifying cutbacks and understanding the reasons for them

Nothing about the fundraising climate today is business as usual. Giving is down, and, although an upswing is certainly on the way, nobody knows when with any certainty. This basic fact brings us to three stark realities that every fundraiser needs to recognize in times of economic challenge:

- ✔ **Reality 1:** Giving is down.
- ✔ **Reality 2:** Personal income is down.
- ✔ **Reality 3:** Government expenditures are down.

As a fundraiser, these three realities add up to the realization that unless your organization hits it big with a major event, gets a huge grant you've been working on for a while, or suddenly discovers a sleigh full of major donors who are intact financially and ready and willing to give, your donations are likely to be lower than forecasted during an economic slump. The main reason for this slump in donations is Reality 2, the fact that personal income is down — no matter where or how you make (or made) a living. People actively working in every industry work harder and make less because costs are elevated. People who had counted on investment income have taken a big hit and may be more concerned today about making major gifts. To top it all off, if you're an organization that relies less on people for donations and more on government support for your programs and services, you may find that your program has been reduced, underfunded, or even cut off from your source of state or federal funding.

To help you navigate these choppy waters, we've included information in Chapter 8 on how to connect with your donors in a variety of low-cost, high-impact ways. Chapter 11 helps you think through your approach for writing engaging, inspiring grant proposals, and all chapters in Part IV focus on specific campaigns you can use to approach your donors in different ways.

Coping with staff reductions and shrinking budgets

Watching contributions slip and investment values fall inevitably strikes a cold fear in the heart of every nonprofit leader and fundraising team. Sure, the idea of reducing programs and services is a difficult one. But the toughest calls of all — for organizations founded on the idea of people helping people — are the ones that impact the lives of the people you serve and the friends and colleagues you work with. Does a decision you feel you have to make to cope with the current economic state mean that staff won't get a raise this year? That some open positions will go unfilled? That layoffs are on the horizon?

Ready for the good news?

Are you ready for some good news? In his book *Democracy in America,* Alexis de Tocqueville wrote that people generally rise to the occasion presented to them. Most people have seen evidence of this phenomenon in their lives, whether it's in a neighborhood rallying for a sick child, a community raising funds for an after-school program, or dramatic and personal humanitarian efforts like the many people who dropped everything to help the victims of Hurricane Katrina.

On the one hand, you have to face the facts and figures and deal with the dire predictions and circumstances that accompany down economies. But on the other hand, you've got the history and culture of what countless people have done in America to combat bad times in the past. Somehow or another, when times are tough, individuals and organizations alike develop more compassion for those in need and for those causes that are important for society. Your organization can do the same today as you figure out how to do a better job of working with what you've got — doing more with less.

All the hardship you're dealing with now offers you countless lessons to learn, and it may even result in a more efficient, focused, and stream-lined organization. As your make your way over the many hurdles, you gather lots of wisdom from the experience. Plus — and this is icing on the cake — when things begin to get better, you'll have one heck of a good story to tell.

In Chapter 5, we show you how to help your board tackle the tough decisions so you know what to plan for and what to expect. You may be surprised to find a little breathing room and discover that you can chart a course that is open and honest and that builds trust throughout the entire organization, even — and perhaps especially — in the midst of trying times.

You may not be able to give staff a raise this year, but you can offer other benefits to offset that loss. Depending on the way your organization is structured, you may be able to offer flex time, give an extra personal day, or change other perks that don't relate to an increase in the bottom line.

Dealing with hard times that linger

One of the biggest challenges in economic uncertainty is that the forecasting models that worked in the past don't seem to fit — and you don't know exactly what to expect. What can you do to prepare and preserve your organization if digging out of the recession takes longer than expected? What if your donations are down for another 6 months — or 12, or 24?

Whether recovery comes quickly or eases in slowly over time, the smart thing to do is begin where you are today with a good, clear look at the building blocks of your organization. We show you how to prepare and preserve your organization with your case statement in Chapter 4, and then we show you how to use it to build a full fundraising plan in Chapter 6.

Finding reliable sources

One of the big shocks — and even bigger lessons — of the recession of 2009 is that as a society we need to be willing to look more closely at where we place our trust. Large corporations that seemed to be operating ethically and efficiently floundered and fell when bad lending practices put everyone at risk. As we begin to pull together our recovery, the question of where we place our trust remains. Donors will be asking you the same thing. Who's a reliable source? On what information will you base your major financial decisions? Can your organization be counted on? Will your organization be around tomorrow? Next month? Next year?

In Chapter 3, we offer a number of resources to help you steer your organization effectively using ethical principles in fundraising. In that chapter, you discover a number of organizations that are designed to uphold the best ideals in fundraising, made up of people who work to guarantee that — troubled times or not — fundraising remains a noble endeavor.

Finding Your Opportunity: A Crisis Is Too Good to Waste

Even though at times the challenges you face as a fundraiser may feel more like mountains than molehills, you cross all challenges the same way: one step at a time. Wherever your organization finds itself — in financial peril, in economic uncertainty, or with lower-than-expected donations and few prospects for grant funding — you can find a path to more solid ground. Use the measures presented in the following sections to begin to restore a sense of stability.

Revisiting your mission

Your current situation offers you opportunities to look more closely at the programs and services you offer and to get clear about your priorities and positions. You can fine-tune your case statement, revisit your mission, get your board engaged, and maybe bring in some great new volunteers.

In Chapters 4 through 6, we show you how to shine a light on your programs and services and reprioritize so the programs that meet the biggest need in your community right now are the ones that get your attention. By getting clear on your mission and exploring creative and innovative ways to deliver the programs and services that meet your goals, you streamline your efforts, which helps you do more of what works — and less of what doesn't.

Paring your services (or pairing up to provide them!)

By definition, focusing on some services means giving less attention and effort to others. How can you help your organization decide what to keep and what to drop? Chapter 5 offers an exercise to help you evaluate your options.

In some cases, you may be able to fulfill your mission by keeping all your programs and services alive through a creative partnership or merger. Today organizations are teaming up like never before to share costs, reduce overhead, and get more done. Find out more about teaming up with other organizations in Chapter 6.

 Collaboration isn't a new idea in nonprofit work, but many organizations still like to run their own shows when it comes to delivering programs and services. If you can team up with another organization to meet the needs of a greater number of people at a reduced cost, go for it. Besides helping you serve more people, working together with other organizations also improves your overall image in the eyes of _grantors_ (the organizations or foundations who offer grants to organizations like you), which can significantly boost your bottom line. After all, foundations like to see cooperative efforts on the grant proposals you submit. (Find out more about grants in Chapter 11.)

Nurturing the donor-agency relationship

In down economic times, it's more important than ever to know your donor. Research the giving patterns of your constituents, find out what life is like for your regular donor, stay in touch with your major givers, and use your messaging to reassure, inform, and invite donors to stay engaged with you. Check out Chapters 7 through 10 to discover everything you need to know about researching and cultivating your relationships with your donors.

Make sure your messaging is empathetic and honest — but stay away from crying "Wolf!" too often. However, when the need is real, dramatizing a community crisis can be an effective way to gather new donors and encourage those who have given in the past to give again. For example, a food pantry recently discovered it was going to come up short in supply of its needs, so the board enlisted the support of the local mayor. This added support resulted in lots of free media and an uptake in giving.

 Crying "Wolf!" may work once in a while (especially when someone in your community is truly in dire need), but overusing dramatic urgency can leave your donors underimpressed. Better to be straightforward, present the opportunities, and invite your donors to be part of your cause.

You can reduce the anxiety your staff and donors may be feeling for any number of reasons simply by being candid (although being candid does take a little courage). When you use candor with kindness to address the situation directly, people feel relief to know the straight story — even if it's not good news — and they usually feel they can trust what you're telling them.

Turning to cost-effective processes

In the middle of a thriving economic time, people tend to build on programs and services, layer new ideas over the tried-and-true, and take on expenses in a generally optimistic frame of mind. When money gets tight, people constrict that expansiveness and begin to look more closely at what they spend and why. This kind of close evaluation is really a good thing for your organization to do periodically, whether or not it accompanies financial hardship.

By scrutinizing the giving patterns and donation flow in your organization, you can get a sense of which campaigns during the year have worked in the past and make some estimation of what may work again. You can also find out more about the who, what, when, where, and how of special events and explore areas in your organization where you tend to spend a lot of your money (in four-color print pieces, for example). After you identify what processes you've been using to fulfill your organization's mission, you can look for ways to make those processes more cost effective.

In Chapters 14 through 17, we show you how to build community, get your message out, increase the visibility of your brand, and build your online presence by using free or low-cost tools that reach an ever-widening audience (for literally a fraction of the cost you're paying for print pieces).

In Chapter 19, we show you how to use another low-cost tool — Webinars — to share your organization with potential donors. Webinars provide a great opportunity to reduce heavy travel expenses for everyone in your organization while making meetings more flexible and time-effective. For a low cost, you can host an online session with presentations, a whiteboard, video, and other programs, while your organization's leaders talk by phone.

Talking Up Your Successes and Building Relationships

It's been said that it is human nature to create — we create with our ideas, our thoughts, our words, and our actions. When you talk up your recent successes, no matter how small they might be, you inspire the people listening to think positively about your organization. When you're the voice of stability in a time of great change, you paint the possibility of better times in your listeners' minds. When you make a real effort to build relationships with your donors — simply to build the relationship, whether they choose to donate or not — your donors realize that you value more than their financial contribution, which makes a huge difference in the amount of goodwill they feel for your organization and perhaps for you personally. One day that goodwill may convert to a dollar amount — or it may lead other potential donors to your door. The following sections discuss some key points to keep in mind as you promote your organization.

Telling your story well

Especially when daily news is filled with negativity, people love to hear a good story. Lucky for you, your organization likely gives you lots of positive stories to tell — people who have been helped by what you do, volunteers who love their work, improvements you have made, lives you have changed. Although these good things may happen against a backdrop of short-fall funding and delayed grants, share your successes out loud with your donors, your staff, and your public.

In Chapters 12 and 13, we show you how to tell the stories of the good things that are going on in your organization. We explain how to make a splash in print (through your annual report), take your stories online, and even post them in videos.

Whether you're a lone fundraiser in your organization or you work with a team or committee, prepare a weekly dashboard that shows what donations came in, what expenses went out, and what kind of progress you're making. This simple data serves as a quick-look guide to show your progress week by week; plus, it gets your whole team engaged in the effort of recognizing and talking about your organization's successes — big or small.

Engaging people who care

People who cared about your organization before the economic downturn still care about it today — they just may be less certain about their own abilities to give. You can help your donors recognize the many ways they can give to your cause by staying in touch with them through e-mail, phone calls, and the Web — even during economic downturns. Stick with your normal pattern of communication, whatever that may be. Consistency is important in building donor relationships, and your donors will be paying careful attention to the way you navigate through this rocky time.

You can be creative about the ways in which you invite your donors to participate in your cause by increasing the number of giving options, spotlighting volunteering, offering matched-giving opportunities, or hosting low-cost, service-related events that enable donors to socialize and find out more about your organization. Chapter 8 shows you how to get to know your donors in a way that makes helping out your organization a natural next step.

Developing relationships with key businesses and funders

Corporate philanthropy takes a hit just like everything else in tumultuous economic times, but the corporate citizen also has a vested interest in doing good — both for tax reasons and for the general goodwill and morale of employees. Continuing to develop good relationships with businesses in your area or industry is important, and continuing to talk with potential major givers is a given. Chapter 22 takes a closer look at corporate philanthropy, and Chapters 9 and 21 show you what you need to do to cultivate those important major givers and secure their gifts.

Meet as usual with your potential business sponsors and constituents — communicate, communicate, communicate. If you can find that perfect match — just the right fit for a particular corporate-giving program, for example — you may be surprised to discover how many people truly want to give, even though they feel limited in how much they can give right now. Over time, a $15-a-month donation may increase to five or ten times that amount.

Doing Your Best to Bring In the Dollars

Just because the numbers are down and people are forecasting difficult days doesn't mean you can't keep trying. During economically tough times, it's more important than ever to ramp up your fundraising energy, double your efforts, and stay in a positive frame of mind. Spending just as much time and energy as you always have in cultivating relationships, telling your story, looking for good fits, and managing your expenses effectively will pay off in the long run. Here are just a few of the ways you can make your hard work pay off in tough times:

- ✔ Reduce costs on your annual fund drive by replacing most or all of your print appeals with e-mail.

- ✔ Improve your Web site and make it possible for donors to give online.

- ✔ Participate in community events to help keep your organization in the public eye.

- ✔ Be willing to partner with other organizations who have similar or complementary missions.

- ✔ Say thank you — graciously (even if you're only getting a portion of what you'd hoped for).

- ✔ Come up with creative, low-cost special events that help people socialize while doing something good for your organization.

- ✔ Be willing to share your challenges with others and enlist their help in reaching your goals.

 Chapters 14 through 17 show you how to reduce your print costs by moving many of your fundraising efforts online. These chapters also explain how to get listed in charity portals and work with online affinity groups. Chapter 19 is all about creating attention-getting special events (while keeping an eye on your budget).

Preparing Now for When Things Start Looking Up

As you can see, many of the challenges fundraisers face right now are really opportunities in disguise. A chance to streamline programs and processes. An opportunity to focus on what *really* matters. An invitation to take a look at the mission statement, goals, and objectives of your organization to see whether you need to update them, renovate them, or throw them out and rewrite them completely.

You can position your organization to be prepared for the good times that will return (sooner or later) by completing some of the tasks we present in the next section. If you're still unsure about how your organization will face the challenges ahead, the final section in this chapter may provide the encouragement you need to forge ahead.

Laying the groundwork to take advantage of an economic recovery

What can you do now to get your organization ready to make the most of the good times when they return? Here are just a few ideas:

- ✔ Get your case statement in sterling shape (see Chapter 4).

- ✔ Take a look at your organizational chart — is your organization set up to run efficiently?

- ✔ Build your donor relationships, day by day (see Part II).

- ✔ Make sure your communications are clear, honest, and mission-driven (see Part III).

- ✔ Figure out how to use social networking technologies to build community and goodwill (see Chapter 14).

- ✔ Consider partnering with another organization to share costs and increase visibility.

- ✔ Consider adding a contingency fund in next year's budget.

- ✔ Replace much of your print expenses by using e-mail for letters and newsletters (see Chapter 15).

- ✔ Expand what you offer on your Web site, and provide more information for donors and readers (see Chapter 16).

- ✔ Build your brand and use it everywhere (see Chapter 17).

- ✔ Invite donor feedback to welcome your donors' engagement with your organization (and be sure to acknowledge and use the feedback you get).

As you prepare your organization for the recovery that's sure to come, be sure to take a look at Chapter 24, which offers a glimpse into fundraising in the future. Optimism is in order — better days are ahead!

In Chapter 5, we invite you to plot the history of your organization. What you likely discover as you create your organization's timeline is that you or your predecessors have survived downturns before like the one you're in now. Your organization has, indeed, risen to difficult times in the past and overcome them, and, ultimately, things did improve. What's more, the difficult times in the past and those you experience today give your organization the chance to witness the creativity, compassion, and collaboration that shows up when people face challenges together.

Moving forward with hope

Before we jump headfirst into the many fundraising approaches available to you, we take a look at two stories that offer slightly different approaches to fundraising in tough times. Consider what these two organizations did to survive the challenging trials that faced them, and then read the rest of this book to find out what you can do to help your own organization make the most of fundraising in both good times and bad.

Giving from a belief in abundance

A local church decided that good work isn't done only by churches but rather is done by lots of nonprofit organizations. As a result, the church decided to set aside 10 percent of the collections it received each Sunday and donate that amount to a local nonprofit. The immediate reaction of the leadership team and the pastor to this idea was "We're barely making it now — this is a hand-to-mouth organization!" However, after considering the options — and trying to answer honestly the question "Do we believe we live in an abundant society?" — they went ahead with the plan. To this day, this church has never missed a payroll and continues to donate 10 percent of its weekly donations to local nonprofit organizations. The minister used to call John (one of the authors of this book) and say, "John, I had to write that check and I thought, 'I can't do it . . . I can't do it!' But I did it anyway, and the money came."

No matter what your mission may be or which constituency you serve, taking a good look at where your principles align — as individuals and as an organization — gives you the opportunity to see whether your actions are in alignment with your beliefs. Do you believe your good work will ultimately be funded? Are you generous to other organizations with missions similar to your own, in terms of sharing community interest, expressing goodwill, and being willing to collaborate when possible? Examine your own attitudes about nonprofit work and consider what kinds of belief statements your organization makes through its daily operating practices.

Creativity and the power of collaboration

When John took on the role of lieutenant governor for the state of Indiana in 1980, the nation was deep in an economic downturn. Everything was in double-digits: inflation, unemployment, and interest rates. As the new administration sought creative ways to respond to the widespread challenges, it realized that helping communities develop their economic potential was a powerful way to plant good seeds during a time of struggle. In communities all over the state, John and his staff gathered the nonprofit community (including faith-based organizations), the business community, and government representatives and presented a plan for a local economic development initiative that helped communities (1) identify the community's assets; (2) identify the people in the community who could be enlisted to help (volunteer leaders who get things done); and (3) identify funders who could contribute to the initiative. More than 165 Local Economic Development Corporations (LEDOs) were born during that difficult time, and they're still operating today. The inspired idea helped these communities stop wringing their hands and begin to move forward by recognizing their assets, mobilizing their talent, and beginning to build for the future.

When dire times call for creative measures, you can trust the fact that people rise to the creative challenge. In your organization, you may be fretting about many things, but one thing is certain: If you're inviting and listening to the input of people who care about your cause and are dedicated to your mission, new ideas will arise. And you will know you have a winning idea when it includes the creative and collaborative effort of many people and brings the best to the table for both your organization and the people you serve.

Weathering the storm

As you know well, the fundraising landscape today is full of sand traps and snake pits and unseen twists and turns. Eventually, the way will feel easier and the path will look clearer, but when you encounter moments of challenge, you find the resources — internal and external — that you need to accomplish your mission. People mobilize to help you. Opportunities pop up unexpectedly. New programs bring new donors. And the good work continues.

It's your job as your organization's fundraiser to put all the ideas you get from your donors, your board, your volunteers, your staff, and yourself to work through fundraising approaches that honor your mission, respect your donor, tell your story, and invite dedication and commitment to your cause.

Chapter 2

Identifying the Fruits of Your Fundraising Passion

In This Chapter

▶ Finding the spark that first brought you to nonprofit work

▶ Building service with passion

▶ Plugging in with social media

*F*undraising folks have an old saying: "People don't give to causes. People give to *people* with causes." This saying means, in essence, you're one of the most important parts of the fundraising process. Your inspiration, your perspiration, your passion. So now comes the hard part: What are you passionate about?

Chances are good that passion for a particular cause led you to fundraising in the first place. Oh, sure, you find professional fundraisers out in the field who are interested first and foremost in turning a fast buck. But those people are few and far between in our experience. People are drawn to organizations because they see a need — perhaps up close and personal — and because they feel compelled to do what they can to make a difference. When you're part of a mission that's close to your heart, the potential for creative effort and action increases and others are inspired and attracted to what you're doing.

Not only is that spark of passion the driving force behind your desire to help, but it's also one of the best tools you can use as you fan the embers of possibility into a full fundraising flame. When you're trying to fundraise in uncertain economic times, plugging in to your own passion — why you do what you do — is a vitally important part of telling your organization's story with the energy that captures people's attention.

In this chapter, we take a look at having and staying in touch with that initial spark that brought about the birth of your organization, that keeps it going, and that you caught and are helping to flame. We also show you how to fan the flame to ignite others for your cause, give you the rundown on some basic fundraising lingo, and reveal just how many nonprofits you're competing against to raise funds (so you know just how vast the industry is). And for those of you who are just breaking into the nonprofit world, we give you some advice on maintaining the buzz. Finally, we give you a taste of how to use social media to build excitement about your organization.

Sparking Fundraising Action

As anyone who's ever had any experience with trying to raise money can attest, *fundraising* isn't a pretty word. In fact, it's a tough term to confront, a kind of oh-no-here-comes-the-pitch word. Some people say that fundraising is really *friend-raising,* but saying that is like putting a bit of polish on an otherwise slippery surface.

Nonetheless, fundraising is a necessary part of any nonprofit organization — the part that puts the hinges on the doors so people can open them and the part that keeps the blankets on the beds and the food in the pantry. It pays the salary for the midwife, helps the senior citizen find affordable medication, and provides the day-camp scholarships for inner-city kids.

But fundraising isn't the main objective of a nonprofit organization, although you may sometimes feel like it gets the bulk of the focus. Fundraising is the means to an end, the way to fulfill your mission, whether that mission is reaching people who are homeless or in need, healing the sick, or promoting the art or music you're passionate about.

Taking the time to think through beliefs about money in general and fundraising in particular is important because your unexplored ideas may — for better or worse — affect your overall success in your role. When you consider the biases, apologies, and reactions that you battle against — within yourself and from the general population — when you set out to raise funds, you will be better informed, have a deeper understanding of donors, and be more likely to be successful in your role.

In this section, we touch on what you need to do to spread your initial spark and passion about your cause to your potential donors. (Chapter 3, which deals with the ethics of fundraising, covers how you think about what you do.) We also introduce you to the nuts and bolts of the fundraising language so that you can talk the fundraising talk to the donors you're trying to attract.

Remembering why you signed on

You may be involved with fundraising today, or you may be considering a request for involvement, but, either way, the initial spark that got you interested in your cause is what we're talking about here. Like the Olympic flame, your spark gets carried from person to person and warms the very lifeblood of your organization, whether you're a volunteer, staff member, or board member.

You've lost that loving feeling

If you feel that you've lost your initial spark or haven't really analyzed what brings you to the cause you're helping to promote, ask yourself the following questions and see whether that spark reignites (and if it doesn't, you probably need to find a different cause to get involved with):

✔ When did I first become involved with this organization?

✔ What brought me here?

✔ What did I think was important about this cause?

✔ Why did I decide to help?

✔ What was going on in my life at the time that this cause appealed to me?

✔ What is my favorite success with this organization? A client's happiness? A problem solved? A new connection made?

✔ What do I need in order to reconnect with my passion for this cause?

✔ How can I help others see what I see?

Knowing your spark story is important for several reasons:

✔ When you share it, it inspires others.

✔ When you remember it, it inspires you.

✔ When you recognize its importance, it helps you remember your priorities.

✔ When you keep it in mind, it provides a common ground where you can meet — and enlist help from — others whom you bring into your organization's cause.

Helping your donor catch the spark

We talk in this chapter about the importance of knowing what brought you to nonprofit work in the first place. That initial spark shows in your eyes and your smile. It carries in your voice and makes your story ring true. It shows in the manner in which you promote your organization and in the personal pride you take in your relationship to your work and your cause. This section presents a few key fundraising philosophies and tools that can help your donor catch the same spark that inspires you. For more specifics about working with donors, visit the chapters in Part II of this book.

The best thing you can do for your donors is believe in the mission you're representing. When you're gung-ho for your cause, others see the importance of it and are encouraged to join. They start to imagine themselves working for a solid cause, a good effort, a positive change.

How many people volunteer?

Do you think volunteering is only for those few people who don't have any other commitments? Well, think again. According to *Volunteering in America*, a research brief published in 2008 by the Corporation for National & Community Service, between September 2007 and September 2008:

✔ More than 61 million adults (26.2 percent of the population 16 and over) volunteered.

✔ More women than men (29.4 percent versus 23.2 percent) volunteered.

✔ Volunteers donated 8.1 billion hours of service to nonprofit organizations.

✔ The average amount of volunteer time offered was 52 hours per year. Seniors (over age 65) offered the greatest amount of time at 96 hours per year.

✔ More than 43 percent of volunteers became involved with an organization after being asked to volunteer.

✔ Long-distance volunteering is a growing area of interest. More than 3.7 million adults traveled long distances to volunteer, often mixing vacations with volunteer opportunities.

Philanthropy as a right

Although philanthropy isn't a new concept, U.S. residents get a perk when they give to worthy causes that residents of other countries don't: The United States is the first country in the world to include a fundamental philosophy that encourages charitable giving. When you give, you get a tax break. This break isn't some loophole that someone figured out how to wriggle through — it's intentional. Lawmakers highly regard the practice of philanthropy — it's part of your heritage, part of your right — and, some say, part of your obligation.

One of the reasons philanthropy is so important in the United States has to do with the diversity of the country's population and the foundational principles at the heart of the American ideal. Nonprofit organizations help lift and address needs that can go unrecognized and unmet in groups focused on the majority; through nonprofit organizations and the programs they develop, minorities can be heard and helped.

For example, John (one of your humble authors) was serving as a board chairman when the AIDS epidemic broke out, calling for a wave of response from leaders across the country and around the world. Many businesses and large nonprofit organizations were so concerned about the controversial nature of the cause that they failed to take action. But the Damien Center, a Catholic-based organization, took the need to heart and started an organization to provide basic life necessities free of charge to AIDS victims. This compassionate action broke through the barrier and enabled caring people to give and receive to lessen the suffering that AIDS causes. Within a year, the AIDS cause became a major philanthropic goal for organizations who previously wouldn't consider it.

Thus, you can see a major potential benefit philanthropy offers society at large: Philanthropy gives individuals and causes a voice, no matter where they fit on the spectrum of humanity.

Today's philanthropy realizes that you can't always see or touch the person who needs the help. Nonprofit organizations arose to help you help others, whether they live down the block or on the other side of the world. These organized bodies provide the channels for your help to get to families living in poverty in Jakarta, AIDS orphans in Africa, or families experiencing homelessness in your own town, which, in turn, enables you to do something concrete to help change the world for the better.

As a fundraiser, you're the all-important link that helps a caring donor give to others. When you view what you do in this way, you recognize the importance of your role as a service provider. You also see how your initial spark can pass from one person to another. And suddenly, the conversation is no longer about simply raising funds.

Talking the fundraising talk

At first blush, fundraising may not seem like a fashionable profession that people *oooh* and *aaah* about at dinner parties (in fact, until people know you, they may avoid your gaze to avoid being asked for a contribution!). But when you come from a point of passion, your efforts take on the nobility of working for the greater good.

Like any industry, fundraising has its own language, and to spread your spark effectively, you need to understand and use the terminology naturally. You no doubt see and hear the following terms again and again as you raise money for the causes you believe in, so try to familiarize yourself with their meanings:

- **Philanthropy:** Actions and giving that attempt to improve the lot of people.

  In the fundraising field, one standard definition of philanthropy is "voluntary action for the public good," meaning any action you take — with or without a financial component — to make life better for someone else. When you tithe at church, you're taking part in philanthropy. When you drop coins in the container on the counter at the local convenience store, you're being a philanthropist. When you include your local theater or your alma mater in your will, you're practicing philanthropy.

- **Annual fund:** A yearly fundraising effort.

  Most organizations run a yearly fundraising campaign in addition to any program-specific efforts. This annual fund is often earmarked for ongoing operational expenses. See Chapter 18 for more about annual funds.

- **Endowment:** A substantial fund that generates ongoing income from its investment.

  An endowment is usually a large sum of money that's invested. The appreciation from its investments and the interest the money generates help to support an organization. See Chapter 23 for more about how endowments work.

> ✔ **Restricted funds:** Funds designated by the donor to be used for a specific purpose; for example, for a particular program or fundraising drive.
>
> ✔ **Nonrestricted funds:** Funds that haven't been designated by the donor for a particular purpose and can be applied as the nonprofit organization sees fit.

Three nonprofits built from passion

Looking at examples of how passion has been at the core of fundraising efforts can be enlightening and inspiring. Here are just a few examples:

✔ When **charity: water** founder Scott Harrison signed up for volunteer service as a photojournalist with an organization called *Mercy Ships*, he had no idea what lay in store for him. Mercy Ships is a humanitarian organization that brings — via floating hospitals — free medical care to some of the poorest nations in the world. During his service, Harrison met courageous and compassionate people whose lives were shaped by heartbreaking poverty, illness, violence, and more. Out of Harrison's desire to be part of the effort to improve quality of life through simple service, charity: water was born. The organization works to raise awareness and provide clean, safe drinking water to developing nations. The charity: water Web site shares the statistic that one in six people in the world don't have safe water to drink — a very basic life necessity many people take for granted. You can find out more about charity: water at www. charitywater.org.

✔ **MADD (Mothers Against Drunk Driving)** was created when mom Candy Lightner lost her 13-year-old daughter Cari in an accident caused by a repeat-offender drunk driver. Though the organization benefited from a few large corporate gifts at its inception, it continues to be largely a grass-roots organization calling for heightened awareness and tougher punishments for alcohol- or drug-impaired drivers. MADD has more than 400 affiliates worldwide because of Candy's original passion, her perceived need for an organized effort to combat drunk driving, and the initial spark that spread to others. MADD illustrates perfectly what passion applied to a cause can do: Beyond simply growing in numbers, MADD grew in voice, becoming instrumental in changing the values and perspectives with which people view drinking and driving in today's culture. You can visit the MADD Web site at www. madd.org for more information.

✔ **Habitat for Humanity** grew out of a passion sparked in the mid-1960s when founders Millard and Linda Fuller visited Koinonia Farm, a small, cooperative farming community in Georgia. There they began discussions with farmer and scholar Clarence Jordan about the possibility of partnership housing, in which those in need of homes would work together with volunteers to build solid, affordable homes. Since Habitat's founding in 1976, more than 200,000 homes have been built in more than 100 countries. Check out the Habitat Web site at www. habitat.org for more information.

Some years ago, John had the good fortune to meet Millard Fuller. Fuller shared his vision of how people become unified in a good cause. When the volunteers, who range from doctors to construction workers to healthcare professionals to stay-at-home parents, pick up the tools and drive the first nail, they're joined together in work that helps build a life. Millard said his challenge was to get people to hammer that first nail.

A mixed bag of contributions

Many nonprofits receive funds from a variety of contributors. An arts organization, for example, raises a percentage of its funds by selling tickets for its exhibits, applies for grant monies from selected foundations, solicits charitable contributions and in-kind gifts from corporations, and develops a planned giving program to help long-time donors work out bequests that continue to fund the organization after the death of the donor. (See Chapter 21 for more on planned giving.)

In some agencies, especially those involved in health and human services, government funding is also part of the package. Other nonprofits sell a product and thereby are responsible for some taxable income in addition to their charitable contributions.

Whatever the funding patterns for your organization may be, get to know your income sources. Evaluate them, assess them, and know where your strengths and challenges lie. Strengthening this part of your program can help you discover major funding possibilities that you may be missing now.

Building on Passion in the Nonprofit World

The nonprofit organizations (NPOs) you care about were born from passion — a response to an identified need in the local, national, or international community. The very frame of philanthropy rests on the idea that "when people work together, they are stronger" — when you share your resources, whether those resources are your wealth, time, effort, or ideas, others benefit. Basically, when people provide help, comfort, education, and more to people in need, society as a whole benefits. But putting together solutions is hard work — and passion and hard work are essential ingredients to carrying the idea from that initial spark of recognized need to the realization of a program that achieves its mission.

And of course, you're not alone out there — your organization is competing for funding with many others. In this section we explain how that competition makes drawing on your passionate sense of mission even more important for the overall success of your organization.

Competing for dollars

Even though changing economic times bring adjustments in the giving world, fundraising totals haven't dropped as much as you may think. Although *Giving USA 2009: The Annual Report on Philanthropy for the Year 2008* reported that the total number of fundraising dollars is down from 2007, this is only the second time on record that the annual amount of contribution has decreased from one year to the next. On a more hopeful note, organizations with religious and international missions actually witnessed an increase in their donations in 2008, in spite of the challenging times. So if billions of people are still giving even in an uncertain economy, doesn't it follow that many people are also receiving?

Whether your organization's numbers were up or down last year, you still may be wondering about your competition. How many people are doing what you do — raising funds for various NPOs? How many of these organizations exist today, and how does that compare to a decade ago? In other words, what does your competition for fundraising dollars look like?

According to the National Center for Charitable Statistics (NCCS), the number of nonprofit organizations rose from 1,084,939 in 1996 to 1,478,194 in 2006. That's a 36.2 percent increase in only ten years! Today it's easy to understand why many organizations are feeling a greater demand for their services with a seemingly ever-decreasing pool of available resources. Missions overlap. Different organizations seek to serve the same populations. Donors are pulled in different directions, recognizing that their dollars may be coveted by a number of similar organizations addressing similar needs.

The sad fact is that a nonprofit mortality rate does exist. Each year, nonprofits fold up their 501(c)(3) umbrellas and disappear. The level of competition for today's fundraising dollars means survival of the fittest. To survive, you need to stay on your toes and be ready for anything. Sometimes you may even ask yourself, "Is this service worthwhile? Are there other organizations repeating our services?"

Keeping your organization going

What does this competition mean to you? For starters, if you want to keep your organization active and growing, you need to

- ✔ **Know your mission statement inside and out — and make sure it's relevant.** A crystal-clear "why are we here?" mission statement (also called a *case statement*) helps keep everyone focused on the organization's vision. See Chapter 4 to learn about crafting a case statement that speaks to today's need and touches people's hearts.

- ✔ **Be different.** Know what you offer that is unique to your organization. Be active in local fundraising groups — know who else serves the population you serve. When possible, work with, as opposed to against, other agencies so that you can complement and not duplicate each other.

- ✔ **Know what's out there.** Make it a part of your regular research to know who is funding similar organizations, where leaders in the nonprofit world are migrating, which topics are in the public mainstream right now, and how your mission connects with what's happening in the world.

Stay engaged through social media, e-mail, discussion boards, and every opportunity for a good conversation (see Part III for more on using these resources). You never know where or when great connections will arise. The *Chronicle on Philanthropy* is one publication that should be in any fundraiser's toolkit. Check it out at `http://philanthropy.com/`.

✔ **Be responsive to the people you serve.** The ever-changing world presents you with opportunities for refocusing and retooling at every turn. If the social ill you battle is no longer viable, step back and reconsider your clients' needs and your organization's options.

✔ **Consider partnerships and new initiatives.** Today traditional nonprofits with a long history and good backing are expanding their missions in ways you may not think of — sometimes partnering with other groups and sometimes adding on to or revising their missions. For example, Goodwill Industries was originally designed to help physically and emotionally challenged adults learn job skills and contribute to society through meaningful work. Their successful program grew and, in the process, the organization discovered that there was a market for the "gently used items" they offer. Today Goodwill Industries is a nationwide organization, and all their activities spring from the heart of their mission. When you're considering next steps, remember that keeping the doors open or shut aren't your only two options. Through creative partnerships and mission extensions, you may be able to add new energy — and attract new donors — in the midst of a challenging time.

✔ **Ask the tough questions.** Does your organization meet today's needs? For instance, 50 years ago, an agency created to provide lodging to unmarried pregnant women was much needed. Today programs exist in many places to help young single mothers, and single pregnancy no longer carries the same social stigma it once did. An organization that asks itself the hard questions, such as whether what it's doing is really necessary, and then changes based on the answers won't be left in the dust when the world around it continues to grow.

✔ **Be willing to change.** Yep. You read it right. After you answer those tough questions about your organization, you have to be willing to make necessary changes. Especially in large organizations with vested power structures and bureaucratic bends, change is often resisted at the board table. But populations, needs, and services change, so you need to be willing to change with them. Doing so can help protect your agency's existence.

✔ **Set deadlines.** Especially when tough decisions are in the air, people may prefer to talk and talk — and *talk* — about what to do but never really get anywhere. You can set a deadline to help establish the expectation that all this discussion will lead to action at a specific time. A deadline helps bring you to a conclusion and positions you to take the next step, which may be just what your organization needs.

> ✔ **Put your best foot forward.** People generally dislike crisis appeals — if you're always crying "Wolf!" to bring in funding from various donors, sooner or later people are going to tire of the continual pleas. Instead, if you can show your donors that you're part of a winning organization, a force that works for good in the world, you may not only keep their interest but also inspire them to join you in your winning campaign. (See Chapter 8 for ways to show and tell your cause to donors.)

Demonstrating Your Connection with Social Media

Today a new kind of conversation is going on in the nonprofit world and around the globe. And it's happening in real time, via short sentences, status updates, and tweets as people participate via computers, cellphones, PDAs, and voice. *Social media* — as these communication outlets are called — is quickly becoming a staple of everyday communication for people of all ages, providing organizations, funders, volunteers, staff, and clients a way to connect easily and quickly all over the world.

Social media is a broad term that describes the various technologies used to connect people with like-minded people across the globe. Facebook is the star on the social media platform stage, with more than 200 million active users — half of whom log on every day. Other social networking sites include MySpace, LinkedIn (which has a more professional look and feel), and various industry- and organization-specific social networking options that service providers can customize for your personal use. Although the younger generations adopted social media right off the bat, today social media is quickly becoming a staple for all ages. In fact, Nielsen reports the fastest growing Facebook demographic is users aged 35–49, and the number of users aged 50–64 is growing at twice the rate of the 18-and-younger crowd.

Twitter is another new voice in the conversation, offering organizations and individuals a way to provide continuous updates to those who subscribe to their Twitter feeds. Participants trade small amounts of information as well as links to Web pages for more details.

What can your organization do with social networking technologies to share your passion and build your fan base? Here are just a few ideas (for more detailed ideas and techniques, see Chapter 14):

> ✔ Create a Facebook page to post photos, events, announcements, and more to grow your online constituency in hopes of gaining more volunteers and potential donors.

> ✔ Use YouTube to share video clips, public service announcements, program pieces, and more with a large, public audience.

✔ Use Twitter to keep in quick contact and share updates with donors, staff, board members, and the public.

✔ Add a blog to your organization's Web site to talk about issues your organization cares about. For example, an education organization can post links to stories about academic leadership, budget cuts, new education programs, or other opportunities donors care about.

No matter which social media tool you use, the underlying message is all about connection. Social media enables you to stay in touch with all the people who care about your mission. Like an ongoing conversation, you can use your social networking tools to share fun, interesting, or compelling stories with those who care. This connection helps others see the work you're doing in the world, and, if your message is successful, they'll care more about becoming a part of your effort.

Chapter 3

Finding the Right Perspective: Fundraising Issues and Ethics

In This Chapter

▶ Taking a look at the great fundraising debate

▶ Getting familiar with the ethics of fundraising

▶ Replacing fundraising myths with realities

*T*he happiest fundraisers love what they do. They believe in their causes, and an air of invincibility surrounds them. They may not be the biggest moneymakers on the block right now, but something inside them recognizes that one day they may be. They have the power of belief, the pride of profession, and the inner conviction that what they do makes a difference.

This chapter explores the issues that you may face when you first begin fundraising. Not only do you have to combat the understandable dread of asking someone for money (nobody we know is too fond of rejection), but you also have to battle against a kind of built-in stigma — deep in the unspoken attitudes people in today's society have about money — that comes with the territory. Here you find out how to face some of those demons head-on and recognize that, for the most part, they're simply misguided impressions you may have about fundraising. Money isn't the root of all evil; rather, the *love* of money — at the exclusion of all else — is the real problem. When you shine the light on the misconceptions you have, they disappear like the illusions they are, and the positives of this profession can really shine.

Inspiring or Selling: The Fundraising Debate Continues

Part of the stigma of fundraising is a social issue. Even though many Puritanical values are fading in today's world, most people are still shy when it comes to talking about religion and money (sex has become okay). Taboos keep the reins on too much familiarity, keeping you from asking "prying" questions about another person's finances and barring you from being so bold as to glance at another person's checkbook while you're standing in the checkout line at the grocery store. The person who breaks past these reins for a living is, according to the unspoken perception, violating a kind of personal privacy everyone wants.

Another part of the stigma is simply a bad reputation. To illustrate this stigma in action, here's a story:

Jimmy is a part-time used car salesman. He knows every trick in the book for getting you to buy that car. He overlooks the fact that the car has *lemon* written all over it. He somehow blinks away the idea that he's trying to sell you a two-seater and you've got a family of five. He nods understandingly when you tell him that you were barely able to pay your electric bill last month and certainly don't need a little yellow sports car that will put you even further into debt. As you sign the purchase agreement, he smiles a big smile, assuring you that all your troubles will just blow away as you do 90 mph through the desert. His gold tooth gleams.

Jimmy isn't a fundraiser. And he's not an ethical car salesman, either. Jimmy is interested in one thing: getting your money. And, contrary to popular belief, that isn't the goal at the front of a fundraiser's mind. All the textbooks and professional organizations tell you that fundraising is a noble endeavor. People who have been in this business for the span of their careers affirm it: Organizations do good work, open doors, help, heal, feed, and house because of the dollars their fundraisers raise.

In business, you don't blanch when you read books that exalt the salesperson. A sale, after all, provides the lifeblood of a business. In sales, you may argue, you have an exchange of goods or services. In fundraising, on the other hand, you have an opportunity for people to walk the talk of their beliefs. In the following sections, we explain how to balance your responsibility of asking for money with the negative public perceptions you may encounter and show you how sales skills and ideals really do fit together.

Living with the stigma

If fundraising is such a noble profession, where does the fundraiser's black eye come from? Unfortunately, for some people, the word *fundraising* means, "I'll try anything to get your money." This mentality taints the fundraising process for all fundraisers who then have to get past that stigma when approaching possible donors.

What about political fundraising?

You may notice that in this chapter (and even in this book) we rarely mention the fundraising your favorite political candidate does to secure your vote and fund his or her trip to office. Everyone has seen the amazingly adept communications and fundraising techniques of modern political campaigns; new technologies — and the willingness to use them thoughtfully — bring opportunities for donors to choose the *who, what, when, where,* and *how* of their giving practices. Political fundraising is the unappreciated stepchild of the fundraising field. Because of widely publicized political fundraising abuses, people sometimes blame fundraising for corrupting or, at least, preoccupying the minds and intentions of candidates.

In fact, if political fundraising more openly applied the good practices and ethics used in charitable fundraising, the standards would improve, the money would be raised, and good people of varying income brackets would have the chance to get into office. The areas of political and nonprofit fundraising aren't so different, after all: When you raise funds in the nonprofit world, you're working for a cause you care about. When you raise funds for a political candidate, you believe in the person or the platform. The skills you discover in nonprofit fundraising are directly transferable to the political arena — and may lead you to contribute to the public debate and, thus, to the political system.

For ethical fundraisers, doing whatever it takes to get money couldn't be farther from the truth. Instead, as an ethical fundraiser, you offer potential donors not the sale of a product or a palpable "warm fuzzy," but rather the opportunity to join a group of people working in an area you — and hopefully the donor — care about. You offer a chance to make a difference, an opportunity to "start where you are, use what you have, and do what you can," as the saying goes.

An ethical fundraiser doesn't sell a lemon of an organization to a donor. So, to be an ethical fundraiser, you need to remember that

- ✔ The match needs to be right between the donor and the organization.

- ✔ The donor needs to have the ability to give (for example, if the electric bill was a problem last month, major philanthropic giving is out of the question this month).

- ✔ The value exchange that takes place has to be a good one for both parties because it's the beginning of a long-term relationship, not a hit-and-run experience in which the fundraiser stuffs the check in his pocket and heads on down the road, grinning his gold-toothed smile.

Combining sales and ideals

Parts of fundraising are similar to — and informed by — good salesmanship. For example, to be a good salesperson, you need to develop certain sales skills that enable you to connect with your potential customer and understand his or her needs. Fundraising builds on those skills and adds the sense of contributing toward a bigger purpose. Take a look at Table 3-1 to see how some basic sales skills relate to key activities in fundraising.

Table 3-1	From Sales to Fundraising
Sales Skills . . .	*. . . Applied to Fundraising*
Communicating with your customer	Communicating your mission and passion to the donor
Being a good listener	Listening to your donor's concerns and interests
Helping a customer find the right fit	Helping your donor find the right giving level and program
Closing the deal	Receiving the donation so it can start doing good right away

Use tools of research to help you find the people who will care about your cause (find out more about these tools in Chapter 7). If you identify people who have a real interest in your cause, approaching them isn't selling them something they don't want; it's providing a connection they crave.

Do some people work for organizations they don't believe in? Sure. But if you're reading this book and want to grow in your professional or volunteer ability to fundraise, we assume that you're willing to make the investment of time and effort you need to master the art of fundraising. Even if you're not crazy about what you do right now, you can benefit by acquiring the skills you need for the day when you're working for a cause that really ignites your passion.

Understanding the Ethics of Fundraising

As a noble endeavor, fundraising has standards to help you determine the "right" ways to fundraise. If you're new to the area of fundraising, perhaps involved for the first time through volunteer efforts, board membership, or a new development job, you may be starting to soak up some of the major ideas present in the nonprofit sector, two of the most important ones being ethics and accountability.

Ethics is basically the study of what's right and wrong and the development of a moral code you can live by. Everybody in every walk of life at some time or other has to measure what they do for a living with what they feel is right and wrong. Some organizations focus on the ethics of fundraising; in the following sections, we introduce you to a few of these groups and explain how their work can help you better understand the ethics of what you do as a fundraiser.

Finding ethical standards organizations

So who sets the ethical standards for fundraising, and how are they governed? A number of professional organizations have formed to help set the standards that guide ethics in fundraising. Table 3-2 offers a select group of organizations you can contact to find out about membership and meetings in your area.

Paid by commission: A hot ethical topic

One issue that professional fundraisers — those working in development for an organization and those serving as consultants — continually argue about is whether a grant proposal writer should be paid by commission. Industry ethics say no. In fact, the 501(c)(3) provision says "no part of the net earnings of which inures to the benefit of any private shareholder or individual." In at least one interpretation, this phrase means that fundraisers' income should *not* be directly tied to the funds they raise.

The argument for paying grant proposal writers a percentage comes from the situations in which a small organization needs a good grant writer to secure major funds to keep the doors open. (Other things should be in place here, but we'll stick with the percentages discussion.) If a grant proposal writer is paid a percentage after the grant is made, the organization can defer payment until it secures the funds and the grant proposal writer is paid what he or she's "worth."

Although this argument continues and many consultants — especially for small organizations — do agree to work for percentages, this position is considered unethical by professional fundraising organizations.

Table 3-2	Ethical Standards Organizations	
Name	*Description*	*Contact Information*
Giving Institute	Giving Institute (formerly the American Association of Fundraising Counsel) works for ethical principles in not-for-profit consulting agencies. Member firms are carefully screened to ensure their practices meet AAFRC standards.	4700 W. Lake Ave. Glenview, IL 60025 847-375-4709 *www.givinginstitute. org*
Association of Fundraising Professionals (AFP)	AFP is a professional association for fundraisers with more than 200 chapters and 30,000 members.	4300 Wilson Blvd., Suite 300 Arlington, VA 22203 703-684-0410 www.afpnet.org
Association for Healthcare Philanthropy (AHP)	AHP is an international association in healthcare philanthropy, developing competency, professionalism, and productivity of its members.	313 Park Ave., Suite 400 Falls Church, VA 22046 703-532-6243 www.ahp.org
Council for Advancement and Support of Education (CASE)	CASE is an international professional organization that offers resources and training opportunities to its members.	1307 New York Ave., NW, Suite 1000 Washington, DC 20005 202-328-2273 www.case.org
Council on Foundations	Council on Foundations is a member organization serving grant makers and supporting high standards of ethical behavior.	2121 Crystal Dr., Suite 700 Arlington, VA 22202 800-673-9036 www.cof.org
Certified Fund Raising Executive (CFRE) International	Certified Fund Raising Executive International offers certification for fundraisers who demonstrate high standards of ethics, skills, and knowledge.	4900 Seminary Rd., Suite 670 Alexandria, VA 22311 703-820-5555 www.cfre.org

Name	*Description*	*Contact Information*
Independent Sector	Independent Sector has been a leading voice in bringing together the leaders of more than 600 organizations and representing the nonprofit view to the U.S. Congress and the IRS.	1602 L St., NW, Suite 900 Washington, DC 20036 202-467-6100 `www.independent sector.org`
Philanthropy Roundtable	Philanthropy Roundtable brings together donors, corporate giving officers, foundation trustees, and staff and offers meetings, guidebooks, and networking to members.	1150 17th St., NW, Suite 503 Washington, DC 20036 202-822-8333 `www.philanthropy roundtable.org`

Your transparency inspires donor trust

Your donors have virtually infinite causes and organizations they can choose to support, so what factors will influence them to donate to your organization? The ethics with which you operate are very important — perhaps even more so as donors think carefully about the charities they continue to support when economic stresses are high. As your donors decide whose name to write on the "Payable To" line, your transparency also helps build trust.

In the United States, two organizations provide information to help donors explore the health of the organizations they're considering supporting. Visit these sites yourself to get a feel for the type of information provided, and add links from your Web site to these sites as a donor service to those who visit you:

✔ Charity Navigator (`www.charity navigator.org`) is an independent evaluator that reports on the financial health of America's largest charities. Even if you don't qualify as one of the big organizations donors may be looking for, you can use the information on Charity Navigator to find out how large, successful organizations are running their agencies. (You can learn a lot from other organizations' success stories.)

✔ Guidestar (`www.guidestar.org`) gathers extensive data on nonprofit organizations in a large, comprehensive database that donors can use to guide their gift decisions. They can find information on missions, programs, goals, success stories, leadership, and more — all for free. Check your own listing on Guidestar regularly to see how your organization looks in the public eye.

Familiarizing yourself with the fundraiser's credo

As you continue thinking about ethical and responsible approaches to fundraising, you may want to familiarize yourself with the following industry standards:

- **"A Donor Bill of Rights":** Developed by a number of professional organizations (including the AAFRC, AHP, CASE, and AFP), this document gives you an idea of the type of exchange valued in an ethical relationship between donor and organization. You'll find the document at `http://tinyurl.com/yjgnlog`. Notice how many of the items have to do with clear, honest communication between parties.

- **"Model Standards of Practice for the Charitable Gift Planner":** Established by the National Committee on Planned Giving (NCPG), this document details the practices that ethical charitable gift planners should follow. Find a copy of this document on the NCPG Web site: `www.ncpg.org`.

What about ethics in cyberspace?

The reality of fundraising online brings with it new challenges in the ethical domain. Using social media, Web pages, blogs, and more to increase visibility with your constituents may be a good thing, but you may need to take extra pains to make sure you're as transparent and forthcoming as possible. Individuals who overstate results, create new personas, or otherwise use the relative anonymity of the Web to veil real identities and intentions have no place in ethical fundraising. As an organization seeking to serve the public good, you need to make ethical practices a must for your online connections. Here are a few suggestions for how to do so:

- Be transparent about your mission, methods, funding, and allocations.

- Provide site visitors with the information they need about you, your organization, your staff, and your plans.

- Only use secure, vetted sites if you choose to fundraise online.

- Provide donors with regular status reports to demonstrate your commitment to accountability.

- Moderate any open forums or discussion boards available on your site.

- Respond quickly to any donor or potential constituent's concern regarding your online practices.

Debunking Fundraising Myths

This section exposes four myths of fundraising that may be holding you back from top-dollar fundraising. Building on the ideas that fundraising is a noble profession and that your passion for the cause is guided by professional ethics, you need to get rid of some of the attitudes that may get in your way. The attitudes reflected in the following anecdotes aren't unethical; rather, they're close calls you have to make that depend on how you view what you do and how clearly you understand your priorities. Following each myth, we propose some ethical guidelines that can help you maneuver smoothly and ethically through each type of situation.

Myth 1: It's all about the money

Some people say fundraisers care only about money, while others think fundraisers care about helping others. Which is true?

Making money is the whole point

You have a lunch appointment with Mrs. M. You've spoken on the phone with her twice in preparation for this face-to-face meeting, and both times Mrs. M. sounded pleasant but cautious. You review your notes from your donor files as you drive to her house. As you pull into the landscaped drive, you return the donor file to your briefcase — no need for her to see your resource materials as the two of you drive to the restaurant.

At the door, Mrs. M. smiles and extends her hand. You introduce yourself and then compliment her on the dress she's wearing. She flashes you a wry gaze. Perhaps the dress comment was too much, you think. *Oh come on,* her glance tells you. *We both know this is all about money.* What can you do to show Mrs. M. otherwise?

Sharing concerns and a willingness to help is the main goal

Instead of being all about money — seeing the donor as a dollar amount — fundraising is really about the relationship you create with another person — a hand extended, saying, "Come join our cause."

Not everyone shares your concerns about recycling, music, or the college of your choice. Some people care more about political activism, fighting cancer, finding homes for the marginalized, or getting runaway teens home. When you find someone who shares your heart and welcomes your cause, you have a potential ally. With some good communication from you and the right conditions for the giver (including a link to your cause, interest in what you're doing, and the ability and willingness to give), helping is a natural next step.

Find the right connection with Mrs. M. — one that benefits her as well as your cause — and you can easily demonstrate that this relationship is about much more than money.

Myth 2: You lie to get what you want

Sometimes you may be tempted to exaggerate to try to get to your goal. In fundraising, insincere tactics don't get you far in the long run. Is a short-term leap in honesty worth a long-term donor relationship? See what you think as you read this anecdote.

A white lie for a good cause is okay

You're with a board member at her house, sitting in on a personal call with a major donor. The conversation isn't going as well as you had hoped. The potential donor is firing questions at you left and right about specific uses of his gift and about guarantees that it will be used the way he wants it to be used. The focus from the board was specific about where lead gifts would go, but this donor wants a personal guarantee from you that he will be able to determine how his money is used. You glance at the board member; she says nothing. You decide to fudge a little, hoping you can figure out what to do later. "Okay," you say, finally. "If you're willing to agree to this lead gift today, we'll let you choose the designation."

What will you say to the board member when you get back out to the car? How will you handle the situation when the donor realizes he can't control the way his funds are applied?

Slick may sell, but authenticity wins the day

The truth is, fundraising is actually a long-term activity. A firm hold on your ethics and priorities, along with a clear statement from your board about what to accept and what to resist, helps you fight the temptation to give in when a gift you've been pursuing is right in front of you and is yours for the taking — if you just bend a little.

The right thing to do with Mr. Major Donor in the preceding situation is to be honest about what you can and can't do; if you think the board would make an exception, offer to ask them and get back to the donor the next day.

Myth 3: Your donor owes the world something

Do you go after donations with the attitude that people with money owe you something? Or do you try to build a mutually beneficial relationship where you and the donor help each other?

It's about time the rich started giving to the poor

Elias Q. Smith has been the richest man in town since he inherited his family's fortune. He has a reputation for being miserly, and other fundraisers who have approached him have come back with their tails between their legs.

When you arrive at his office, his secretary informs you that Mr. Smith is tied up in meetings all afternoon and won't be able to meet with you after all. You tell the secretary you'll wait. She shakes her head and returns to her work. You sit there, stewing about Mr. Smith's miserly ways. It's about time he gives something back, you think. It's not right to sit on all that money and do nothing with it.

What do you say when Mr. Smith opens the door after his current meeting adjourns? Does the look on your face show your feeling of entitlement? How much respect have you shown for Mr. Smith and his choices by not rescheduling your appointment?

The best donations benefit both the giver and the organization

People give money for all kinds of reasons. Maybe they want to be part of your organization because of a good experience they once had with the same type of organization. Maybe your cause is good for their business. Maybe they want the recognition a named donation presents. Maybe they're trying to prove something to their parents. It's not your job to question motives.

It's your job to give Mr. Smith the chance to find out what your organization does and respect his right to make his own choice about whether your organization matches his interests. If he doesn't find a match, thank him for his time to protect any future relationship if he has a change of heart and move on.

Some donors are shy

Some people have problems with the idea that if they give to your organization, their name may be added to the engraved nameplate in the foyer. Some people aren't comfortable with banquets and recognitions and fountains and programs named in their honor. These people make great anonymous donors.

Myth 4: Wining and dining donors is all you do

Some folks think fundraisers spend too much time and money on lengthy lunches with major givers. The fact is that most fundraisers are accountable for the money they spend and how they spend it. Which side of the debate do you find yourself on?

Fundraisers schmooze for a living

You have a lunch scheduled every day this week. On your way to one of the lunches, you try not to think about the look on your executive director's face when you told her your lunch schedule. "I'm concerned about the amount of money we're spending to make money," she said. "I'd like to talk about this later."

You shrug off the concern and have a pleasant lunch with the new donor, who's actively involved in children's issues and made a trip to Namibia last year to visit an orphanage. The waiter brings the check and you pick it up quickly. Your prospective donor glances at the credit card you pull from your wallet. "Is the organization paying for this?" she asks. "Oh, of course," you respond. Her next question blindsides you. "Is that where my donation will go?"

Fundraisers are accountable for what they spend

Before a foundation makes a grant in your direction, it wants to see what you do with the money you have, what you've done in the past, and what you're planning to do in the future. Likewise, before a donor even gets close to giving a major gift, she's going to have her financial advisors and lawyers check you out and look closely at your financial statements, your tax filings, and the giving levels of your board members.

The donor in this situation has a legitimate concern. To address it, consider the extra expenses that draw from your fundraising dollars and be willing to explain the structure of your fundraising budget.

If you take a potential donor out for lunch and he offers to pay, let him. You want your prospective donors to know that every dollar is dear to your cause and that your donor's generosity saves the organization money. In addition, buying your lunch sets a precedent for the donor's giving pattern. Now that he's already supported your organization, you just need to build the giving relationship from there.

Chapter 4

Writing Your Case Statement: Your Agency's Reason to Be

*I*f you're new to fundraising, chances are that you're also new to the case statement. Your organization's case statement is an all-important vision document that spells out the major aspects of your organization's story, from your mission, to your program goals and objectives, to board members, staff, and key volunteer leaders. Think of your case statement as the fabric you use to create all your other messages — promotional pieces, letters to donors, grant proposals, and more.

You may not be — or have any intention of becoming — an attorney, but there's something to be said for being able to make your case. And when the economy is pitching and swaying around you and you're trying to stay afloat (or, in better financial times, trying to navigate the squalls of abundance pouring your way), a well-developed, clear case statement is your map and guide. Your ability to describe the mission of your organization, your goals, your objectives, your programs, your staff, and your plans all in one cohesive, well-thought-out document (in other words, your case statement) will impress your donors. It'll also impress the people working with you, as well as others in the fundraising community. And even more important than impressing your donors and partners, your case statement will help them understand why you exist, why you do what you do, and why they want to join you in doing it. This chapter shows you how to put together a top-notch case statement and what to do with it.

Stating Your Case

Before you can write your case statement, you need to understand what your case is and how you use the case statement after you've written it. You also need to know how to get started (see the "A Step-by-Step Guide to Writing the Case Statement" section for details on how to write your statement). This section lays the groundwork so you're prepared to state your case effectively.

Understanding what the case statement is and how you use it

A *case statement* is a clear statement of the need your agency addresses, how you address it, what makes you unique, and how others can help. Done well, the case statement provides the basis for all your other published materials, as well. The message you generate in the case statement speaks for itself through presentations, brochures, newsletters, annual reports, and more. The tone, flavor, style, and focus of this information, carried from one piece to the next, help build the overall identity for your organization. The fact that you don't say one thing one way in this brochure and say it another way in that brochure isn't lost on your potential donors. Consistency carries a message: dependability, clarity, and honesty.

Another use of the case statement — especially a good-looking case statement — is the effect it leaves behind. You can't be everywhere at once, and you can't always be the one to represent your organization, so it helps to have a document that gives the potential donor the facts of your organization — in more detail than you can or would offer in a face-to-face meeting. In putting together a case statement, your board and staff have to come together to communicate with each other about the central vision of the organization, which brings everyone involved to the same page.

Getting started with your case statement

Unfamiliar with case statements? Don't worry — here are some questions people often ask as they begin to draft case statements for the first time. These inquiries give you a quick glance of what goes into a case statement:

✔ **How long should the case statement be?** This is easy to answer: As long as it needs to be. Now, before you start groaning, check out the steps in the "A Step-by-Step Guide to Writing the Case Statement" section later in this chapter for a listing of the items you need to include in your case statement. How much you have to say for each item determines how long it has to be.

✔ **How often should you write a case statement?** Theoretically, you write a case statement one time from scratch — and then you update it as needed. Because you have sections for programs, budget, and more, some parts of your case may need revising every year. Other parts, such as the staffing section or the history section, need revisions less often, only as changes warrant them. (See the "Overhauling an Outdated Case Statement" section for more advice.)

✔ **Who should write the case statement?** Ideally, a person who has a clear sense of the vision of your organization — someone with spark — should write the case statement. But this type of writing can be difficult, and the drier the text, the less likely donors and evaluators are to make it all the way to the end. If you have someone on your board or your staff who is a talented, lively writer, solicit that person's services; otherwise, have the person most likely to get the job done write a draft of the statement and then have a committee of reviewers go through the draft and offer opinions, make suggestions, and add information as needed.

✔ **Should you include pictures and charts in a case statement?** Your board or leadership group should decide the way in which you publish your case, but, in general, it never hurts to look good. Don't overwhelm your readers by providing too many charts, using too many or conflicting fonts, or shouting at them with headlines that are too big. Simple and understated are best. But a few photos — especially of a program in progress, your new facility, or your cheerful staff — can help hold the reader's interest and build a bit more recognition for your agency. (Check out the "Formatting your case" section for more pointers on making your document look good.)

✔ **Should you make your case statement into a video?** Today you can use video for all kinds of storytelling — and your case is no exception. You can show the spark you want to communicate to your viewers by linking images — emotional, hopeful, or heart-wrenching — with your cause in your donor's mind. Telling your case visually can be helpful when you're filling out corporate and foundation grant applications, as well as when you're introducing your organization to potential donors in another state or country, or on another continent. You can post your video on your Web site so that it plays whenever somebody lands on your home page, or you can post your video case statement on YouTube or Facebook. (See the "From paper to online posts: Putting the case statement to work" section for ideas about what to include in the video.)

✔ **Should you make your case statement available in PDF format on the Web?** Absolutely! The more information about your organization you provide, the better — for both your donors and your organization. One suggestion, however: Hold back any sensitive financial data from the general public eye. Provide a link so that any visitors who want to see your financial data can send you an e-mail request.

Making the Case Compelling

The case statement does more than provide the basis for the message you use in your grant proposals, PR materials, and other documents. The case statement gives you the opportunity to think through all the aspects of your organization, from mission to governance to program delivery, and to make sure you connect all the dots along the way.

Times of economic challenge and change — whether the financial landscape seems to be improving or worsening — provide a great opportunity for you to revisit your case statement and assess whether it really speaks to the current needs of your community or constituents.

What makes a case compelling for one group may leave another cold, so knowing what your donors care about — and explaining clearly how your organization gives them the opportunity to help in that particular area — is key to writing a compelling case. This helps donors make the connection between the cost of the unmet need and their ability to make a difference. For example, an educational organization might include in their case statement something like, "Nearly 70 percent of prison inmates in the U.S. today can barely read or write. We can invest in children now, or pay a far greater price later."

The following list offers suggestions for the types of information you can include in your case to demonstrate the need and set the context for your services:

- **Animal welfare:** Tell today's story of issues that connect with what's on your readers' minds. Include national statistics — such as the number of dogs euthanized each year, the number of abandoned animals, or the number of kittens that would be born without your spay and neuter clinic. Share stories of specific animals and families whom your organization has helped, and be sure to include stories of care, advocacy, and passion when you introduce your staff and volunteer corps.

- **Art organizations:** Explain how the current economic climate is affecting art organizations as a whole. Find recent statistics on the number of closings or program suspensions in your area of specialty. List how many other nonprofit art centers are closing; describe how the symphonies of neighboring cities are faring; tell the stories of theaters under siege. Find out whether art programs are being cut in your local schools. Connect the local need for arts advocacy to the very real benefit your art organization brings to your community, and tell compelling stories to fan the fire of advocacy in the hearts of your readers.

- **Education:** It's no secret that governments change how much money they spend on education in times of economic change. Everyone knows the vital importance of education, but people often think funding comes from elsewhere — which can lead your potential donors to ask, "Why should I give? You get money from the government." To tell your story compellingly, you need to have both facts and figures — national statistics about funding cutbacks, teacher layoffs, and program suspensions, as well as data that demonstrates the needs of the people you serve. Connect the facts with stories of the difference your organization has made in the lives of real people touched by the services you offer, and invite the readers to see how your organization is an important part of the broader education landscape.

✔ **Environment:** Today you can find all sorts of statistics on global warming, climate change, conservation measures, and domestic and international efforts to make positive changes for the environment. When you're considering what story to tell in relation to your organization, choose your facts and figures carefully and be sure to begin and end with the facts. Because the environment is a relatively new focus in society's conversation, you still find a wide range of opinion about what's happening, what's needed, and what the long-term effects may be. Know where your organization stands in terms of key issues and take the extra effort to make your stance clear for your potential donors. Understanding your story in the context of developing science helps your donors find their connections to your cause.

✔ **Healthcare and social service:** In times of economic downturn, the need for services in all human services organizations — from healthcare groups to advocacy of all kinds — goes up at the same time that funding decreases. Whatever your focus may be, know the national and international statistics in your area. Be able to share stories of real people impacted by the cause you address and show — with compassion and care — how your organization has helped families meet their challenges. Make sure your stories are current and real; help readers get to know and identify with the real people you're asking them to help.

If your organization mobilizes to respond to a crisis — for example, a shortage at your food pantry, the emptying of your supply of flu vaccines, or the impact of a devastating storm — tell those stories in your case statement. The crisis may be temporary, but the story will capture the reader's imagination and demonstrate your ability to fulfill your mission.

✔ **International organizations:** People have been saying "It's a small world" for years and years, but just recently — perhaps at least in part because of the advent of the Web — this mantra seems to have become true. Today people from all over the globe can get involved in advocating for people in countries they've never visited; they can feel drawn to make a difference for children in Africa; they can be inspired by art in Sweden; they can want to help support an ecovillage in the United Kingdom. If your organization has international appeal, include both big-picture and person-to-person stories in your case statement. The international donor cares about initiatives in which people and organizations work together in peace to reach a common goal, so be able to share the vision and collaboration of your organization, while at the same time telling powerful stories of individual lives and communities that have been impacted for the better by what you do.

✔ **Religious organizations:** Faith is an ever-important — but often unseen — component in the lives of individuals, groups, and nations. Fundraising for a faith-based organization, beyond any national affiliation or tithing program, is still a challenge for congregations of all types. Although your programs provide the channel for the good you accomplish in the world, be sure to tell the human story — who's impacted by what you do, how many people you've helped, and what your community would look like if you weren't present to meet the need you see. Connect these facts with the story of your faith, and tell how your specific response to the need is providing a much-needed ministry. Telling the story of how you meet the universal need to alleviate suffering and help others move forward from your own particular tradition can provide a compelling invitation for others to support you whether they're part of your tradition or not.

When you're brainstorming ways to tell your story in the case statement, invite others in your organization — from board members to staff to your favorite donors — to share their favorite stories about your organization. You may wind up with a few great stories to include, and, at the very least, you'll have some great content for your Web page or PR materials.

A Step-by-Step Guide to Writing the Case Statement

Okay, it's time to get started with the case. In this section, we assume that you're the person responsible for writing the case statement — the first draft, anyway — and that your board, your focus group, and any staff members you've selected to help with the review process will then review your draft, making revisions and suggestions as they go. Of course, if your organization does everything by committee and you're drafting the document as a team, take the steps we describe in this section, multiply them by the number of people on the team, and pad whatever schedule you set for your tasks (which varies depending on your goal and the size of your organization) to provide extra time for each additional team member.

In the following sections, we walk you through the process of writing a case statement, using the organization StreetReach, a young nonprofit that serves teenagers who are homeless, as an example.

Step 1: The mission: Why are you here?

The first step is to draft your *mission statement.* The best mission statements share the following characteristics:

✔ They're clear, concise, and easy to understand. The shorter the better — fine-tune your mission message so you can deliver it in the time it takes the elevator to move from one floor to the next.

✔ They capture and hold the reader's interest.

✔ They include a call to action that gives the reader a reason to respond now.

Your mission statement should draw readers in and hold their attention. Start out strong. Describe the issue you're addressing; explain your solution; then specifically describe your organization and show how it uniquely addresses the problem you opened with. The process looks like this:

✔ Big picture (problem)

✔ Zooming in (solution)

✔ Close up (the specific ways in which your organization addresses the problem)

Write with passion, and your words will read with passion. For example, consider this introduction from a case statement: "The masterful chords of Rachmaninoff sounded through Sandinsky Hall, pounding powerfully from the fingers of 14-year-old piano prodigy Anna LaFuentes. . . ."

Getting a clear view of your mission

Perhaps even more important than what the outside world thinks of your organization is what your organization understands about itself. Drafting a careful case statement helps bring a wide range of thoughts into a focused purpose, which enables everyone connected with your organization — donors included — to get a better picture of what you do and what you need.

When people have different ideas about what the organization does, they may be pulled in different directions, which can mean wasted effort, money, time, or worse. When you define and stick to a clear, specific mission for your organization, you make sure everyone's efforts are spent in pulling the organization down the same path.

Thousands of nonprofit organizations are out there today — what's special about what you do? If you can't answer that question for yourself and your agency, you're going to have a hard time convincing someone else to join forces with you and fight for your cause. As the competition for fundraising dollars becomes fiercer (which it has — and continues to do), the need to determine "What's special about us?" grows ever greater.

Seeing how StreetReach defines and refines its mission

To get a better idea about the importance of defining your organization's mission, imagine that you're a part of the nonprofit organization StreetReach. As a fundraiser for the organization, you know that StreetReach's mission is "to identify and reach out to disenfranchised teenagers in the Baltimore community, offering fun, educational, and safe activities that help them build better relationships with peers and parents." But when potential donors and others ask your board members about the mission of your organization, here are some examples of how they respond:

"We're here to serve the needs of youth."

"We help teens in trouble."

"We get kids off the street."

Although none of the board members is dead wrong in the summary of your mission, none of them hit the nail on the head, either. They all have different ideas of what the agency is all about. To improve StreetReach's fundraising efforts, the agency hires Jane as its first full-time *development director* (who's in charge of fundraising for an organization) and asks her to draft a case statement. Consider how Jane handles each of the elements we describe in the preceding section in the StreetReach mission statement:

- ✔ **Big picture:** Homeless teens living under bridges, in abandoned tenements, in boxes and doorways in every major city nationwide. Homeless teens often run away as young as 12 years old, learn the prostitution trade weeks later, and eat only every other day, surviving on the scraps left by those who have homes, families, and futures.

- ✔ **Zooming in:** You may want to think a city as progressive as Baltimore doesn't have teenagers living on the streets. You may want to think the best about our city, but you'd be closing your eyes to a real problem facing our city today. Last year more than 350 teenagers lived under bridges, in abandoned buildings, and in the doorways of our community. They lived on the streets along with the shadows of drug addiction, horrendous poverty, illness, depression, and the haunting nightmares of sexual abuse and exploitation.

- ✔ **Close up:** StreetReach is a 501(c)(3) organization that began with the simple mission of getting help for these kids — whether that help is connecting them with their families, giving them bus fare home, finding sufficient counseling services, providing occupational training, or moving them into transitional housing. StreetReach reaches out and offers a hand and a heart to hurting teens, giving them a home, a chance, and the skills they need to create a life free from the horrors of homelessness.

The resulting mission statement that Jane draws up your organization looks something like this:

Homeless teens. Not a problem here? Better look again. Come join us and help us get these kids back home to their beds, their rooms, and their families. And for those kids who don't have a home to go back to, you can provide a means for them to complete their education and pick up the tools they need to enter the workforce, which gives them a real chance to succeed in the adult world.

Step 2: The goals: What do you want to accomplish?

After you've established the *why* of your organization — the mission — you need to think about the *what.* What are you trying to accomplish? Your organization's response to the need you focused on in the mission statement makes up the *goals* section of the mission statement.

When writing about your goals, try to paint pictures in your reader's mind. Images last longer than abstract figures, so, for example, describe the light in the eyes of the elderly patient, not just the medical supplies she receives.

Jane, the development director of the StreetReach organization (for which we compose the mission statement in the preceding section) came up with the following goals:

- To get teens off the street
- To help teens get home whenever possible
- To enable teens who can't return home to become self-sufficient

Remember to think *organizational* goals here. For example, instead of describing the new programs you want to offer, focus on the larger challenges you seek to address through your organization, such as helping to preserve the natural waterways in your area, improving the reading skills of recovering addicts, or taking arts education into private schools by the year 2011.

Step 3: The objectives: How will you reach your goals?

Objectives give you a way to tell the people who read your case statement how you will accomplish the goals you define in the preceding section. While your goal may be to get homeless teens off the street, your objective may be to work with local agencies to find housing for 25 teens a year.

Make your objectives specific, measurable, and attainable.

The objectives Jane comes up with for StreetReach (the example organization from the preceding sections) show specifically how the organization plans to work toward each of its goals. For example, the first goal is to get teens off the street, so the objectives are as follows:

- Research and report on the extent of the homelessness problem among teens by June 1, 2010.

- Develop a trained volunteer group of 30 adults to begin outreach services by September 1, 2010.

- Provide, as of September 1, 2010, transitional housing, food, and clothing to ten teens coming in off the street.

Here are some questions you should be able to answer "yes" to as you write your objectives:

- Are your objectives brief?

- Are your objectives measurable?

- Did you set a date by which the objectives will be achieved?

- Do the objectives answer the question "How will we meet this particular goal?"

- Have you included specific program information?

If your organization is using an existing case statement, find out when the objectives were last updated. Because objectives are measurable and tied to programmatic responses to your organization's goals, they will — and should — be revised every year.

Similar but not the same

When you first begin working with the mission statement, goals, and objectives, the different areas may seem to mesh together in your mind. Don't panic — that's normal. Each of these areas has an important, albeit subtle, difference that distinguishes it from the others:

- The *mission statement* explains the need that your organization addresses.

- The *goals* are general ways in which your organization seeks to respond to that need.

- The *objectives* list the specific, measurable ways your organization will meet its goals.

And although not a defined section in your case statement, your organization's accountability needs to come through loud and clear throughout the entire document, including these first three sections. Your donors and other major stakeholders will get a sense of your accountability, especially in the sections about the leadership of your organization, evidence of financial responsibility, and long-range planning.

Although your organization has only one mission statement and a few goals, you may have several objectives for each of your goals.

Step 4: Programs: What exactly do you provide?

In the *programs* section of your case statement, you get to pull out the stops a bit and toot the horn of your organization. What are your most effective programs? What are you most proud of? This section enables you to talk about what your organization does and how it helps the people it serves.

Use "alive" language. The verbs you choose carry the movement of the images. Flash strong words wherever possible, for example, "The Clean Needles program brings *healing* to an *ailing* neighborhood in downtown Detroit. . . ."

In Jane's case statement for StreetReach, she writes about the TLC program that StreetReach currently offers, taking medical supplies and basic food and clothing items to kids living on the street. The major parts of this program, which include creating links to area agencies, reuniting teens with families, and providing residential training for kids who can't return home, are all projects StreetReach plans to launch this year to further its mission.

Be sure to include a paragraph about each of the programs your organization offers. Then when you need to use selected paragraphs in a grant proposal, for example, you can simply remove the paragraphs that don't apply and leave those that do (we discuss grant proposals in Chapter 11). Thus, you have a minimum of effort and an economy of work. The case statement helps you say what you need once — powerfully and succinctly.

Step 5: Governance: What's the anatomy of your board?

Not all prospective donors are board-savvy, but you can be sure that any donor considering giving you a large gift or any foundation reviewing your grant proposal will want to know how your organization is governed. Who comprises your board? What different areas and interests do they represent? You answer these questions in the *governance* section of your case statement.

Be sure to include the following elements in your governance section:

- The legal status of your organization (501(c)(3) status if you have it)
- An overall picture of your board, including the number of members, member selection process, terms of service, and committee structure
- Specific information about key people on your board
- Information about the administrator, or executive director, of your organization

In the governance section, Jane lists the executive director and all board members, their board titles, and their current professional affiliations. She also lists key volunteer leaders who have been part of special events and fundraising campaigns or who have served in an advisory capacity.

Step 6: Staff: Who are the people behind your services?

The next important step is to include information on who actually provides the services to the people you serve — in other words, your *staff*. In the staff section of the case statement, you need to include both general information about how your staffing system is set up and specific information on the duties of key roles. You may want to include summarized job descriptions to give readers an idea of which tasks go with which roles.

In addition to describing the different hats your staff members wear, you need to talk about the staff members themselves. We suggest that you stick to the key staff members in your organization — people in roles unlikely to change often, such as the executive director, the director of development, and so on. Also introduce key volunteers and people who have been ready, willing, and able to take on leadership roles for your organization's cause.

In the staff section of StreetReach's case statement, Jane includes brief bios of each of the key staff members, including the program directors and staff members directly involved in program delivery. This section shows the range of talent and experience staff members bring to the organization.

You may want to request copies of your staff members' resumes as you create your case statement so that you have them when you need them later. After all, staff will be an important part of all the grant proposals you submit, too, and you want to attach the resumes of key people in your programs along with your grant proposals.

If you're a startup nonprofit organization, you may not have staff yet. That's okay. In your staff section, mention that you're a startup organization, describe any current staffing conditions, and mention where you envision your staffing to be a year from now.

Step 7: Location: Where do you live and work?

The *location* section of your case statement describes where you provide the services you offer. You may have a traditional office in a traditional part of town, or you may be an Internet-based 501(c)(3) that does its work in the home offices and computers of various board and staff members. Or you may even work out of a museum or out of a delivery van.

Wherever your location is, describe it. Explain how the location is right for the services you provide and how many people you can serve there. Show how it helps you meet your goals. Include any plans for improvement and/ or enhancement you have for the facility (and be sure to illustrate how these improvements will help you better meet your service goals).

The location section in the StreetReach case statement details the physical location of the StreetReach main office, as well as three small satellite offices that are hosted on local college campuses and run by volunteers.

Step 8: Finances: Is your organization financially responsible?

Although the *finance* section certainly includes your current financial statements, one of the most important things a donor looks for is an explanation — a summary — of your financial picture. As part of this summary, you want to include information about your current income and expenses, the overall financial picture today, and your projections for tomorrow.

Most importantly, make sure you write your finance section in understandable terms. Not everybody is an accountant, but everybody knows that $1 + 1 = 2$.

Talking about money is a tough thing to do, and writing about it can be even harder. If you keep in mind that you're still telling your organization's story — explaining the need, but this time with numbers — you can move beyond financial phobias and get the important information down on paper. In general, remember to do the following in the finance section of your case statement:

- ✔ **Fight the desire to detail to death.** Especially when talking about money, people tend to show specifics to the nth degree. It's more important in this financial narrative to give the reader a big picture of your finances. The financial statements you provide can fill in the details for those readers who want them.

- ✔ **Focus on people, not numbers.** Numbers and people aren't mutually exclusive — talk about your numbers in the context of the people they help. For example, Jane of StreetReach uses a statement like, "We were able to help 102 teenagers return home or find suitable housing, at an average cost of $65 per child," in her case statement's finance section.

- ✔ **Show and tell.** Charts are helpful in giving readers a quick impression of your overall financial picture. Create charts that are easy to understand, and be sure to title and label them in such a way that readers can get the message quickly.

✔ **Evaluate and revise.** Your board will be reviewing your entire case statement, of course, but you may want to have your financial advisor review the finance section before the initial review. Having a professional take a peek at the numeric data can help you catch any errors or inconsistencies early.

Step 9: Development: What will you do in the future?

Anyone thinking of contributing to your cause wants to know that you'll be around tomorrow. If they donate $1,000 to your symphony today, they want to know that they'll be able to come hear Mozart in the summer series. The *development* section of your case statement is where you show your prospective donor that you'll be here tomorrow, and you do so by explaining the following:

✔ That your organization has a vision for the future

✔ That you have a specific plan for carrying out that vision

✔ That you have checks and balances in place to ensure accountability

✔ That you have credible people monitoring programs, finances, and growth

✔ That you have the means for evaluating your own progress and revising goals as needed

Getting input from your stakeholders

A *stakeholder* is someone who has an interest in your organization — whether that person is a donor, a volunteer, a staff member, or a board member. When you begin to discuss case statements, testing the primary ideas — such as your mission statement — with a sampling of your stakeholders is a good idea. Be sure to have clients represented as well as the people who serve them. One arts organization that was created to support a local symphony forgot to count the musicians among the stakeholders from whom they invited input. Oops. Be sure that when you ask for opinions and suggestions, you ask a wide range of people who care about what you do — not just the people responsible for securing the funding for it.

One way to find out what your stakeholders think is to create a *focus group*. In essence, a focus group is any group of people you bring together to focus on a particular task, document, program, or problem. Although focus groups can help you get a feel for issues you need to address in more depth, don't mistake them for a representative sampling of public opinion. If four out of six people in your focus group think that your idea is a great one, for example, you can't take that to mean that the same percentage of the general public will feel the same way. Test your ideas, throw them out in a focus group, and listen carefully to the ideas and suggestions offered. Then use the preliminary information you've gathered to target and launch a more in-depth investigation, if needed.

For the development section of the StreetReach case statement, Jane includes a new program currently in the planning stage, as well as a write-up of an expanded Web effort and plans for a new special event.

This section requires big-time board input. If you're the lone development person or a volunteer putting together a case statement for the first time, you may not be able to address these issues for your particular agency. Not all organizations have a system of self-evaluation, although everyone seems to agree it's a much-needed facet of nonprofit management. If you're in the dark about the details of your organization's development plan, request a meeting with your executive director and/or board chairperson. Asking and answering questions about the way your programs get evaluated may just start a domino effect that causes your board to think about these development issues seriously for the first time.

Step 10: History: What successes are you building on?

Many charitable organizations — especially the ones that have been around for a long time — want to tell you all about their histories. They can keep you rooted in your seat for hours, describing great people, events, and influences that came about because of their existence in your community. They're glad to show you photos of past volunteers and produce a timeline of significant achievements.

The only thing wrong with this approach is that it puts your donors to sleep. Today's donors want to know the highlights that show you have momentum and accomplishments to build on, but their focus is all about *today's* issues. History is all well and good and is important as a means for gauging how your organization has lived up to its promises in the past, but people giving money today want to know where the money will go *today*. They want to join with you in solving a need *today*. They're interested in doing something *today* that will help make things better for tomorrow. For this reason, the *history* section comes at the end of the case statement; however, don't let its position in the case statement fool you into thinking that your organization's history is unimportant.

History gives your organization a power that new organizations don't have — a reconnecting energy that summons the best of the past with the hope for tomorrow. Your past successes are essential in convincing donors that their money will actually accomplish something. The people involved with your organization catch the spark first ignited by your agency's founders when they relive the history of the need, the mission, and the people. But the viability of your current request doesn't lie in your organization's past. You're raising money today because there's a need for what you do — today. Speak to that need. Put real faces on the need, describing people whose lives improve because of your mission.

The history section of the StreetReach case statement includes the story of the organization's beginning — the compassionate wish of an individual to do something for teenagers in trouble. Jane writes a compelling section sharing how the organization has grown thanks to a dedicated and passionate volunteer corps.

Overhauling an Outdated Case Statement

Maybe you already have a case statement, but you're looking for ways to breathe new life into the old document and hopefully attract more funding at the same time. Put on your reviewer's hat (you may want to invite input from colleagues as well) and consider the following questions:

- ✔ Is the need you address in your case statement compelling? Does it connect with today's real need?
- ✔ Are your programs described fully, with measureable outcomes?
- ✔ Do your objectives seem realistic?
- ✔ Does the description of your board sound like it has a lot of energy, as though your organization is ready for growth?
- ✔ Is your staff section current, spotlighting talents and abilities that meet today's need?
- ✔ Is your financial section up-to-date and written in understandable terms? Have you demonstrated support from major donors and foundations?
- ✔ Does your history section connect with today's lively story of your organization?

If you hesitate in answering any of these questions, consider doing an overhaul of your case statement. Bring in fresh new stories. Include new developments in technology. (Do you use Twitter? Are you blogging now?) Add phrases or stories that show that your organization really does address a real need in your community today. An hour or two spent reworking an old case statement can go a long way toward helping your donors recognize why they want to support your efforts.

 Always keep a master copy of your case statement updated with changes, revisions, and ideas that others suggest. You may find that as the years go by, some ideas work better than others, some programs are explained better than others, and some foundations request more information in certain areas because your case isn't quite detailed enough on some points. You can make those adjustments over time, improving the case as you go along. Your case statement, like your organization, is an evolving, growing entity. Remember to keep it up-to-date as your agency evolves.

Sharing Your Case Statement

After your board reviews the case statement and you make any last-minute changes, you're ready to begin sharing it with the world. How you go about sharing your case depends on who your potential donors are. Today's donors are more technologically savvy than donors in years past — so they may prefer to receive your case statement electronically, either by e-mail or simply via a link to a file you've posted online in document, video, or presentation format. Of course, your older donors may not be too keen on all the newfangled Internet stuff, so being prepared to provide good, old-fashioned print versions of the case statement is important, too.

Formatting your case

Whether you decide to offer the case as a print or electronic document, you need to put some time and effort into making the format of the document as pleasing as possible. A well-formatted document is easy to read and helps the reader understand the main points quickly (through the use of headings and bullet points). Here are a few suggestions for formatting the case statement:

- ✔ **Use a readable font.** Remember that the people reading your case may be young, old, or anywhere in between, so don't make the typeface (or *font*) too small. Generally setting your word processor to 12-point Times New Roman is a good choice.

- ✔ **Make your headlines stand out — but not too far out.** You need to have headings for each of the major categories, and you need to choose a type size and style that lets readers know you're changing tracks. A larger font, like Arial 16 bold, accomplishes this task. Consider using built-in styles for consistency.

- ✔ **Avoid using too many fonts.** The flexibility of word processing gives you so many different fonts and formatting choices to play with that you can drive yourself — and your readers — batty by using too many bells and whistles in a single document.

- ✔ **Include charts if necessary.** Charts are a great way to show complex information at a glance, but don't include them if you don't need them. Including visual effects gratuitously may seem like a good idea in the name of holding people's attention, but unneeded information in a case statement is just a waste of space.

From paper to online posts: Putting the case statement to work

As organizations become more comfortable with the variety of communication methods available — from traditional reports and brochures to online videos and tweets — they get more and more creative about the ways they tell their stories and provide information to donors.

After you have the case statement in its final form, you can reuse what you've created in several different ways. Reusing your case statement's content is not only a smart use of your time but also helps build the credibility of your organization because all your messages are consistent. You can use the information you created in your case statement in virtually everything you produce for your organization, including brochures, newsletters, grant proposals, campaign plans, appeal letters, speeches, press releases, public service announcements, videos, and your Web site's content.

After you have a finished case statement, you can use the full document in the following ways:

✔ Save an electronic version of the document as a PDF (Portable Document Format) file and post a link to it on your Web site. A PDF file preserves the format of the document and enables readers to print it no matter what kind of computer they're using.

✔ Use the text as a basis for slides and bullet points in a PowerPoint presentation you can give to donors or make available on your Web site.

✔ Print copies of the case statement and include them in informational folders you take with you when visiting potential donors or foundations.

You can also use specific sections of your case statement to create fun and effective identity pieces. For example,

✔ Use the text from the governance section to do a five-minute video introducing your board members to the general public.

✔ Use the basics from your program section to tell the story of your programs by filming a day in the life of one of the families who receives your services. In addition to posting the edited video (on your Web site, YouTube, or any number of other video-posting sites), you can include a link that users can click to download a copy of PR materials (which you can also create using the information from your case statement).

See how easy it is to put your case statement to work for your organization? Oh — and did we mention how efficient it is? Create your case once, and use it many times.

Chapter 5

Organizing Your Team: Board Members and Volunteers

*I*n this chapter, we show you how to work with two of your most valuable assets: your board and your volunteers. Your board helps you set your goals and strategies — and having a good one is truly a magic key to getting things done. Your board can provide tremendous support for your fundraising efforts along with setting the course for the big picture of your organization. Equally important to your organization's effectiveness are your volunteers. Some volunteers lick stamps, go door-to-door gaining support for your cause, and process donations, while others provide leadership in a variety of ways. These two groups of people — your board and your volunteers — provide the answers to the why and how of fundraising and contribute in a big way to the overall success or failure of any initiative you undertake.

Board members and volunteers are crucial to your organization in any time in its history, but they're even more important during times of change. Your board members are often the ones closest to your efforts — they're the keepers of the legacy and the eyes to the future; their experience, wisdom, and relationships help you navigate through both the good and the bad changes that come your way. Volunteers are the people who invest their time in your organization because it means something to them — their dependability, resourcefulness, and generous effort help sustain your mission and make a positive impact on the people you serve. This chapter explores ways to gather these great people around you to help bring in the support — practical, emotional, and financial — you need to be a successful, effective organization.

Seeing the Big Picture: How Boards and Fundraising Fit Together

The board is a very important part of your organization, so you have to understand who your board members are and what they can do for you. Having high-profile members who are also good fundraisers is a dream come true, but chances are your board includes a mix of experiences, personality styles, and comfort levels. You may have a fair amount of educating to do before the board feels comfortable — and can be effective — in fundraising. The following sections explain how a board oversees and directs a nonprofit organization and how your role as a fundraiser fits with the board's mission.

Understanding the board's duties

Being a board member isn't all about prestige and power. It involves vision, dedication, hard work, and all the responsibility a person is willing and able to handle. Some of the most important duties of a board include recruiting and hiring the CEO; approving the mission statement, the budget, and the fundraising plan; developing the policies that make the staff accountable to the organization; and setting the ethical and moral framework for the organization. You can divide the various responsibilities of the board into the following three major areas:

- **Organization governance:** The board of directors for your organization has the responsibility of governing the agency, in terms of both dealing with legal issues and answering the question, "Are we being true to our mission?" Board members are in charge of holding the organization's assets — financial and material — in trust for the stakeholders.

- **Community interaction:** Your board members *are* your organization to the community; they represent who and what your organization is. The choices the board makes — on behalf of the organization or not — reflect on you and your mission. As a group, they're responsible for evaluating and leading the public persona of your organization, which is extremely important when it comes to fundraising.

- **Growth and vision:** Your board not only ensures that the organization is accountable to everyone it serves today but also looks ahead into the future and charts the short- and long-term growth. The board's investment in the future means caring about the mission and programs as well as training its members for fundraising, raising the funds needed for day-to-day programming and long-term sustainability, and finding and hiring key people in your organization.

Who's on your board?

Depending on the size and involvement of your board, you may have several different types of board members, including the following:

✓ **Advisory members:** Members who serve to advise the board in specific areas related to the organization's mission

✓ **Executive or trustee members:** Members who are the voting members of the board

✓ **Founding members:** Members who function as an advisory council to the executive board

✓ **Honorary members:** Members who have contributed effort or income or both at a high level and are recognized for their ongoing involvement

---

Knowing how your role fits with the board's work

As a development person, you may wonder what your role with the board should be. If you're the development director or executive director, the board may have hired you. If you're a volunteer, you may have grown through the ranks into a position of volunteer leadership, which means you have some involvement with your board.

As someone in a key fundraising position, here's what you need to do in relation to the board:

✓ **Share the fundraising.** You are not — nor should you be — the Lone Fundraiser for your organization. The board is responsible for overseeing the mission, development, implementation, and evaluation of the work that your organization carries out. Each person involved in the leadership of the organization — including board members — has to be willing to get involved in securing the funds necessary to fulfill the mission. If fundraising isn't part of your board members' job descriptions, you need to add it.

✓ **Identify prospective board members.** Even if your role doesn't include recruiting board members (some organizations recruit on a peer-to-peer basis), your role is key in identifying people who would add experience and assets to your board.

✓ **Keep the spark alive.** Part of your role as a development person is to help your board recatch the spark when they've lost it (see Chapter 2 to read about the spark); you can do so by providing information, running retreats, or suggesting new roles and committee structures.

✓ **Train and educate new members.** As a member of the development team, you're in charge of training new board members and educating them about fundraising opportunities, keeping them abreast of new ideas and avenues, and apprising the board of needs, changes, and the status of current campaigns.

Finding the right folks to lead your organization

Great board members come from all walks of life. The best board members have a passion for your organization, the expertise or insight you need on your board, some experience in fundraising, and the willingness to commit their time and work hard. As the development person, you may be asked to help the executive director or board chair interview prospective board members. Before you begin the interview process, identify the type of talent you need on your board by creating a skills inventory.

Begin by identifying categories for the experiences and talents your board members have (business experience, financial skills, legal expertise, and so on). Then add a category that tracks personal characteristics that are important to you, like gender, ethnicity, and location. This helps you ensure your board is diverse. Then list your existing board members and map out the qualities you would like to augment or add to your board's skills.

All nonprofit boards are different, and depending on the size of your organization, your relationship with the board may be more or less involved. In a small agency, you may have a close, teamlike relationship with the entire board. In a larger organization, you may work only with the development committee, and even that relationship may have a formal feeling to it.

Enlisting the Board to Help Advance Your Cause

Which board members make the best fundraisers? First and foremost, effective fundraisers are people who care. A board member who has been personally affected by the illness your nonprofit fights or touched by the services you offer makes a great ally. Hopefully, your board members also bring the richness of their experience, the expertise of their professions, and the financial, social, and strategic resources they have to the organization, the board at large, and the individuals served by the organization. Each area of expertise can offer you a fresh perspective on how to find, approach, and connect with donors — whether they're individuals, corporations, or granting programs.

Although you do hear a lot about board members' financial resources in any given discussion on boards and fundraising, note that board service isn't only for the wealthy. True, some board members are selected, at least in part, because they can give the organization access to donors in a certain income bracket. But not all board members are chosen for this reason. A healthy board needs to be diverse, and it needs to include some people who receive the services your organization offers.

In the following sections, we give you suggestions for enlisting your board members' help in fundraising, explain the pros and cons of using a well-known board member to ask for money, and offer some reasons why you may want to think about holding a board retreat.

Helping the board help you in fundraising

As the person responsible for finding funding for your organization, knowing how to work with the board to get the best result is crucial. Your development role is vital to board members, who turn to you for the expertise as well as the day-to-day work in building relationships and raising funds.

In addition to the many oversight roles your board members may play, they can also play a major part in the fundraising. Here are some specific ways you can encourage them to help you in your fundraising efforts:

- ✔ **Set the standard for giving in your organization.** Let your board members know that they can impact the amount others give to your organization just by giving their own donations. Having a 100 percent giving board (meaning that every board member contributes some amount of money to your organization) sends a strong message of support to staff, other donors, committee members, volunteers, and the public. After all, your giving board serves as a model of care for your mission.

- ✔ **Participate in fundraising training.** Invite your board members to sit in on fundraising training sessions to help them feel comfortable talking to others about the mission of your organization. Practice the process of asking for donations so that they're comfortable asking for money if the opportunity arises. (See Chapter 10 for more on the process of asking for donations.)

- ✔ **Open their address books.** Pass out a blank piece of paper at the beginning of a meeting and ask board members to write the names and phone numbers (or e-mail addresses) of three people they think you should contact this week. All board members should be willing to put you in touch with people they know who may be interested in the work your organization is doing.

- ✔ **Help you with the checks and balances.** If you have questions about ethical practices, fundraising approaches, or accounting procedures, know whom to ask on your board. After all, the board is responsible for setting up systems to test the credibility and accountability of the organization.

✔ **Provide input on your case statement, mission, and goals.** Although you may draft your case statement and fundraising plan, you must give it to the board for approval. The board offers suggestions and changes and then holds you to your milestones. (See Chapter 6 for more on developing your fundraising plan.)

Balancing the attraction of high-profile board members

The members of your board who have some visibility in your community or industry area make great spokespeople for your organization. As the development person, realize that you have a golden opportunity to build on board members' visibility and reputation. Both volunteers and donors — and prospective future board members — may be drawn to your organization because of the presence of a well-known board member.

A fundraiser's guide to board committees

Depending on the size of your organization and the amount of time you spend working directly with board members on matters of fundraising, you may find it helpful to have a working knowledge of the types of committees that may comprise your board.

Whether you're dealing with a large or small board, having a committee structure enables the board to divide up responsibilities and make more effective use of its members' already-limited time. The executive committee may meet quarterly throughout the year, while the other committees, which are organized to fulfill different parts of the organization's responsibilities, meet in the interim as needed or as scheduled to accomplish their specific goals. Here's a quick guide to what the various committees on your board may do:

✔ **Executive committee:** Acts on behalf of the board when the entire board can't meet

✔ **Development committee:** Establishes, leads, and evaluates fundraising efforts for the organization

✔ **Finance committee:** Oversees the financial commitments and investments of the organization

✔ **Nominating committee:** Identifies, recruits, and nominates prospective board members and officers

✔ **Governance committee:** Oversees the way in which the organization is run, evaluated, and supported

✔ **Program committee:** Oversees the organization's programs

✔ **Public relations committee:** Acts to establish and build the organization's identity in the community through public relations

---

A board member's fame can go two ways. On the one hand, an experienced, high-profile board member can be a great advantage to your cause — depending on the nature of the member's personality and renown. On the other hand, a board member's public popularity can overshadow your cause or even take your message in directions you hadn't intended.

To keep things in a positive framework, consider these simple guidelines:

- ✔ Recognize and acknowledge the benefit your organization receives because of the involvement of all your board members.

- ✔ Cultivate good relationships with all board members and strategize ways to bring visibility to the organization with the specific purpose of attracting funds and supporters.

- ✔ Invite honesty and open communication set in a framework of collaboration among all the board members.

- ✔ Help boost the visibility of all your board members by listing their names on your organization's letterhead and Web site and inviting them to serve as spokespersons on projects that have a public component.

Walking your Board through Tough Decisions

In times of economic challenge, your board members, as leaders of your organization, will face some tough decisions. Charged with both the stewardship of your organization's legacy and a plethora of decisions that reflect today's realities, your board may have to focus only on the essentials.

The first priority is survival. As the development person, you may be asked to make a presentation to the board on the status of current and projected fundraising campaigns. This information helps the board develop a timeline for the future when cuts in programs or cuts in staff may be necessary.

Doing this kind of analysis with the staff present gives them confidence in the organization's approach and builds trust that your board makes plans affecting the entire group thoughtfully and in the open.

Getting down to brass tacks on the key issues — and knowing where your organization draws its line — can bring an important (and, we hope, catalytic) point of clarity to your board. The conversation may go something like this:

> "Last year our fundraising brought in this much. This year we got this much. How long can we function with our current income stream without making substantial cuts?"

"... without cutting staff positions?"

"... without closing locations?"

"... without eliminating part — or all — of some programs?"

"... without reducing the number of individuals we serve?"

Identifying clear trigger points gives you a plan for action in case the organization's assets drop to one of the trigger levels you've identified. When a particular trigger point shows up in the monthly report, the board and staff both know the action they need to take. And if that trigger point never comes and you never need to make the associated reductions, great! But having the plan in advance empowers your board to act when and if they need to make some difficult calls.

Especially in challenging economic times, getting your board together — away from the office — can spark creative ideas and renew energy and commitment. A few simple guidelines will help your retreat be effective:

- ✔ Plan well in advance so all board members can adjust their calendars and be present

- ✔ Hire an outside person to facilitate so that you can participate in the brainstorming

- ✔ Keep your costs down by creating a nice but not luxurious environment

- ✔ State the results you expect, going in. This helps you focus your collective vision and come out with renewed passion and vigor for leading your organization in the months ahead.

The following sections give you pointers on choosing what areas of your nonprofit are the most important to maintain and when dipping into your endowment nest egg is a good idea. You also may be faced with new opportunities, so we help you figure out whether the time is right to take advantage of them or whether you're better off waiting. Finally, we explain how you can help your team see that you'll all get through the current rough patch eventually.

Slating and prioritizing your issues

Knowing the answers to the questions about your income stream and operating and program costs gives your organization a game plan to follow if your current economic situation continues. It also helps you know where to begin making changes when changes are necessary. For instance, instead of reducing positions, you may choose to suspend or cancel one of your programs, look for alternate ways to deliver services that cut costs, or find a partnering organization to share services and overhead. For example, to cut costs in response to challenging times, two arts organizations in the same city decided to share the same administrative staff, and two ballet companies in two different cities decided to share the same scenery.

You can use a number of analytic models to help you determine what your organization has to work with and what it needs to work on. SWOT (strengths, weaknesses, opportunities, and threats) is one such method of evaluation that helps you and your board brainstorm about the various assets and liabilities in your current organization. Using the SWOT method gives you the information you need to develop an informed and effective strategic plan for your organization.

Understanding the relationship between your organization's income and costs also helps you revisit and reevaluate the various priorities your organization holds dear. Whom do you serve? How do you serve them? Are your mission, service, and programs in alignment, or is your organization reaching into new areas that are beyond the scope of your focused goal? Slating and prioritizing your procedures and programs shows you clearly what's negotiable and what's not — and helps your board make clear decisions about what should continue in tough economic times and what simply can't.

Be aware that you may encounter sacred cows as you start the prioritization conversation among your board members and staff. You're likely to hear people say, "Oh we can't stop doing that — we've been doing it for 50 years. . . ." But the question is, will your organization still be around 50 years from now (or even 5) if you continue that practice?

One fairly simple change that can bring a big return over time is changing your messaging about the type of funding you invite. No organization can get far without operating funds, and yet major giving programs, endowments, and special campaigns often attract donors who want to give to specific programs, not just to operating costs. Increase your messaging around your annual fund campaign so that donors understand why their nonrestricted gifts are vital to the long-term sustainability of your organization.

Knowing when to use reserved funds

When donations drop, some organizations turn to their endowments and look for creative ways to draw more income without invading the *corpus* (original value) of the endowment. Invading the corpus is a serious matter. First, doing so breaks your promise to the donors who gave to the endowment as a perpetual investment for the organization, and, in some cases, invading the corpus might mean breaking the law. Typically, organizations draw down 5 percent of the endowment, based on an amount taken from the endowment's value averaged over the last 36 months. In times of financial hardship, some organizations increase the percentage of the draw to 6 or 7 percent.

Note that in some states, increasing the percentage of the draw from endowments may be a violation of law. Check the laws in your state to determine whether increasing your draw is an acceptable practice in your area.

One governance idea that helps manage changes in using reserved funds involves having a separate board (or in a smaller organization, a committee) to oversee the endowment. This separate entity provides a kind of check and balance for the endowment.

When an organization's income is substantially down and programs and fundraising campaigns aren't bringing in the needed revenue, questions about other possible revenue streams are sure to come up. If your organization's financial statement shows extra cash — perhaps because your programs have not been well attended and you have money in your budget for program supplies — you can reasonably use that money to sustain your programs.

Figuring out when to launch into unchartered waters

If your fundraising is flat and the economy is flatter, how do you know when the problem is your organization's image and when it's just the fallout of a bad economy? Knowing when and how to extend your mission or add a program (in an effort to build fundraising capacity) is an act of faith, art, and will.

Being aware of the area you serve, as well as the changing needs and interests of the world around you, can help you and your board take advantage of opportunities that come your way. Here are a few questions that can help you determine whether a new direction is a good option:

- Does the new direction you're considering extend your mission in a logical way?
- Will you be adding service for an audience you already serve, or will you need to find a channel to an entirely new audience group?
- Do you have systems in place to support your new initiative?
- Can you easily secure support in terms of partnerships, funding, talent, and visibility? The more natural the fit, the better. Partnerships can extend the visibility of your organization and bring new energy and attention to your cause, while reducing your costs and helping you meet your mission more completely.

At first it may seem counterintuitive to launch a new program in the midst of a challenging financial time. But depending on the factors you identify as influencing your drop in fundraising, you may be able to find smart new opportunities that you overlooked in more abundant times. You may discover, for example, that you could be offering your services to a group that would be a more natural fit (and require less marketing) than the group you're serving now. For example, perhaps in a time of skyrocketing job loss, your occupational program for senior citizens could be easily — and inexpensively —

expanded to include all job seekers. With minimal investment, you could share your program with a larger group, meet a critical need in your current landscape, and greatly expand the number of people who know about and have access to your organization.

As a general rule, donors get tired of emergency calls for help — if your organization seems to be continually in crisis, sooner or later constituents wonder how well your association is managed. So when the money isn't coming in as fast as you need it to, it's okay to cry "Wolf!" sometimes. But if a specific situation needs immediate attention — for example, homelessness is reaching crisis proportions and the weather forecasters say the temperature will be dangerously low this week — getting the word out to your donors that you need help is a good thing.

Helping your organization find clarity in challenging times

Leading a nonprofit organization is an awesome task. The board is charged with holding in trust the legacy of the past, working for success in the present, and thinking and planning for the future.

One way to help your board members plug into a common organizational identity — past, present, and future — and mobilize them for positive, creative action, is to use a nonprofit timeline. You can create a timeline with the board and staff to spotlight key moments, challenges, changes, and people in your organization's history; then set that timeline against a backdrop of what was happening in the economy and culture at the time those key events were happening. To get started, on big pieces of butcher paper, write the start date (when your organization was founded) and the end date (the present), and then plot the following items on the timeline:

1. Events of significance in the organization

2. Dates when employees joined and left the organization (these dates are great for your staff to see)

3. Important historic events that occurred in your community and nationally (for example, you might add "Beatles come to America," "Moon landing," or "Hurricane Katrina hits" to your timeline at the appropriate dates)

Divide your board and staff into teams and have each team talk about what they know of major events in your organization's history; then come together and assemble the timeline together. This activity gives you a sense of history as well as the realization that you've come through tough times before . . . and you will again. Even better, this exercise may spark some creative ideas that can help you chart your course out of the rough waters.

Bad news and nonprofits

Nonprofit organizations are in the news all the time — sometimes because of great, need-meeting programs, altruistic acts of service, or innovative approaches. Occasionally, though, an organization makes the news for less uplifting reasons: broken promises, mismanaged funds, or questions about ethical (or unethical) practices.

When an organization experiences a run of bad news, the board helps frame a response and set a course of action. In general, the board deals with one of two kinds of negatives. In the first case, an organization fails to fulfill its promises, which in times of economic downturn is a fairly common story. In the second case, an organization gets bad press — and rightly so, we think — when it uses illegal or morally questionable fundraising techniques. The first case is regrettable and may require a forthcoming message from the board explaining the steps that the organization is taking to correct the problem. The second case is the more dire circumstance that calls for direct and visible action from the board — otherwise, the news may damage the organization's reputation and have a negative impact on the entire field of fundraising.

A now legendary fall from grace in the non-profit community happened almost 15 years ago at United Way. The CEO at that time had served a number of good years with the agency when he lost sight of his mission and began making unethical and unwise choices. When the fiscal abuses came to light, the United Way movement — and, in fact, the entire nonprofit community — was tarnished. Donors wondered whether their money was going to fund actual programs or hidden agendas.

An extensive evaluation of the situation revealed that the board, which had appeared to be the best possible board an organization could have, dropped the ball. No one knew what was going on. No one asked questions. The board as a whole had abdicated its role as guardian of the ethical standards for the organization, and in doing so, had paved the way for a situation that had a very negative impact on public perception.

Today, the Sarbanes-Oxley Act (2002) helps to ensure best practices in governance for publicly traded companies, but it also suggests to nonprofit organizations that voluntarily adopting best practices for board governance is the best way to ensure long-term, ethical oversight. To find out more about the impact of Sarbanes-Oxley on the nonprofit community, see Independent Sector at www.independent sector.org.

Discovering the True Value of Volunteers

If you've worked with — or volunteered for — a nonprofit organization in the past, you know volunteers are at the very center of the work you do. Volunteers are the hands, eyes, and hearts of the service you offer; their passion tells your story; their belief in your organization helps it grow. By developing a healthy, growing, appreciated volunteer corps, you not only provide people to perform your organization's mission, but also bring together a group of people who will carry the spirit forward, which is especially important in challenging economic times.

Even though volunteers are, well, volunteering, they should feel good about the role they play, and they have to be willing to be professional about their commitment to your organization. Your volunteers need to go through an interview process and a complete training program before they commit to a volunteer schedule. (We give you the lowdown on finding and recruiting volunteers in the next section.)

Happy volunteers are the ones who get to use their gifts and talents in the roles they play. So if you have a volunteer who has a knack for or an interest in fundraising, assign him or her to your fundraising committee or give the volunteer an active role in your next special event. (More on this topic in a minute.)

Do your volunteers wear many hats in your organization? In small organizations, a single volunteer may be worked so hard she burns out in a short amount of time. Watch out for the 80/20 rule — which is when 20 percent of the people do 80 percent of the work. People carrying the 80 percent can tire quickly, which doesn't do you or the volunteers any good. If you find yourself in the middle of an 80/20 situation, review the talents and interests of your less-involved volunteers and see whether you can inspire some of them into more active roles. Sometimes a thoughtful invitation and a little appreciation go a long way toward helping a lukewarm volunteer feel important to your organization.

Seeking volunteers

Finding wonderful, dedicated volunteers is no small task: Whole committees exist with the sole purpose of building, leading, and growing volunteer bases. We hope you've already acquired a thriving volunteer group that you can continue to grow, but if you haven't, here's what you need to do to find good volunteers:

- ✔ **Know what — and whom — you need.** Identify the areas in which you want to enlist volunteer help. Have specifics — jobs, times, tasks, and relationships — in mind. The more you plan these areas, the better your chances of finding and keeping just the right volunteers.

- ✔ **Plan where you want to look for volunteers.** Think about where you can find good volunteers for your particular charitable organization. Looking in a vet's office for volunteers for an animal shelter is a logical match. Contacting schoolteachers or local writers may be your best bet if your organization focuses on increasing literacy.

- ✔ **Start with your board.** Introduce the idea of building your volunteer group at a board meeting. Ask board members to suggest people they know who may be interested in serving on a committee or volunteering their time.

  As part of your board, you may have a nominating committee that's in charge of identifying and recruiting volunteer board members. Additionally, depending on the makeup of your particular board and the size of your organization, you may have a committee that identifies, builds, and trains your other volunteer staff. Make sure these committees are in communication. After all, a volunteer who isn't willing to take on all the responsibilities of a board member may be willing to take on a smaller task.

✔ **Review your volunteer list.** Take a look at your existing volunteer list. Do you see patterns in the volunteers' other activities that may provide access to other volunteers? For example, do some volunteers belong to a gardening club that may be a good place to make a presentation for your organization? Do some belong to a fraternity? A civic group?

✔ **Target families of volunteers.** Often the families of volunteers are a good place to find not only donors, but volunteers, as well. For example, volunteerism among teens is growing and presents a great opportunity for progressive-minded charitable organizations. In fact, according to the U.S. Bureau of Labor Statistics data for 2008, 21.9 percent of all volunteers are in the 16–24 age range.

✔ **Look at your personal network of friends and associates.** Ask somebody who owes you a favor if she can help out your organization. If you volunteered for another organization, maybe someone in that group is willing to return the favor. Scan your own personal mailing lists. Take a look at your holiday card list. Look for anyone who may be interested in helping out your cause.

✔ **Consider the people your organization serves.** Have you considered your clients as a possible source of volunteers? For example, if you work for a small business development center, someone who has mastered valuable business techniques (thanks to your program) may be interested in passing them along. If your immunization program for preschoolers reaches neighborhood parents, you may find that moms and dads who have benefited from your services want to help others do the same.

In times of economic downturn, you may find that the unemployed or the underemployed are more motivated than ever to volunteer with an organization they see as having a worthwhile mission. Volunteering gives them the opportunity to network, meet new people, and learn new skills. And yes, volunteering does have a spot on a résumé.

Establishing a productive relationship

After you've found the right people to help your organization perform its mission, it's time to put your volunteers to work (in the nicest possible way, of course).

One of the most important parts of building working relationships with your volunteers is being clear about what you want them to do. Give them specific requests for action. Don't say, "I want you to do a mailing." Instead, say, "I'd love it if you could spend two hours a week on Tuesdays stuffing envelopes for us." Sure, being that direct takes a little gall, but it's absolutely necessary — after all, if you don't ask for what you want, you won't get it.

If a volunteer tells you she can't do what you asked her to do, be willing to bargain down. If you ask a volunteer to put up 500 yard signs, for example, be willing to bargain down to perhaps just 25 signs if she says no initially.

Another way to build a productive, working relationship with your volunteers is to have regular report meetings a couple of times a year so your volunteers can see all the other people who are also volunteering. These meetings build *esprit de corps* and help individuals feel like they're an important part of a larger effort. And, finally, don't forget the all-important thank-you meeting — after all, you can ask your volunteers to sign up for the next project at that meeting!

Using your volunteers as fundraisers

As you become more aware of who your volunteers are and what they're doing, you may notice that a select group of them may be of great help to you in fundraising. Volunteers can be very effective as fundraising team members. In fact, at one point in our fundraising experience, we brought in a team of volunteers to raise $125,000, giving each of them the responsibility of raising $5,000 through their own donations, friends, families, and peers. We selected and trained each volunteer carefully, and every one met his or her fundraising goal.

Ways to say "thank you!"

You can find countless ways to recognize especially dedicated and helpful volunteers. If you're creative and genuine in giving your thanks, your volunteers are sure to feel appreciated. Here are just a few examples of how to say "thanks!"

✔ Say "thank you" with a smile and mean it.

✔ Send a card with a personal note.

✔ Invite the volunteer to lunch.

✔ Have a recognition dinner for special volunteers.

✔ Give out certificates of recognition.

✔ Submit a thank-you note to your local paper.

✔ Mention your volunteer's work in your organization's newsletter.

✔ Ask the volunteer to speak to a group of new volunteers.

✔ Give a plaque of recognition.

✔ Dedicate a publication or event to your volunteers.

✔ Throw a volunteer party.

A volunteer can get directly involved in fundraising in many different ways, including serving on a development committee; helping you find sponsors for special events or publications; writing, printing, or addressing letters; serving at a special event; meeting donors during a donor visit; or hosting a donor luncheon.

How do you know which of your volunteers would be helpful in your fundraising efforts? Look for the following qualities in your fundraising candidates:

✔ Contagious passion

✔ Ability to lead others

✔ Strong organizational skills

✔ Friendly, open manner

✔ Ability to follow through

✔ Talent for working on a team

Fundraising isn't for everyone. Even if a specific volunteer is a great speaker, an outgoing person, and a valuable member of the community, if she isn't comfortable asking for money, the donors she approaches won't be comfortable either. Part of respecting the volunteer-agency relationship means using the talents volunteers want to offer, which doesn't involve coercing people into roles they don't want to play.

Making use of baby boomers: Retirees as volunteers

In the next 20 years or so you may find yourself in the midst of a gold mine of volunteer talent. Baby boomers are now entering retirement years and have skills you need (think computer and business skills), good health and energy, and ample time to commit to your cause. As a generation, baby boomers are industrious, capable, independent, and value driven. Those people comfortable with money — and people — will make absolutely great fundraisers; they have the confidence, tact, and personality they need to succeed. This generation is also mission driven; they've paid their corporate dues and are now looking for ways to get back to the altruistic orientation of their younger years.

As you try to attract senior volunteers to your cause, keep in mind the following tips:

✔ Retirees want to feel their continued value to society. Volunteering is a structured way to feel like part of something worthwhile.

✔ Some retired people use volunteer work as a way to reproduce the role they played in a paying job.

✔ Older volunteers may need special considerations in terms of doing certain types of work (lifting 50 pound boxes is out!) or needing handicapped access to your facilities.

✔ People in their 60s and 70s are much more active and productive than they have ever been, and they are not only comfortable as volunteers and program leaders but good fits for online services as well. Never underestimate these vital, energetic, and intelligent people who are smart and have life skills to contribute to your mission.

How do you reach out to retirees and seniors and attract them to your organization's cause? First, make the effort to go to them. Find out about organizations, neighborhoods, and causes in your area that baby boomers are involved in. Make a speech at a community center, meet folks at an arts organization, or see whether you can have a few minutes' time at local service club meetings of Kiwanis, Rotary, Lions, and Elks. Reaching out to them directly is definitely your best bet for bringing these talented people closer to your mission.

Chapter 6

Creating a Winning Fundraising Plan

*W*hat exactly do you need to have before you can start raising funds? No organization can exist for very long on good intentions alone. To be a successful fundraiser, you need to be able to demonstrate to your donors (1) what you have, (2) what you need, (3) how you plan to get it, and (4) how you plan to account for it after you receive it.

In this chapter we talk about the fundraising plan — your road map and the modus operandi for your short- and long-term fundraising strategies. Not only will a good plan help you attract support from people inside and outside your organization, but it will also provide a chart for you to steer by as you navigate through uncertain economic times.

Drafting the Perfect Plan

When the economy is pitching and swaying and you aren't sure how long you can even keep the doors open, putting time and energy into envisioning the future of your organization 12 or 18 months down the road may seem like a waste of time. But creating a well-thought-out fundraising plan is more than an empty exercise of wishful thinking. The time and energy you invest in creating a well-ordered, thoughtful plan can pay great dividends by helping you assess all the potential revenue streams you have and figure out how you can develop each of those channels more fully.

Your fundraising plan needs to include the following items:

- **Clear statement of your mission:** Your case statement.
- **Fundraising goal:** What program or other goal you're raising money for.
- **Needs statement:** Description of your fundraising market and resources.
- **Financial target:** Goals you want to reach. You may want to set targets at different intervals, such as six months, one year, two years, and five years.
- **Selected fundraising method(s):** What types of fundraising campaigns you plan to use to reach your goals.
- **Targeted markets:** The different donor groups that different campaigns may appeal to and how you plan to reach them.

When you write up your fundraising plan, you need to include specific information, such as the overall time frame, the benchmark goals you want to make during that period, the resources you plan to use, some information on campaign leadership, and the fundraising budget for the campaign. Don't have a budget yet? No worries; we give you the scoop on creating a budget in the "Budgeting Your Fundraising Efforts" section later in this chapter. The following sections get you started with your fundraising plan.

Make sure the people who will carry out your fundraising plan are part of the creation process. Nobody wants to hear, "We just decided that our goal is to raise $1 million this year. Do you think you can do that?"

Starting with the case statement

The first step in building your fundraising plan is to write your organization's case statement — your carefully expressed reason for being — which we discuss in detail in Chapter 4. If you don't have a copy of your organization's case statement in front of you, get one. We'll wait.

Starting with the case statement is a must because this statement includes the goals and objectives you set for your organization, which are essential parts of your fundraising plan.

Identifying your goals

After you've identified your organization's mission with the help of the case statement, it's time to describe what your organization wants to fund — in other words, it's time to draft your *goals.* You may need to generate money for programs, raise funds for operating costs, cover the costs of expanding your offices, or build an endowment. Or you may want to do all of the above.

Most nonprofit organizations have four primary fundraising goals. They need funding for

- ✔ **Programs:** These enable you to fulfill your mission.
- ✔ **Everyday operations:** These include all the costs involved in running your organization day to day.
- ✔ **Capital enhancements:** These include building renovations and other facility improvements.
- ✔ **Building an endowment:** An endowment enables you to provide for your organization's long-term future.

In times of economic turbulence, you probably have a fifth fundraising goal: survival (keeping the doors open and the lights on). Achieving this goal may mean looking for creative partnerships or putting your general operating fund front and center.

Identifying your specific fundraising goals is key to setting up your plan. Just saying "We have to raise money — for everything!" isn't going to get you very far. Whatever your fundraising goals are, apply these three questions to each goal:

- ✔ Why do we want to achieve this particular goal?
- ✔ What benchmarks are involved in achieving this goal?
- ✔ How much will achieving this goal cost?

Your answers to these questions need to be focused and specific. What you come up with eventually becomes your goals statement.

Building a needs statement

After you get clear on your mission and identify your specific fundraising goals, you're ready to consider how you plan to reach those goals. The following five questions help you define the big picture of your fundraising plan:

- ✔ What resources do you have?
- ✔ What resources do you need?
- ✔ Where have you come up short recently?
- ✔ Which fundraising method is the right one for you?
- ✔ Which *market* (the people or groups you turn to for money) do you want to approach?

Armed with the answers to these questions, you can create your *needs statement,* which summarizes how you'll go about raising funds. This statement helps you get a clearer picture of what you have and what you need.

Assessing your existing resources

So far you've been laying out your overall fundraising approach. The next step is to gather specific information for your fundraising plan and identify the people who will help drive it. If you already have a lot of information about your organization's previous plan and the people available to help make it work, you may not need to start your fundraising plan from scratch. Either way, here are the essential items you need to include as you consider your organization's existing resources:

- The donor list
- Histories of the amounts your donors have contributed in the past
- Fundraising strategies your organization's previous fundraisers used — and how much money they raised
- Any market studies done by your organization gauging public awareness of your organization
- Public relations materials used in the past (membership brochures, annual reports, copies of press releases, and so on)
- A list of potential donors
- A list of the volunteers or staff who participated in past fundraising efforts
- A list of the board members experienced in fundraising
- A detailed description of a specific program or campaign that directly addresses your needs statement

If your agency has done fundraising previously in any sort of organized way, you may already have some of this information available to you. If you're new to the organization or the fundraising role, ask someone who's been with the nonprofit for a few years to help you round up this data.

Before you start writing your fundraising plan, you may need to do some research. Taking some time now to investigate what's been done before can save you valuable time later and help you focus your efforts and resources. If you discover, for example, that a program appeal fell flat two years ago, you can carefully investigate the whys behind that bomb before you launch a similar program. The economic climate may have been much different two years ago, but you can still benefit from looking carefully at a campaign postmortem. Also remember that you aren't limited to financial statements and donor reports; you can engage long-time volunteers and board members to get some great stories and insights about previous fundraising efforts and their results.

Determining what you need

After you have a sense of the resources you already have, you can determine what you still need as you get organized for fundraising. The following list provides a few possibilities:

- ✔ **Updated mission statement and goals:** If your organization already has a mission statement and a list of fundraising goals, you still need to look at them carefully to update them to fit your organization's current situation.

- ✔ **Development committee:** This committee isn't a must, but it's helpful if you have the people power.

- ✔ **Complete slate of board members:** This list includes all your board members, not just those with fundraising experience. And don't forget to incorporate training for the members who are inexperienced in fundraising.

- ✔ **Donor list:** This all-important list is the database of all donors who have ever given to your organization in any capacity.

- ✔ **Assessment of public opinion regarding your organization:** You might think of this as your "brand" — what do people think of when someone mentions your organization?

- ✔ **Clients or previous clients:** Your clients are the people who need what you offer or who have benefitted from your programs in the past.

Setting your financial targets

The leadership of your organization — the board, the executive director, and the program director — are responsible for telling you exactly how much money you need to raise as your organization's fundraiser. You may be in on the discussions, of course, especially when they get to the "Do you think it's doable?" part, but the financial targets are really up to them to decide.

If you've seen a big decline in revenues or you've recently seen your investment values plummet, you may be understandably wary about setting specific financial targets. When the economy goes topsy-turvy, gauging when things will stabilize is anybody's guess. Even when times are tough, however, the best approach is to keep your eyes on your goal and keep moving forward — this is no time to lessen your expectations for fundraising. You can create the targets with the best information and insight you and your board can pull together, knowing that some factors, like the economy, may be outside your control.

Plan your fundraising targets for

- ✔ **The present:** Funding for current expenses, such as a summer program, the acquisition of a van, or the salary of a special speaker.

- ✔ **The short term:** Funding for upcoming expenses, such as for the next semester, the next year, or until a specific program ends.

- ✔ **The long term:** Funding for a three-year plan or an endowment plan.

- ✔ **A cash reserve:** Funding to help you navigate through uncertain financial waters. Plan to tuck away three to six months' worth of operating funds for a potentially rainy day.

Some organizations do extensive testing before they set and announce their fundraising targets. In a capital campaign, for example, your fundraisers and staff do much of the work — and raise a good portion of the money through major lead gifts — before the campaign is even announced publicly. Why? Because success breeds success, and people like to give to a campaign that's going well. When you can announce your new campaign and present graphs that illustrate that you're already 35 percent of the way to your financial goal, you inspire others to give.

Putting the all-powerful giving pyramid to work

One tool that's extremely helpful in planning for the realization of your financial goal is the *giving pyramid.* The giving pyramid helps you visualize (and communicate) how you make your revenue. It can also help you determine how many large gifts you need to obtain to reach different benchmarks in your target amount. For example, suppose that the first benchmark of your three-year fundraising plan is to raise $250,000 the first year. The giving pyramid can help you find out how many gifts at various levels you need to reach that goal. Figure 6-1 shows you what the giving pyramid looks like.

Not long ago, while we were working on an annual campaign for a major non-profit organization, we were aiming at a goal of $300,000, which was made up mostly of small gifts. But twice during that campaign, people walked into the office, took out their checkbooks, and said something like, "You know, I've been coming here for more than five years and just love it. Here's a check for $25,000." We were floored both times. The moral of the story? Count on the smaller gifts, but don't forget to cultivate major gifts along the way (see Chapters 9 and 10 for more about major gifts).

Goal-setting tips

Goal setting in tough times isn't easy because you may not know what the financial landscape will look like 6 or 12 months down the road. Here are some tips to help you set workable goals for your organization no matter what the economy looks like:

✔ Make sure the people involved in the fundraising are involved in the goal setting as well.

✔ Be specific about how much you want to raise. Don't use vague phrases, such as "as much as we can get."

✔ Consider setting two goals — a lower one that the staff realizes is what you need to bring in to keep operating, and a higher goal you share with the public. That way you cover your bases in a shifting economy, and if you reach your higher goal, great — but if not, you still have what you need to keep the doors open.

✔ Set benchmarks for the campaign to motivate you and your fellow fundraisers. Know how many $1,000 gifts you want to obtain by a certain date, for example.

An old fundraising joke goes, "It's easy to raise a million dollars! Just find a willing millionaire to write you that one big check." In reality, though, it's the multitude of smaller gifts, along with those well-cultivated major gifts, that bring you to your goal.

Total raised: $250,000

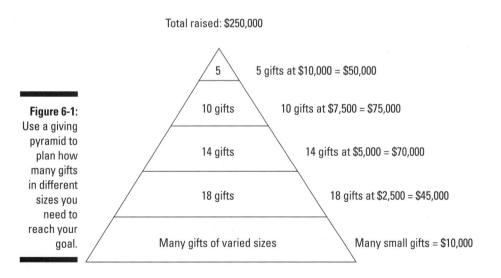

Figure 6-1: Use a giving pyramid to plan how many gifts in different sizes you need to reach your goal.

5 gifts at $10,000 = $50,000

10 gifts at $7,500 = $75,000

14 gifts at $5,000 = $70,000

18 gifts at $2,500 = $45,000

Many small gifts = $10,000

Getting started with the right methods

Your fundraising plan includes all the campaigns, events, grants, and so on that you use for your overall fundraising strategy. When you begin a fundraising campaign, you first have to decide where you want to go — what your fundraising goals are. Then you have to choose which fundraising *method* (or means) you want to use to reach your goals. If you know you want to increase your donor base by 12 percent and reach a fundraising goal of $300,000 by year's end, for example, you've already established the end point. What you need to do next is choose the right fundraising method that'll get you there.

Understanding the different fundraising methods

The standard fundraising methods are

- ✔ **Annual campaign:** A yearly fundraising campaign to raise support for operating expenses (see Chapter 18)

- ✔ **Major gifts:** A one-time gift or repeated large gifts given to support a particular program or campaign, project, or improvement (see Chapter 21)

- ✔ **Capital campaign:** A fundraising campaign that adds to an organization's assets — providing money for a new building, for example (see Chapter 20)

- ✔ **Planned gifts:** Gifts that either add to the endowment of the organization (see Chapter 23) or are scheduled to be received in the future (see Chapter 21)

Which fundraising method you use depends on your needs statement. If you're raising funds for day-to-day operations, you want to create an annual fund campaign to reach that end. If you're focusing on building an endowment for your organization, think more along the lines of planned giving.

What about special events? We didn't forget the black tie and tails you have hanging in the back of your closet. Special events can be great fundraisers when done right. Unless you've publicized that your organization will use the proceeds of your special event for a particular purpose, the moneys you raise at your event can go wherever you need them: the operating fund, the capital campaign, a special project, a particular program, or the endowment fund. We talk more about special events in Chapter 19.

Creating a method comparison worksheet

If you have a track record to use, look back through your fundraising budget for past campaigns. How much did you raise for your annual fund? How much did you spend raising that amount? Compare and contrast similar numbers for your direct mail campaign, your donor renewal program, your special events, and so on. Where did you break even? Where did you make significant money?

Where did you take a loss? Use Table 6-1 to help compare the effectiveness (or lack thereof) of the fundraising methods your organization has used in the past. Doing so can help you choose which methods to use in the future.

Table 6-1	Method Comparison Worksheet		
Method	*Income*	*Expenses**	*Percentage (Income Divided by Expense)*

*Include staff time in the expenses

When you calculate the expense of putting a particular method into action, don't forget to include the staff time. You may need to estimate the number of hours staff members dedicated to working on a specific campaign or method and then use the hours multiplied by their wages to calculate the cost. Having even ballpark figures related to cost-per-hour can help you evaluate the effectiveness of the method.

Discovering fundraising markets

The next step in creating your fundraising plan is to identify your *markets:* From where do you raise the majority of your funds? Again, if you're an existing organization, you have data that gives you the answer pretty quickly. Look through the data carefully, but don't get stuck in the past. If you're just starting up, you need to put some thought and planning into where you should begin. Think about current economic trends, community issues, and the cultural climate before deciding on the right market and the right method for your effort.

The best fundraising plans don't focus too heavily on any one market; instead, they mix and match constituencies to make sure they're continually raising both short- and long-term funds. Consider the markets in Table 6-2, and think about the amount of time it takes to receive a gift from each.

Table 6-2			Markets and More
Market	*Short-Term*	*Long-Term*	*Description*
Individual donors	✓	✓	Individual donors comprise the biggest category of givers, providing 75 percent of all philanthropic contributions. *Giving USA 2009* reports that individuals gave an estimated $229.28 billion dollars in 2008, in spite of the shaky economy. Your short-term donors may contribute to the annual fund, while long-term donors (who may develop into major givers or donors interested in making planned gifts) may give through a cultivated relationship with the agency. Your goal for individual donors is to get repeated gifts to the annual fund and to cultivate donors into other giving programs, as well. In 2008 in the U.S., charitable bequests — gifts left to nonprofit organizations in donors' wills — weighed in at $22.66 billion, which is 7 percent of all giving.
Affinity groups	✓		Affinity groups, such as professional associations or special interest groups, are usually a source of short-term, programmatic funding; they usually apply a specific time period to their donations.
Churches	✓	✓	Depending on your relationships with sponsoring churches, you may receive specific program support or ongoing operational support. Although you may receive small to medium gifts from many churches consistently, the likelihood that you'll get a major gift from a church is small. Even so, the best market for major gifts — individual donors — may come to you through a church contact.
Corporations	✓	✓	Corporations are often more interested in funding a specific program — something they can see their name on or something that aligns with their product or service — than in providing for operational expenses or endowment concerns. Corporations provided an estimated $14.5 billion in 2008 contributions to nonprofit organizations, which is 5 percent of all giving. For a short-term relationship, corporations may supply program or equipment grants — over the long-term, expect to cultivate a partnering relationship. In times of economic upheaval, corporations may pare down philanthropic giving substantially while they work to shore up and stabilize their own operations.
Foundations	✓		Foundations, by and large, are interested in helping provide solutions, which means programs, programs, and more programs. *Giving USA 2009* lists grant making by foundations at an estimated $41.21 billion in 2008, which is 13 percent of giving totals. Generally, foundations don't want to fund either annual fund campaigns or the "bricks and mortar" of capital drives. In thinking about your funding needs, coming up with a grant proposal for a specific program that fits the mission of a particular foundation is a great way to meet short-term funding goals.
Government	✓	✓	Similar to corporations (but with a lot more red tape), the government may be able to provide your organization with program-related moneys, staff salaries, and perhaps even ongoing operational support. Long-term involvement is possible, although you won't build a sizeable endowment from the support of government grants.

Giving circles: A new and promising approach

In the last decade, a new kind of citizen philanthropy has brought a hopeful new opportunity for fundraisers. *Giving circles* are groups of individuals who pool their money and other resources (like time) and decide collectively where to donate their funds. A 2009 study by Dr. Angela Eikenberry and Jessica Bearman found that donors in giving circles

✔ Give more than average donors because they're aware of the impact their collective gift makes and because members inspire each other to give more

✔ Think more strategically about where they give because the group as a whole makes the decision

✔ Tend to be more engaged than average donors in the communities where they live

✔ Are more likely to talk about the causes they support with others in their lives

✔ Are likely to give to organizations that support women, the arts, and ethnic and minority groups

Giving circles often have their own processes that they use to determine what they'll fund and how you can get your organization on their radar screens. Do some research to find out about giving circles in your area that may be open to receiving new proposals or hearing your presentation (or just having a conversation!). You can use the Giving Circle Directory created by the Forum of Regional Associations of Grantmakers (www.givingforum.org) to get started.

According to an article published by the American Enterprise Institute, low-income working families may be the most generous givers in America (as of 2008); they reportedly give charitable organizations an estimated 4.5 percent of their income.

When you start small, you may not be able to work from an established or tried-and-true plan. Begin with the people closest to you — people you see often, vendors you work with, community organizations that work with you in similar causes. As your circle widens, so does your market. Although shooting for the big grant from the major foundation is a worthwhile and perhaps profitable act, your overall fundraising plan will be healthier in the long term if you build the steady support with gifts from a variety of sources — many of whom should be close to home. Plus, foundations may want you to demonstrate your ability to raise funds before you approach them for a grant. If you submit a proposal too early in the process, they may ask you to work at the program for a while before they consider your request for funding.

Avoiding Plan Busters like the Plague

Throughout this chapter, we talk about what you can do to put together your fundraising plan and begin working toward its success. One of the challenges of fundraising in tough times is that even the best plan may take a while to come to fruition depending on the economic climate and other variables outside your control. In the meantime, here are a few red flags that you can — and should — watch out for along the way:

- **Choosing the wrong leadership:** The leadership for your fundraising effort has an enormous effect on the way others perceive their roles in your campaigns. Make sure you have positive, can-do people with willing attitudes and strong connections in your leadership roles; they can make a huge difference in the effectiveness of your fundraising campaigns.

- **Not knowing your mission:** Knowing your mission seems pretty basic, doesn't it? Well, it's not only basic; it's essential. You aren't going to be able to raise any money for your organization unless you know why your agency exists and whom you serve. Make sure you have a strong, clear case before you even think about fundraising.

- **Having unrealistic expectations:** Be realistic in your needs statement and in the goals you set as a result. If you raised $100,000 last year, you may be shooting too high to aim for $300,000 this year.

- **Dealing with bad timing:** If your organization has recently suffered a setback in the news — a board member resigned in anger; a legal suit is pending; a large funder just denied a gift — now may not be the best time to launch a fundraising campaign, but that doesn't mean you should just drop out of the market. Think through your messaging, focus your campaign, and tell your story honestly and clearly to call attention to what really matters — getting your programs or services to the people who need them.

Can you run an annual fund and a capital campaign at the same time? Sure you can — and many organizations do. But in shaky financial times, this kind of undertaking may be impractical, impossible, or even dangerous. People and corporations who normally give to your annual campaign may think that their capital donation takes care of that contribution, as well — and as a result, your annual fund may come up short this year, especially given the fact that individuals in a shaky economy are looking at their checkbooks with more concern than usual. See Chapter 18 to find out more about annual funds; for capital campaigns, see Chapter 20.

Budgeting Your Fundraising Efforts

You've no doubt heard the phrase "it takes money to make money." Well, this phrase holds true for fundraising just like any business endeavor. Essentially, you have to spend fundraising dollars to raise funds — a fact that may concern some donors if your fundraising efforts seem too extravagant. And because you're in the business of raising money, you better go about it in a businesslike way. To meet your goals most effectively, you need to carefully plan, budget, and account for all the money you bring in and spend.

A *budget* is a financial plan that shows how you intend to use your resources to pay the expenses you incur to fulfill your mission. Your fundraising budget, which your board approves as part of your organization's overall budget, is an important planning instrument for you, as well as a great way to show your potential funders — whether those funders are individuals, corporations, or foundations — the black-and-white details of your fiscal responsibility.

 Your organization's budget requires a team to complete it. If you're the executive director, you may do the first draft of the general budget, but the board will review — and likely revise — it after you're done. As a development person, you may have to draft the fundraising portion of the overall budget. But, as with the case statement, be prepared to answer questions and make changes after the board review. And know that it's never a bad idea to fly your proposed budget past your financial officer first, just to make sure you didn't miss anything.

The following sections help you estimate how much money you need in order to raise the money that keeps your nonprofit going.

When opportunity strikes . . .

Out of the blue, a bolt of awareness may electrify your cause. For example, take the current heated conversation in the United States about healthcare. This issue has stirred up (and rightfully so) discussion on issues that touch all levels of family life, from the youngest to the oldest members of society. If your organization's mission relates to healthcare or social services, the current debate may help call attention to your cause.

Although you can't prepare for such occurrences when you're setting up your fundraising plan, be aware of the pulse of your environment. Identify issues that are related to you, and keep your eye on them. Take advantage of stories in the news — when the link is genuine — to help potential donors understand better than ever how your organization can help address the topic they're concerned about.

If you think taking advantage of current events sounds distasteful to you — as though it's in some way exploiting a big need in your society — think again. With a topic as seemingly basic as good, universal healthcare, opinions get polarized, views grow stronger, and a wave of frustration — both personal and cultural — ripples through the culture. At times like these, society has a natural need for balance and action, and stories showing that good work is still being done, that people care, and that the people most in need are being cared for are more important than ever. If your organization can be a legitimate part of that healing and help provide some of the answers, you're not exploiting anyone — you're simply taking advantage of a real opportunity to further your mission.

Making sure you include everything in your budget . . . but don't overbudget

The categories in your fundraising budget vary depending on the type of work your organization does, but a few basic ideas take effect across the board. First, make sure fundraising has its own section in the overall operating budget of your organization. In that budget, be ready to put down numbers for the following items:

- How much time you're allocating for fundraising
- How much staff time will be spent in support of fundraising
- What the real expenses are for running your fundraising program

Second, when you're planning out the expenses of your fundraising program, be sure to consider costs in all the following areas (the top four are likely to apply only to larger agencies and organizations; smaller organizations or community groups may have only one or two paid staff, if any):

- Salaries and wages
- Pension plan contributions
- Employee benefits
- Payroll taxes
- Supplies
- Telephone and Internet access
- Web site design and maintenance
- Utilities
- Postage and shipping
- Rent
- Equipment costs
- Printing and publications
- Travel

In times of economic transition, it can be a challenge to gauge how much you need to allocate for the various expenses your organization incurs. Two rules of thumb to keep in mind: First, include in your budget everything you're likely to need for the year (including a cash reserve fund for emergencies), and project what you need, taking the current rate of inflation into consideration. Second, go over your budget carefully — with the help of your board and key staff members — to weed out all unnecessary expenses and qualify the costs you project. A lean, effective budget based on your real needs and best-educated projections is much easier to track and manage in the long-run than a budget that is woefully underfunded or one that includes amounts earmarked for noncritical extras that tie up funds that could be used to reach more people and effect more good.

You may be familiar with Form 990 — the IRS form that nonprofits use to provide full disclosure of their activities and finances. While you're putting together your budget, think about data you need to complete your 990 and plan your budget categories accordingly. (You can get a copy of the Form 990 online at www.irs.gov.)

Figuring out the cost of raising money

So how much money does it take to make money? Different types of fundraising methods require different investments, but the range can run anywhere from a few cents on the dollar for major gifts, planned giving, and capital campaigns to upwards of 50 cents per dollar raised for special events. This wide range of costs is another reason why you need to make sure you select the right fundraising method for your campaign.

You may have heard stories about charitable organizations that take huge cuts for themselves — paying exorbitant salaries and taking huge liberties — from the dollars their supporters provide. These few organizations have created a cloud of suspicion that every fundraiser must overcome — today's donors want to know where their money is going and to see evidence that it is, in fact, going where you say it's going. And when times are tight, your donors will want to be doubly sure the donations they give are going to good use. For this reason, you need to be open and forthcoming with your financial information and keep your fundraising and overhead costs as low as possible. This open communication is an important part of creating a solid, respectful donor-agency relationship, which is essential if you want to be successful.

Turning Elsewhere for Assistance

Fundraising is all about creating and cultivating relationships — with your board and staff, donors, volunteers, constituents, and the public. Much of the best work you do will be in partnership with others as you brainstorm plans, evaluate campaigns, come up with new initiatives, and design your approaches. As you put together your fundraising plan and test it out with those who know your organization best, you may want to consider using outside resources — including fundraising consultants or fundraising software — to help fill in any resource gaps you may identify.

The miracle of the development office

Years ago the Lilly Endowment was greatly concerned about the financial plight of theological seminaries in the United States. They did a survey of seminaries and found that almost no seminaries across the board, from liberal to conservative, had development offices.

In response, the Lilly Endowment created a granting program in which they funded for three years a development office in a number of seminaries — and a virtual miracle occurred. Nearly all the seminaries involved in the grant program earned back the cost in the first year of having a development person. And not only did contributions continue to grow, but an entirely new field in fundraising developed as people began to prepare to become development professionals for seminaries.

Knowing when to outsource

Every nonprofit organization has more than enough fundraising work to go around. Whether that work goes to someone like you — hired to serve in a development role or volunteering to help the greater good — or to someone outside the organization is a very important decision that affects the overall effectiveness of your fundraising and your organization.

If your organization's budget won't yet support a salaried development person, you do have other options available. You can train a corps of volunteers, but doing so can be a hefty responsibility if you're thinking about doing a substantial fundraising campaign. Another option is to contract with a third-party company or consultancy to help you do the fundraising work. From feasibility studies to campaign strategies, from plans to event management and reporting, third-party businesses are ready, willing, and able to take over campaign leadership and planning when you need help.

Good reasons to outsource may be

- You feel the time is right to launch a fundraising campaign but you don't have the necessary leadership for the campaign on staff.
- You're preparing to start your first fundraising effort and want to benefit from the expertise of an experienced consultant.
- You have a close working relationship with a third-party agency and feel that its objectivity would help you create and run a better campaign.

We urge you to think carefully about the pros and cons of putting your fundraising work into the hands of people who may not be working from the same point of passion that you and your board are coming from. Consider a few compromise solutions: Hire a third party to work closely with your board to design the campaign, and then let impassioned volunteers do the actual fundraising work. Or work with a consultant on the development of your mission statement, the planning of a specific campaign, the feasibility of a campaign's success, or the training of key fundraising members of your board and staff. Taking either of these actions can help you build the foundation you need to pursue a successful fundraising campaign.

People who have a passion for your mission must do the actual execution of the fundraising plan, or you'll fall short of your goal and perhaps lose some good relationships in the process.

Using fundraising software

Fundraising software can help you organize your fundraising plan and donor lists and provide valuable reports and analyses of your results. Should you make the investment not only to buy the software but also to transfer all your data into it? The answer is yes, yes, yes!

First, the odds are you don't have to reinvent the wheel here. You can import the donor lists you now keep in a spreadsheet or word processing program into most mainstream fundraising software programs. After you transfer your current data into such a program, here are the areas in which you can expect to reap benefits:

- ✔ Donor management, including cross-references among family members and co-workers

- ✔ Volunteer management, including scheduling and tracking of hours worked

- ✔ Membership management, including keeping track of renewal notices, membership cards, and more

- ✔ Pledge processing with cash-flow projections and delinquent notices

- ✔ Major-gift management, including tracking memorial gifts and generating automatic acknowledgements

- ✔ Direct mail, e-mail, and other campaigns, including helping you organize your lists, personalize communications, and weed out duplicates sent to the same address

Yes, you may have to spend some time inputting data into the software, you may have to spend some money purchasing the software, and you may have to spend some more time training volunteers and staff to use it. But, in the end, fundraising software helps your organization keep track of all the details more efficiently, and because your organization profits from keeping a record of its activities, the software, in turn, helps you develop and grow.

Here are some fundraising software products worth a look:

- ✔ **DonorPerfect:** This program has a robust set of features for small to mid-size organizations; you can purchase the software or buy a monthly subscription online at www.donorperfect.com.

- ✔ **FundRaiser Software:** This simple-to-use donor management program helps you manage your donor lists, keep track of all communications, and create reports based on activity in donor accounts. Check it out online at www.fundraisersoftware.com.

- ✔ **eTapestry:** This Web-based fundraising software makes it easy for your donors to give online and easy for you to update your records from anywhere — not just from a single office location. In addition, eTapestry helps you create and send e-mail campaigns. Check it out online at www.etapestry.com.

- ✔ **Raiser's Edge:** This comprehensive fundraising software program gives you a sophisticated system of fundraising tools, from donor contact management to relationship cultivation, operational management, and much more. Raiser's Edge is a bit pricey for smaller nonprofits, but it has a big user base among large nonprofit organizations. You can find out more at www.blackbaud.com/products/fundraising/raisersedge.aspx.

Many companies offer free trial versions of their software that you can download and try out to see whether they're right for you. See Chapter 17 for more about online fundraising techniques.

Part II
Finding — and Winning Over — Donors

In this part . . .

This part focuses on the donor — the most important person in your fundraising effort. Meet your donor and find out how your organization's needs and your donor's interests connect. Discover how to research everything from your donor's interests to giving trends.

Don't worry about asking for gifts — major or minor. When you really get to know your donor and establish a relationship based on trust, asking for that all-important donation feels like a natural part of your conversation. Even when your donor says no, you have the opportunity to turn that no into a yes down the road. This part shows you how to do so.

Chapter 7

Getting the Lowdown on Your Donors

In This Chapter

▶ Identifying your stakeholders and types of donors

▶ Eliciting help from your board members to find potential donors

▶ Investigating prospective donors

▶ Creating an up-to-date donor information system

▶ Keeping donor research confidential

*T*his chapter is all about the "who" in your fundraising plan. Your donors — whether they're individual givers, couples, affinity groups, or even foundations or corporations — all believe in the work you do and contribute to your cause. Cultivating relationships with your donors and starting new relationships with people who are likely to catch the spark of your mission and involve themselves in your cause require a dedicated effort and a well-thought-out plan. And rest assured that your work — in good times and bad — is likely to be rewarded.

Finding Your Stakeholders

A *stakeholder* is anybody who has a stake in what you do. In other words, your work impacts your stakeholders in some positive way; the existence of your organization makes a difference to them. Your stakeholders are the people you want to research as possible donors (if they aren't already); they may be board members, staff, volunteers, clients your agency serves, vendors, or contributors to your cause.

Different agencies have different types of stakeholders, including the ones we describe in the following list. You may recognize some of your own donors in this list.

✔ **Your clients:** Your clients are the beneficiaries of your services. Who can better understand how worthwhile your mission is than those who have experienced it firsthand? For example, the family of an Alzheimer's patient who found a daytime caregiver and developed better coping skills through your organization is a potential contributor to your organization. The patient's family members believe in your cause because they've had a personal connection with it, and, thus, they may be more than willing to give back to your cause in some way.

✔ **Current and past donors:** Current donors believe enough in what you do to donate their money and possibly their time, energy, and talents to your cause. Past donors gave to you in the past but, for whatever reason, may not be giving now. At some point, your cause inspired them to give, so it's reasonable to expect that they will give again.

✔ **Major donors:** Your major donors give at a high level and are already aligned with your mission and your message. They have made the connection between spark and action and already support you, perhaps with their time and effort as well as with their dollars. See Chapter 9 for more about major donors.

✔ **Your staff:** Your staff members are the champions of your cause. You know your staff members believe in the work they do because they commit a significant amount of time and energy to fulfilling your mission. Staff members are in the unique position of being able to see the results of what you do and have a sense of the continuing and far-reaching possibilities of your organization. For example, staff members of a research think tank see the research being done, the people benefiting from that knowledge, and the possibilities for the future. Staff members in an arts organization see increasing support for the arts, productions of exciting programs, and strong and growing arts education programs. Your staff, who believes so strongly in the mission, makes up a logical potential donor pool for your organization.

✔ **Your board:** Your board members are the people who steer the course for your agency. So who should believe in the work you do more than them? Your board members care enough to commit their time, their effort, their vision, and often their professional and personal resources; they should also be giving financially.

Chapter 5 talks about the importance of having a board committed to the cause and the need to get every board member to give. Foundations look for 100 percent board giving as one of the criteria for funding. But beyond that, having a board that includes all-giving members is a good example for all the other stakeholders, from staff to volunteers to clients.

✔ **Your vendors:** Your vendors provide your paper products, your payroll services, your software support, and many other products and services you need to keep your organization running. These businesses and individuals know something about what you do, the people you serve, and the people who work with you. For example, perhaps you buy used vans for a meal-delivery service from a particular van dealership. The dealership is probably glad to get your business and may make a good potential donor. The link your vendors have to your organization is a closer one than the link you're trying to form with a new business you're considering approaching, so put your vendors on your stakeholder list.

✔ **Neighboring organizations:** These organizations are people or groups in your community that benefit from the services you offer. Certainly you have agencies in your area that are glad you exist. If, for example, a local community theater works in tandem with a larger theater arts agency from time to time, the agency may be a good source of donations of money, costumes, or props.

Recognizing Your Bread and Butter: Individual Donors

Individual donors were responsible for 75 percent of all gifts given in 2008 — a whopping total of almost $230 billion. Gathering all those small donations can really add up: In fact, your individual donors' gifts typically add up to more than any single large gift resulting from that grant, corporate sponsorship, or other large donation you've been hoping for.

Nonprofit organizations with effective fundraising plans don't stop when they get the $25 donation from Mr. Smith each year in the annual fund drive. They persist, first securing Mr. Smith's gift for a repeat year and then upgrading that gift to a higher amount. Over time, Mr. Smith gets more involved with the organization and continues to give at a higher level. Ultimately, his involvement may lead to a high-level gift, such as a major gift, a lead gift in a capital campaign, or a bequest for the organization's endowment. What this means — to you (the effective fundraiser), to Mr. Smith, and to your organization — is that over time, through your invitation and gratitude and through Mr. Smith's continuing interest and satisfaction, a trusting relationship develops between your organization and its donor. In this way, creating and honoring your relationship with each donor is at the center of all the work you do for your organization today and in the future.

The following sections help you understand the relationships that different potential donors have with your organization and how to use that knowledge to cultivate them as real donors.

Understanding donor levels

Donors come in all shapes and sizes, as well as in all giving levels. Your organization's fundraising environment is comprised of the following four distinct levels of involvement:

✔ **Level One:** People closest to the heart — and hopefully the passion — of your organization, including members of your board, your agency's managers, and major givers

✔ **Level Two:** People who work with or are served by your organization, including volunteers, staff, general donors, members, patrons, and clients

✔ **Level Three:** People who may have given to your organization in the past but who aren't active givers now

✔ **Level Four:** People in the general population who have interests compatible with your mission but who, as yet, don't know you exist

Identifying possible donors

When you identify potential donors, make a list of specific people who fit into each of the top three donor levels described in the preceding section. The following three steps show you how:

1. **Identify by name those people involved with your organization at Level One.**

2. **List the names of your potential Level Two donors.**

   If you have a small volunteer group or staff, you can list the individuals by name. Otherwise, you may want to write down only the volunteer leaders or names of volunteers who are highly active in your organization. Make notes of any ideas that occur to you about people you think would be a good fit for a particular donor level. Similarly, if you have an inspiring idea about resources — online databases of potential donors, for example — make a note to follow up later.

3. **List your Level Three prospective donors. Record the names of people you know have fallen off your organization's active donor list.**

After you have a list of possible donors, plug the names into your donor tracking system so you can follow up on them later (see the "Keeping Track of Your Donors and Their Contributions" section for more information about this tracking system).

Just because people stop giving doesn't necessarily mean you've fallen out of their favor. They may be feeling the strain of the economic times. Or maybe they simply need a reminder of how much you appreciate them and their gifts. Perhaps they need a "We've missed you!" note. People who have given in the past are more likely to give than those who haven't yet given to your organization, so make the most of your existing resources to help build your list and keep it active. By making the effort to stay in touch, you preserve the donors' connection with your organization and make it more likely that they will eventually give again.

Doing Business with Corporate Donors

Corporations normally give for one or more of the following four reasons:

- ✔ Because they think giving is part of being a good corporate citizen

- ✔ Because they want to support and align with the mission of their business

- ✔ Because your organization's mission resonates with an individual in the company who champions your cause

- ✔ Because companies that are known for giving are considered better places to work by employees (For example, McDonald's employees are proud of the way McDonald's serves families through Ronald McDonald House.)

That being said, however, corporate donations aren't likely to be a major portion of your overall fundraising campaign — especially in challenging economic times. According to *Giving USA 2009,* corporate giving in the United States totaled $14.5 billion in 2008, which is only 5 percent of total giving.

One additional but perhaps indirect benefit of soliciting corporate gifts is that you may attract company executives who turn out to be good personal givers. As individuals find out more about your organization, they may very naturally be drawn to contribute time, treasure, or talent.

There's a lot more to working with corporate donors than what we present here. Flip to Chapter 22 for details about approaching a corporation for donations.

Finding Foundations That Care

Foundation giving can be a great boon to your organization, but winning a major foundation grant is often a time-consuming and lengthy process. Do your homework so you don't waste your time or the foundation's by submitting a grant that doesn't have a chance of succeeding. In other words, find good research sources that help you understand which foundation is likely to be a good match to your mission. (For the details of applying for grants, head to Chapter 11.)

The first step in your search for the right foundation is to get your hands on different foundations' giving guidelines to see what types of organizations and programs they tend to fund. Find out whether your organization fits their guidelines. In addition, check out some of these resources for more foundation knowledge:

- ✔ **The Foundation Center:** Find useful statistics, links, and even online orientations about becoming a successful grant seeker (fdncenter.org).

✔ **Donors Forum of Chicago:** Find useful information about the three types of foundations — independent, corporate, and operating — as well as links to various foundation directories (www.donorsforum.org).

✔ **GuideStar:** This online research site allows you to post information about your organization that donors or grant makers can browse to find matches to their mission. It also offers information about a huge range of private foundations. GuideStar's Grant Explorer product helps you look at historical information on foundation funding (www.guidestar.org).

If you're scouting foundations, you can get a foundation's annual report simply by calling the foundation and requesting it. (You can also order most foundations' annual reports online.) Foundations pay out a percentage of their holdings in contributions. You can find out how much and in which areas these foundations have given simply by asking (this information is available to the public).

Community foundations are another useful resource for you as you begin exploring fundraising channels. Not only is your local community foundation a place to find funds, but it's also a repository of information about all the nonprofit organizations in your community.

Asking Your Board All the Right Questions

Luckily, all the work of identifying potential donors doesn't fall on your shoulders. Your board is instrumental in helping to identify the people and resources that can make your organization grow. One way to help your board help you in advancing funding is to get them away from the daily tasks they do so they can brainstorm about donor research and support. You can hold an inexpensive off-site meeting to enable board members to let go of the operating expense hassles and focus on the long-term picture.

So what questions do you put to the board when you get their attention? You may have a list of your own, but as you explore areas in which you can find donors to give to your cause, don't forget to address the two questions we pose in the following sections.

Where did you forget to expand your donor base?

As you think through your strategic plan, you probably discover some unmet needs you want to address. And if you choose to explore ways to address those newly discovered needs, your exploration of a new area may lead you to some more potential donors — which is one way to expand your general donor base.

The following questions can help you explore donor areas that your organization may not have thought about yet:

- ✔ Do you have new members or subscribers coming in regularly?
- ✔ Is your group growing or stagnating?
- ✔ What areas of activity can your organization consider?
- ✔ Are any of your programs outdated or unnecessary?
- ✔ Have you identified new programs that would reach new populations?
- ✔ What's the average age of your members? Do you need to implement strategies to reach a broader group of people?

For example, a symphony that plays primarily classical and pop music wants to expand its donor base. Its members are worried that its current series isn't bringing in new patrons. The symphony needs to try something different, so its board members get together and ask the preceding six questions. Upon answering these questions, the board recognizes the need to reach a new group of people and decides to take the symphony out into the community and change the musical selections. The idea produces several new venues, including a hugely successful program called Symphony on the Prairie, which brings the symphony out under the stars with audience members listening from their blankets or tables — complete with boxed dinners — in a natural amphitheater in the countryside. As the success of the idea grows, corporations realize the benefit of providing clients and families with a nice night out on the prairie, and as a result, the symphony gains a huge audience in the corporate market.

In the medical field, this idea of addressing unmet needs is beginning to emerge in helping people develop an organized, cost-effective means of managing chronic illness. If your organization has served in a particular health-care area, for example, you may be able to expand your services to include case management, transportation, or another medically related service that helps patients manage long-term treatment more effectively. By expanding your services, you also expand your donor base.

Whom did you forget to ask?

While adding new programs to bring new donors to your door is an excellent way to expand your donor base, you may be (and probably are) overlooking potentially valuable donors who are as close as your boardroom table. To find these donors, remind your board members to think of friends, colleagues, and other contacts they have who may be interested in donating to your organization.

If your board is lukewarm about using its collective contacts, try a little experiment. At the next board meeting, take a set of 3 x 5 cards, and five minutes before the meeting is adjourned, say, "I'm working on donor prospecting this week, and I'd appreciate it if before you left today, you'd list three peers or companies you think could be potential donors to our organization. And while you're at it, put a check mark beside the people you'd like to suggest we interview as possible board members for the future."

Using Table 7-1, list the potential donors your board members come up with and add a few of your own, too. You can then find out more about the potential donors by talking to the board members who recommended them or doing your own sleuthing. Write the donor's or company's name in the Potential Donor column. In the Individual/Corporate column, write *Individual* or *Corporate* to indicate which one the donor represents. Write the contact's name or how the potential donor is linked to your organization in the Link/Contact column. In the Ability to Give column, write *Y* (Yes) or *N* (No) to indicate whether the potential donor has the financial means to give. Finally, write *Y* or *N* in the Links to Major Donors column to indicate whether the donor may be able to open the door to other people in positions of power or affluence.

The key to remember here is that you have at your disposal a number of people — in your organization or on your board — who are likely to know the answers to your questions about potential donors. You just need to ask the questions.

Table 7-1		Data on Level-Four Donors		
Potential Donor	*Individual/ Corporate*	*Link/Contact*	*Ability to Give*	*Links to Major Donors*
Jim Smith	Individual	Cousin uses our services	Y	Y

Take a look at the donor recognition list published in the annual report of an organization in your community that serves an audience similar to the one you serve. Notice the individual donors and giving levels as well as corporate sponsors and foundation gifts, and add any names to the lists you're compiling in the different donor levels.

Checking Out Potential Donors

Say your board comes up with some great names of potential donors for you to follow up on. What do you do next? Or maybe your board comes up with a list of duds. No one seems to have the type of resources you're looking for. Now what? Because these two situations are very different from each other, we look at each one individually in the following sections.

Pursuing promising prospects

You have a list in front of you of 15 of the top givers in your city, with links through the board members who know them personally. Before you get too excited and march up to their front doors asking for major donations, you need to do some homework.

Your homework involves finding out personal, financial, and professional information about the donors before you meet them so you can strategize the relationships you hope to develop. Your strategy includes finding out what types of contribution the donors may be able to make to your organization, what types of investments may appeal to them based on commitments they've made to other causes, and how you plan to approach the prospective donors when you meet them and when you ask for their commitments.

The most effective fundraising takes place between peers, which means that for the best results, the board member who identified Mrs. Van Buren as a good prospect should be the one to call on her. The board member is her link to the organization, he knows her, and he can say, "You know, Gladys, I'm on the board of this organization, and I'm really proud of what's going on here. Would you like to come over for a tour of our facility? I'd like to show you around myself. And maybe we can have lunch together afterward, if you have the time."

Clearly, Mrs. Van Buren's relationship with the board member is a key component in furthering her interest in your cause and in your organization. See Chapter 10 for more information about perfectly executing "the Ask."

Finding the silver lining with unlikely prospects

Even if your board survey comes up dry — which may mean you don't have the best mix of people on your board — you still have plenty of places to start to build your donor list and look for those high-level donors. And in the meantime, you can work on improving your board.

As you build your donor list with little or no help from your board, start by doing the following:

- **Examine lists (public lists, that is) that similar organizations keep of their donors.** For example, an art museum looks at the patron list published by the symphony and vice versa.

- **Keep an eye on your community.** Take a look at your local paper and note the names of local philanthropists that crop up repeatedly in print. Likewise, keep an eye on national, international, and online news if your mission reaches farther than a local constituency. Watching, listening, and taking notes can help you discover potential resources you may miss if you don't keep your fundraising eyes and ears open.

- **Review the list of political donors.** Political donations are a matter of public record; every political campaign committee must file its list of donors with the commission in their state. Somebody who gives $5,000 to a political campaign may be willing to give to you, too — and you may be able to determine what a particular donor cares most about by understanding the key issues of the candidate's platform he or she supports.

- **Visit the places where people go to be seen.** Certain places in your community are equated with a certain status. Perhaps one of the gathering places is a formal garden, an elegant historical inn, or an arts center. Visit these places and read the plaques on the walls; look at the named statues in the garden; pour over the portraits on the walls. This type of sleuthing can show you which families in your area have wealth — and are using it to further causes that capture their imaginations and their passions.

Researching the Internet Way

When it comes to trying to find new potential donors, one of your best research tools today is the Internet. It provides a huge amount of information that is easily searchable, and you can use it 24 hours a day, 7 days a week, whereas your local library or chamber of commerce likely closes its doors every evening.

Here are some of the most useful tools and approaches to use when researching online:

- **Browse Web sites.** Countless Web sites are available to help you build your donor list. For example, if you're researching a potential corporate giver, you definitely need to visit the corporation's Web site. You can also visit the site of your local community foundation to find the latest nonprofit news in your area, read about funding opportunities, and learn about other nonprofit organizations. Check out industry standards like the Foundation Center (www.foundationcenter.org) to find data, links, and articles to help you gather information and resources on fundraising. Visit discussion boards, foundation sites, and social networking sites like LinkedIn to find out more about potential donors.

Bookmark your favorite sites, display history lists of sites you've visited recently, and use research tools to make your browsing experience easier.

✔ **Use search engines.** Search engines abound online, and they're very useful tools. But not all search engines are created equal. Most (like Google and Yahoo!) are capable of providing quick, targeted results in response to search words, phrases, or questions; others (like ChaCha) include the best results from a variety of search engine results in addition to custom vetted information; and still others (like the new Microsoft Bing) provide a variety of related material like product reviews, mapping features, and more. When you search for information on a specific donor, you may be able to discover what the donor's giving interests are, which organizations she supports, and what roles she serves on corporate or nonprofit boards. These pieces of information will be helpful to you as you determine whether your mission is a likely fit for this particular donor.

✔ **Locate people online.** Donor research means finding out information about people, and, lucky for you, the Internet provides great resources for doing just that. You can browse white pages for just about every town online. You can also browse corporate sites that list board members or senior managers by name or search for news about potential donors to find their current organizational affiliations.

✔ **Explore government Web sites.** Government sites offer free information about trends in the economy that may have an impact on future giving and regulations, tax benefits of giving, and more — all of which are important to know as you approach potential donors. As you plan your fundraising strategy, you may find the following government sites useful:

- IRS (www.irs.gov)
- Catalog of Federal Domestic Assistance (www.cfda.gov)
- Combined Federal Campaign (www.opm.gov/cfc)
- USA.gov for Nonprofits (www.usa.gov/Business/Nonprofit.shtml)

Also check out specific agencies related to your mission, such as the Administration on Aging or the Administration for Children and Families.

Keeping Track of Your Donors and Their Contributions

After you identify and research new donors, how do you keep track of all the information you accumulate? You need a system that's comprehensive enough to store all kinds of data from multiple meetings — because you're going to be meeting with potential high-level givers more than once or twice — and to essentially track an entire relationship. Such a system requires a lot of time and planning. We walk you through the how-tos in the following sections.

Creating an effective donor information form

A *donor information form,* whether on paper or in the computer, gives you a place to keep all of a donor's data as you research and find out more about the donor. The following list outlines the most important categories of information you need to include on your forms and in your database records:

- **Administrative data:** The date the form or record is created, the name of the person who created it, and the way in which the donor was referred to you (board member, other donor, friend, mailing, event, and so on).

- **Name and address:** The first, middle, and last name of the donor, the donor's title, and the donor's contact information, including residential and business addresses, phone numbers, and e-mail addresses. If your donor is a business or foundation, include pertinent information about the organization in general and also the name of and information for your contact within the company.

- **Interests and business affiliations:** The donor's professional position and memberships, foundation or philanthropic interests, awards and honors, key relationships, special interests, and political, religious, and military affiliations.

- **Education:** The individual donor's educational background, details of any continuing relationship the donor has with an educational institution, and social or business activities that tie the individual or organization to education.

- **Family:** The name of the individual donor's spouse, children, parents, and pets, including any significant or relevant information such as birthdays, anniversaries, or hobbies.

- **Resources:** The names of the donor's bank, financial planner, tax advisor, and attorney.

- **Finances:** Information on the donor's income, assets, past contributions made, and so on.

- **Gift record:** A listing of all gifts the donor has pledged and made to your organization.

- **Visitation record:** A listing of all contacts made to the donor by you or a member of your development staff or board.

> ✔ **Opt-in/Opt-out:** Give your donors the option of opting in or opting out of your e-mail communications and note their preferences. When donors opt out of your online communications, be sure to honor their requests and remove them from your send lists for messages and e-newsletters.
>
> ✔ **Comments:** Any comments you have about interactions you have had with the donor or mailings he or she has received.

Make your donor form simple and effective. Plan for multiple pages, with the first page collecting quick-look items, like the donor's most recent gift (date and amount) or the program she most likes to support. Make the form easy to follow and understand, and organize the categories of information in a logical fashion. Leave plenty of space for comments so you — or board members who contact the donor — can make notes about the visit or call. Include columns for totaling gifts and pledges so you can see donation totals and dates at a glance.

In time and with some effort, you'll have hundreds of donor information forms, and you'll want to have easy access to them. Create a good storage system of binders (or folders on your computer) labeled clearly so you know which records are kept there (A–D, Corporate Donors, or whatever). Of course, long term you'll want all of this data captured in your donor management software as well so you can use it in searches later. Try to stay on top of your data by entering information soon after you gather it. That way it won't get buried on your desk.

Keeping good donor records

Keeping your donor records up to date and accurate is a vitally important part of a good fundraising system. Whether you use an online donor management system or keep track of your data in a custom database or an Excel worksheet, be sure to track your data consistently. In general, make notes of all the interactions you have with your donors, summarizing what was said and done, what pledges and gifts were submitted, and what your next steps will be in cultivation.

Maintaining Confidence: The Issues and Ethics of Handling Personal Data

When you accumulate information on a person of high status in your community, you have something other people want. People at dinner parties would love to hear about the net worth of Mrs. Van Buren. A con artist would be interested in knowing that you're doing research on wealthy older people in your region.

Fight the temptation to disclose what you're working on — and certainly respect the privacy of the people you're preparing to approach. The information you gather is meant to assist you in finding the right match — both for the donor and for your organization — nothing more. When you find the donor who shares your interest in an issue, who has the ability to give and the motivation to do so, it's an equitable, honorable relationship. You help the donor make a difference in an area she cares about and she helps you further your work. Everybody wins.

Divulging information about the person you're researching is bad business, bad fundraising, and bad news. Giving away personal information to the first person who asks for it destroys the respectful relationship that should be at the heart of any fundraising effort. It makes the donor nothing more than a mark you're approaching to "hit up" for cash. And you certainly won't keep that person as a donor; in fact, you may get a reputation for lack of discretion that scares away many other donors as well.

Here are a few other ethical reminders you need to keep in mind during every fundraising effort you take part in:

- ✔ Make sure your board knows and approves of your methods of donor research.

- ✔ Review the Donor Bill of Rights and Code of Ethics from the Association of Fund Raising Professionals to make sure your approach is ethical from the start.

- ✔ Carefully consider whether a donor would consent to the type of research you're doing or would be outraged to find that such research was being done about her.

- ✔ Keep your computer (and all the information stored on it) secure. Don't post lists on your Web site and don't give access to your records to sharp computer hackers via the Internet — protect your computers with a firewall or other security software.

- ✔ If you're in doubt about a research practice, check it out with your executive director or attorney.

If you leave your position at your current organization and go to work for a similar agency, can you take your donor information with you? The answer is simple. Whether you're legally bound by a confidentiality or non-compete clause in your employment contract or not, information stays with your current organization — no question.

Chapter 8

Meeting Your Donor

*F*undraising isn't for the fainthearted, no matter what the economic climate may be. And you may never be more aware of the need for courage on the job than when you sit down with your donors for the first time. What should you do at your initial meetings with donors? Picture them in their underwear? Imagine successful outcomes to your meetings? Be careful to present just the right image? All of the above?

Smart fundraising isn't a hit-em-fast endeavor. It's about relationship building, which enables donors to grow continually closer to your mission and to help increasingly through their time, efforts, and gifts. This chapter shows you how to think about the motivations and potential hot buttons of the donors you meet face to face. Keep in mind that you won't visit every donor personally, of course. For example, Uncle Joe, who sends you a $15 check every year for your annual fund, doesn't expect you to appear on his doorstep to take him to lunch. But Mrs. Benefactor, who gave a special gift to a program fund last year, makes a good prospect for your endowment campaign this year. As part of building a relationship with her, visits are expected and, hopefully, welcome. In this chapter, we help you focus on the quest of building positive, long-lasting relationships with your donors.

Evaluating the Importance of a Visit

Attentiveness and respect are two keys to building relationships in the world of donor cultivation. Mailings are fine, but you don't draw donors closer to the mission of your agency or higher up on your giving chart by sending them mailing after mailing. Phone calls are more personal than mailings as long as you don't construe them as telemarketing ploys — at least donors hear a warm voice and know they're getting your personal attention — but, for a potentially major, long-term donor, plan to make regular face-to-face visits. After all, you have a shared interest — your organization and the work it does. Take your donor to lunch or visit her at home; bank on the fact that you're nurturing a far-reaching and, hopefully, continuously rewarding relationship.

So when is the appropriate time to begin planning regular visits to a donor? Donors need special, personalized treatment at the special gifts level of giving and above. Your goal is to secure the commitment of donors whose philanthropic goals match those of your organization. The special gifts level of giving is the first indication that the donor is willing to make a serious commitment to your organization. When the donor gives you this first hint, it's up to you to take the ball and run with it. To nurture this important relationship, you need to do more research, make a greater effort, spend more time, and create more opportunities for interaction with the donor.

Visits — and the time they take — let donors know that they're important, their contributions matter, and you want them to be happy. Not to mention, they keep the door open so your relationship can grow.

Preparing to Meet Potential Donors

Some of your donors have probably been giving to your organization for years. Some likely started out as volunteers helping with your big annual event; others may have served on your board for a term or two. Over the years, you may have sent these long-term donors your quarterly newsletter and a few mail appeals — one for your annual fund and another for a special program fund. In general, you can observe the following characteristics about these long-term donors:

- They're engaged with the mission of your organization.
- They have had enough of a good experience to keep coming back.
- They may have increased both their giving and their involvement over the last few years.

These long-term donors are your first candidates as you begin your research for major gift donors. Chances are that you come up with a number of donors' names during this part of the process. As you evaluate the donor files, consider several key points:

- How many times have they already been contacted by your organization?
- What donations have they already given to your organization?

✔ What other affiliations do they have with other nonprofits in your community?

✔ What's their potential for giving (that is, what can you deduce about their financial status)?

Fully armed with the answers to these important questions, you're ready to contact each potential donor for a meeting.

To begin your personal contact with a potential major gift donor, you call her number. After she answers the phone, you say what you've rehearsed many times.

> "Hi, Mrs. Donor," you say. "This is Jamie from New Beginnings. I was going over our volunteer records and I see that you've been giving both time and money to our organization for three years now."
>
> Mrs. Donor takes a minute to process the information.
>
> "Well, we're glad to help," she says. "We've really enjoyed our time there."

As the call continues, you tell Mrs. Donor that you'd like to invite her and her husband to be your guests at lunch, so you can thank them for their involvement and introduce them to new happenings at your agency. Mrs. Donor says she'll talk to her husband about it and asks you to call back Monday. When you call back as requested, you and Mrs. Donor schedule the luncheon.

To make sure your first face-to-face meeting with Mrs. Donor (and all other prospective donors) goes as smoothly as possible, you need to think about the following:

✔ What you offer a donor who gives to your organization

✔ How charitable giving is really a win-win proposition

✔ What motivates donors to give

The following section helps you explore each of these issues in detail to help you prepare for your initial donor meetings.

Examining the Giving Relationship between the Donor and the Agency

Nonprofit organizations and agencies exist and thrive to help real people accomplish good works. Way back when, if someone in the community was ailing, you could rally the support that person needed right there in the neighborhood, in the church, and in the family. In today's world, however, the needs are often great and complex, sometimes spreading around the globe, which is where nonprofit organizations like yours come in to play. Nonprofit organizations exist to help people help others — through giving money, time, effort, or material goods.

In exchange for everything your donors give to you, you and your organization offer something in return. The relationship between you and your donors isn't a one-sided one in which the only dynamic is that the donor gives and the nonprofit takes. Both sides have tangibles and intangibles to offer and receive, with the intangibles probably being the more important. These important intangibles include the following:

- ✔ The donor feels like he's making a difference, like he's an appreciated, valued part of a select group.

- ✔ The organization feels the security of being able to count on the donor's involvement and contribution year after year.

This equal exchange not only helps the organization grow; it also enables the donor to benefit from the relationship. The following sections show what both your organization and the donor get out of the relationship.

Showing donors the value of their gifts

When donors give to your organization, what do they get in return? Hopefully they see the effectiveness of their gifts and feel assured that their money is going where you said it would (through stories in your newsletters, Web sites, or other communications about the programs and services they support). You show your donors that you value them and their gifts by providing them with the following services:

- ✔ **Providing financial information:** When you help a donor find out about planned giving options, you educate him about the various estate and tax-planning opportunities available to him. By working with his financial advisor or tax attorney, you can assist in designing the right giving plan to meet the donor's financial needs.

- ✔ **Evaluating options:** Your donor's time is valuable. When you clearly and simply communicate the mission of your organization — in print, in person, or on the Web — you help your donor make informed choices about the charitable organizations he wants to support. You help your donor get informed and involved with an issue close to his heart by helping him evaluate all his giving options.

- ✔ **Interacting and corresponding regularly:** You need to regularly show donors where their money is going by inviting them in for a visit and enlisting their help, care, and vision in building the organization. As donors get involved in and gain appreciation for your organization, they become part of a bigger system working to solve the problems of the world at large.

✔ **Being accountable:** After you receive that first fundraising gift, you owe your donor accountability. Report on what effect the gift has had on your clients, what good has come of it, and how you plan to continue the growth in the future.

✔ **Demonstrating the good that's being done:** When a donation leads to a good outcome — a person finds a good job or a family moves into an affordable home because of a particular donation — don't miss out on the great opportunity to enable the people who received the services to say thanks to the donors in their own words. Ask the recipients of your services to write a personalized note to the donors, sharing what happened because of the donor's generous gift. These personal notes enable donors to hear directly from recipients how their donations made a positive impact on the lives of others — and that's powerful stuff.

Getting more than money from your donors

What do donors offer your organization? You're probably thinking, "Money!" But that's only partially right — and it's not even the important part. Although your donors do show their involvement through financial contributions (we hope), the most important donation they make is the donation of their belief.

If donors didn't believe in what you do or in your ability to carry out what you promise, they wouldn't spend their time — much less their money — on you. The strength of the belief your donors have in you and your organization may vary over time and circumstances, but it's your job to keep that belief strong and the interest growing. In tough economic times, even though donations may dip for a period of time, you always have the ability to keep the belief and connection strong. So don't make the mistake of thinking your donors offer you only money. Some of the critical intangibles your donors provide are

✔ **Time in voluntary services:** Volunteers provide an amazing amount of service in nonprofit organizations all over the globe. The dedication and sweat equity offered is a huge testament to their belief in your mission and their partnership in your cause.

✔ **Material goods donated:** Some donors may prefer to give your organization supplies, tickets to community events, or materials instead of monetary gifts; these material goods can be a great help for donations ranging from computer equipment to classroom supplies to vehicles and buildings.

- ✔ **Donations of services and resources:** Other donors may want to provide in-kind donations that offer professional services or resources for free. You may be able to secure high-quality legal help, investment consultation, or human resources services through these kinds of donations.

- ✔ **Goodwill in conversations with friends:** Don't underestimate the value of a respected member of your community having a positive experience with your organization. Your donor then shares the story with friends, who suddenly see your organization in a whole new light. This kind of trusted referral — from someone people look up to and trust — makes all the difference in how open they may be to developing a relationship with an organization they don't know.

- ✔ **Visibility for your organization:** If you have a small organization and you're in the beginning stages of building credibility and reputation, here's a tip on how to build that credibility: Go for the Good Fundraising Seal of Approval. In your area, you probably have certain companies and donors who are known for their philanthropic interests. When one of these groups or individuals gives to a nonprofit organization, the rest of the community thinks, "Oh, I guess that organization has a pretty good thing going — otherwise Mrs. Endrow wouldn't give to it!" Look for and identify where the Good Seals are in your area, and organize your fundraising efforts to secure a donation from one of these key people.

The tax benefit for your donors is something important to remember as you talk about the upsides of giving — for you and for them. Donors who itemize can take a tax deduction of up to 50 percent of their adjusted gross income. For those donors who make major gifts, that percentage can add up to a sizable deduction.

Checking out what motivates giving

Why do people give — and why *don't* they? When we threw this question to a classroom full of fundraisers, they gave us some interesting responses, as you can see in Table 8-1.

Table 8-1	Reasons for Giving . . . and *Not* Giving
Reasons to Give	*Reasons to Not Give*
They have an emotional response to a cause.	They weren't asked.
They like the tax deductions.	They're unhappy with the way the organization is handling finances.
They share a belief in the cause.	Their interests and priorities have changed.

Reasons to Give	Reasons to Not Give
The nonprofit's image appeals to them.	Nobody said thank you the last time they gave.
The nonprofit's marketing materials attract their attention.	They no longer have the resources to give.
They want a sense of belonging — joining something bigger than themselves.	They didn't like the manner in which they were approached.
They want to give back to a cause that helped them or someone they care about.	They're insecure about the organization.
They get good seats at a basketball game in return for their donation (personal gain).	The organization doesn't have long-term plans.
Their peers influence them.	They weren't asked for the right amount.
They enjoy donating.	They aren't motivated by the cause.
They have personal experience with the cause.	They haven't been part of a culture of giving.
They want to give in memory of someone.	They have compassion fatigue.
They want to set an example.	
They hope to pass on a legacy.	
They like the honor that accompanies donating one's time and treasures.	
They have spiritual reasons (tithing) for giving.	
They want to have a voice in the larger discourse.	
They feel empathy for the cause and its benefactors.	
They want to make a difference.	
The right person asked them.	

We didn't list these reasons in any particular order. We want to show that, although you may hope people give to your organization because they believe in your mission, tax deductions, marketing, or image may play a bigger role in why a particular donor decides to give or not give.

If you think about how, when, and why you give to the charities you support, you may identify with one or more of the reasons in Table 8-1. People have all kinds of motivations for giving — some people-serving, some self-serving. As a fundraiser, you can't judge givers' motivations — the why is up to them. The what, how, when, and, hopefully, how much is what you need to focus on when your mission matches their motivation.

One of the reasons why people don't give is compassion fatigue, as you can see in Table 8-1. So what is compassion fatigue? In recent years, the term *compassion fatigue* has been used to describe the situation in which the donor is bombarded and overloaded with calls for help. They've been asked by too many different causes, which spread them too thin, especially when they're concerned about finances themselves.

As a fundraiser, be sensitive to any messages your donors give you that indicate changes in their relationships with your organization. Be candid with your observations and ask them whether you can do anything to alleviate any concerns they have about supporting your organization. By inviting the donors to share their ideas and opinions, you may wind up strengthening the bond they have to your cause.

You may find it hard to believe that one of the major reasons why donors don't give is because they're never asked. But it's true! Can you imagine visiting with a donor, having several conversations, having lunch, and then not asking him to make a donation? Hopefully, not! But recognize that rejection is a universal fear, and people everywhere try to avoid it — fundraisers included. Often, fundraisers set up conversations to lead to asking for major gifts but then avoid the direct question at the last minute. Why? Because hinting for a gift (instead of asking directly) is safer when you anticipate a *no.* (See Chapter 10 for how to ask for major gifts directly and sidestep the whole rejection issue at the same time.)

Considering Your Donor's Context

In times of economic downturn — or worse, a recession like the one we lived through in 2009 — everybody swallows a little harder when it comes to writing the big checks. Families, businesses, and organizations all over the world feel the pressure, and philanthropy does indeed experience a dip in overall giving to charitable organizations.

However, the dip isn't as big as you may think. Why not? In large part, because giving has less to do with money than it does with hope. People give because they care and because they want to contribute to improving other people's lives — whether those improvements help families rebuild after a storm, finance a child's education, make prescriptions affordable for seniors, protect the environment, or make a difference in any number of other causes.

That being said, however, considering your donor's context as you prepare to ask for any gift is extremely important. Knowing how your donors may be feeling and thinking can help you communicate — in a way they can understand — why giving to your organization is a good idea, even in tough times. The following sections offer some insights into how your donors may be feeling during a slow economy.

Involve your board as you consider how your donors are responding to your current economy. What do your board members feel is realistic? Are some groups affected more than others? Brainstorm ways to keep the mission of your organization moving forward while considering your donors' realities — and be sure to plan to incorporate these ideas in your communications with donors.

Engaging donors with limited means (for now)

During times of economic uncertainty, people who live paycheck to paycheck struggle to make ends meet, so they're unlikely to feel comfortable giving a major gift to your organization, no matter how much they want to. A large portion of your giving population may fall in this group, and your younger givers may comprise a large percentage. Similarly, people on a fixed income, who may include baby boomers and senior citizens (see the later section for more about these folks), may also be cautious about giving right now. How can you reach out to this group of donors with limited means and encourage them to give, letting them know you value their involvement with your organization — whether they can give $5, $50, or $500?

We've figured out that if you ask the questions you struggle with and listen carefully, people will provide the answers you're looking for. So, if you don't know how to reach people with limited means in poor economic times, try doing a little focus study with some of your donors in this group, and say, "We're in unchartered territory and we need your help. We know you love us because you came to this meeting (thanks!), and we'd love to hear how you think we should approach donors and present ourselves during these tough economic times." And then listen! You're likely to get a gold mine of information about donor practices, language, and expectations. Be sure to incorporate your donors' suggestions into your approaches, and send them a nice thank-you note when everything's said and done.

In the short-term, providing flexible, easy ways for donors to give — and feel good about what they give no matter the amount — is key. You can stress your own need to raise funds for daily operations by translating what the donor's small donation can provide (something a donor can readily identify with). For example, say something like "Your $10 donation buys three back-to-school kits for second graders at PS 103."

In the long-term, tell donors that you know the economy will improve and that people will feel comfortable giving once again at higher levels. Including this idea in your messaging not only lets your donors know that you're adjusting to meet them where they are right now, but also sends a message of belief that things will get better soon (and lets donors know you're counting on them to increase their giving when they're able to do so).

Connecting with affluent donors

The major drops in the stock market during the tough times of 2008 and 2009 put everyone on edge — including your more affluent donors. The major givers in your group may not experience the same level of impact that other donors do during economic downturns, but all people with investments, homes, and futures watch the churning markets with trepidation and worry. The good news is that eventually a sense of solid recovery will spread throughout the economy, and even the investments that suffered a major drop will begin to climb again.

Your major donors aren't insulated from feeling the stress of the downturn, but they do still have resources to contribute to your organization. If you have a donor capable of giving you a half-million dollars, she may still be able to make that kind of gift, despite the economy. Affluent donors still have a tax or giving plan in place, and they're still looking for charitable organizations with a mission like yours. Don't hold back on your plans to approach affluent donors — after all, they're expecting you. Just be prepared to answer questions candidly about how secure your organization is, how you've been meeting financial challenges thus far, and what your plans are for the future.

Meeting reluctant retirees on their level

Of all the groups in your donor list, the reluctant retiree is likely feeling the impact of economic downturn most of all. Unlike younger donors who are just starting out, retirees have often worked their whole lives to arrive at retirement, ready to relax and live on what may be limited means. They may have planned carefully, saved religiously, and invested wisely — only to see their retirement funds drain away over a few nightmarish months.

The long-term good news for the retiree is that their portfolios will recover, but chances are they'll never feel as buoyant as they did before the recession hit. Because of the shock of the drop and the shifting of their expectations, the retiree becomes a cautious donor.

You may be able to meet baby boomers and seniors where they are by bargaining down for now, suggesting that they choose to give $50 a month instead of a larger lump sum. You can offer additional options to help secure the income your organization needs while affording the donor control by offering automatic deductions from the donor's bank account. It's easier, efficient, and both your donor and your organization can budget for it.

Don't underestimate the intrinsic need people have to help make the world a better place, no matter what their finances may say. Giving — even if it's only a fraction of what they used to give — still makes people feel good and demonstrates the reality that no matter how tight things may be financially, good is still getting done.

Cultivating the Initial Relationship

As you continue to talk and get to know your potential donor both personally and financially, you build trust and discover where your shared ideals
lie. If the situation is right, by the end of your first meeting with a donor, you
should offer your donor the following ideas:

- You value the donor's involvement with your organization.
- You want to involve the donor on a deeper level.
- You have ideas for helping the donor meet his estate goals and avoid
  excessive taxation.
- You want to write up a few ideas and meet with the donor to discuss
  them in the coming weeks.

At this point in your blossoming relationship with the donor, it's important
to keep the trust building. At the end of your first meeting, you want the
donor to leave with a good feeling about you and his relationship with your
organization. So avoid the following when you're in this initial relationship-
building stage:

- **Being vague about how the donor's money is going to be used:**
  Today's donor, having grown up in an age of media exposés, is somewhat leery about how nonprofit organizations spend their contributions.
  Be forthcoming with your organization's financial information — it
  speaks volumes about your credibility. And remember that even if you
  don't want to reveal information about the sources of your income and
  how it's used, you have to make this info (which appears on IRS Form
  990) available to the general public whenever it's requested.

  Speak candidly about the value of contributions for the general support
  of your organization. Say something simple like, "We have to turn on
  the lights everyday and get gasoline for the truck." Most people understand that general support — the money that goes to keeping your doors
  open — may be the most important money you raise in tough times.

- **Making assumptions:** Making assumptions can lead to missed opportunities, especially during down economies. For instance, if you assume
  that donors in their 30s aren't interested in an estate-planning option,
  you may lose a major donor because you failed to give him a convincing
  reason to donate. For example, if your donor's father died at age 45, the
  donor is likely to be sensitive to the issues involved with caring for one's
  family long-term in the event of an untimely death. The key here is to
  listen, listen, listen to your donors, and let them lead you to the gift area
  that's right for them.

- **Being afraid to bargain down:** When you're at a point when you're
  ready to ask for a specific gift, don't be afraid to ask for a lesser amount
  if the donor rejects your initial amount. Generally speaking, most people

are flattered that you considered them part of a group that could give the amount you requested, so no harm is done. If your donor says no to $10,000, don't be afraid to say, "Would you be more comfortable with $7,500, given over three years?"

✔ **Promising more than you can deliver:** Some fundraisers get so focused on the goal that they promise the moon to a donor to secure a gift. If you're one of those people, fight the temptation. Every interaction with your donor either builds credibility or detracts from it, and making promises you can't possibly keep only hurts your organization in the long run.

✔ **Forgetting to say thank you:** How can something so simple be overlooked? Easily — organizations often focus on receiving and not on giving. Recognizing your donors by saying thank you, sending cards, making phone calls, or planning a luncheon needs to comprise about 20 percent of your fundraising time. Seems like too much time? Well, it isn't if you recognize that your primary goal is building relationships with your donors, not raising money. *Thank you* are two of the best friendship-building words in the English language, so don't forget to use them.

One way to continue to cultivate your relationship with donors is to recognize your donors for their contributions. A great way to do so is to get your donors together at a dinner or other social gathering. This type of event not only recognizes your donors' contributions, but also strengthens their relationships with your organization.

One nonprofit organization we worked with held cocktail parties for people who gave $5,000 or more. The receptions were a way of saying thank you — and were very popular with the donors. During the evening, donors exchanged ideas and information about the organization, such as why they gave, how they became involved, and what they liked about their involvement, which made everybody feel good about what they were doing. Donors also often met people they admired in the community and felt affirmation for their giving choices, which increased their loyalty to the nonprofit organization. The internal message was, "Wow! I didn't know Mr. Smith supported this organization. This must be a great place!"

If you decide to hold a donor recognition dinner, try getting a sponsor to underwrite the meal for you. You can have a box lunch or a formal fete brought in, rewarding your donors and giving visibility to your sponsor — and it won't come out of your budget! Everybody wins!

Chapter 9

Cultivating Major Givers

*E*very donor who has given to your organization in the past, who gives today, or who will give tomorrow is important to the continuation of your mission. The donor who gives substantially to your organization — in terms of time, talent, or treasure — is one of your primary stakeholders and is close enough to your cause to care in a big way. This chapter takes a look at the special relationship you nurture with major givers, whether they're already giving at a top level or you hope to help them increase their gifts over the years to come.

Cultivating relationships with major givers is both an art and a science — and doing so successfully requires honesty, respect, and an ongoing commitment to long-term benefits for both the giver and the receiver. This chapter helps you think through the process of cultivating major givers and helps you make sure you acknowledge their gifts and commitment appropriately.

Seeking a Major Gift Today for Tomorrow

Asking for a major gift when the economy is pitching and swaying is completely unrealistic, right?

Wrong.

In fact, no matter what the financial landscape looks like, major givers are a breed apart from all others. These demonstrated givers have a history of contributing to your organization, they believe in what you're doing, and they have experience with the work you do and the people you serve. People you identify as potentially able to make major gifts have demonstrated an interest

high enough to give in a big way. It's up to you to determine whether
also have the financial ability to make a large contribution, and then —
's where the science comes in — you need to use the data you gather to
he up with the right amount for which to ask.

cording to the 2008 Bank of America Study of High Net-Worth Philanthropy,
le wealthiest Americans give from a high sense of commitment to their local
communities and tend to be very loyal to the organizations they support.
Thus, even in challenging financial times, organizations can expect major
givers to continue to support their favorite causes, in terms of both finances
and volunteer hours.

Working with major gifts and planned-giving programs requires long-term
cultivation because donors who eventually make a major gift or bequest do
so only after establishing a trusting relationship with your organization. They
get to know you over time, during which you answer all their questions, demonstrate your mission, model good follow-through and ethical behavior, and
show that you care. Gradually, the relationship moves closer to the point at
which you can confidently — and comfortably — ask for a major gift.

When you encounter people who aren't ready to give the major gift at a particular time, one way to encourage them to give something is to invite them
to put your cause in their wills. The idea here is that even though the donors
aren't ready to write a big check at the moment, putting your organization in
their wills gives them a way to contribute to your organization in the future.
Many organizations that develop major endowments and big gifts do so in
this way, over a period of years. Gradually, over time, these major gifts build a
pipeline of giving.

Your donors can put your organization in their wills easily thanks to the
codicil, a legal document that's an amendment to a will, spelling out that a
specific grant of money will be subtracted from the corpus of the estate. You
can draft a codicil for interested donors to use and your donor can then provide you with a letter saying that the codicil has been completed. The letter
enables you to count the contribution toward your organization's funding
without needing to have a copy of the donor's will in hand.

Many years ago, John was one of the founding board members of the
Wellness Community, a cancer support group in Indianapolis. An attorney
who was handling a donor's estate planning contacted John and explained
that his client was looking for a place to make a gift where the organization
put the gift in trust and the trust paid interest and earnings each year to the
charity. At the end of 20 years, the corpus would go back to the heirs of the
estate. After talking to John, the donor put one million dollars into a charitable trust for the benefit of the Wellness Community, and the annual earnings
sustained the organization during up and down times. The gift literally saved
the Wellness Community during difficult times and ensured its long-term
viability.

Finding the Holy Grail of Fundraising — The Major Gift

So now that you're fired up to begin cultivating major gifts no matter what the financial climate looks like, you may be wondering what qualifies as a *major gift*. Well, no matter how hard you look, you won't find a hard-and-fast rule about what constitutes a major gift; a major gift in your organization may be completely different than a major gift in another organization. The following sections show you how to plan for major gifts and build a relationship with those donors who may be willing to donate the big gifts you're seeking.

Does your agency have a gift program that enables donors' gifts to keep on giving? People want their money to be used for something good, something that creates change for the better. For this reason, scholarship programs, research for cures, and programs that battle the recognized ills of society (like poverty, drug abuse, and illiteracy) are good candidates for major gifts. Who wouldn't want to be able to say, "I gave the money that led to a cure for multiple sclerosis?"

Soliciting major gifts for human services organizations can be challenging because human services are ongoing, dynamically changing services, which means a donor can't always give a major gift and know exactly where it's going to be used. For human services organizations, one successful area for major gifts is in the endowment area. In this case, the organization sets up an endowment fund to produce an ongoing source of funds, which guarantees that the service will continue for future generations. We cover endowments in Chapter 23.

Planning your way to major gifts

Although you may think — and logically so — that the best (and perhaps only) time to receive major gifts is when donors feel like giving them, realize that a lot of planning on the part of the fundraiser goes into acquiring major gifts. For instance, fundraisers often plan to secure major gifts when they gear up for specific fundraising campaigns — and begin cultivating the relationship with the donor months, if not years, before they're ready to ask for the donation. In fact, a major gift often serves as the very foundation of a campaign, ensuring the success of the campaign before the organization launches it completely. For example:

> ✔ You're planning a capital campaign and you need to determine how many major gifts you need in each of several ranges to meet your goal. (Creating a giving pyramid can help you determine what you need to know. See Chapter 6 to find out how to create a giving pyramid.)

ou're starting a new scholarship program and you ask a board member
o donate a major gift as a challenge grant to get other members to give.

You're building an endowment fund and you plan to use major gift strategies and planned-giving opportunities to bring in the funds you need.

u can have a major giving program even if you're a small organization just
arting out because you need to cultivate low-level donors over time and
grow them into major donors. The normal progression of fundraising is to
bring the donor closer and closer to your cause over time, which also means
increasing the amount of giving along the way. If you haven't thought about
your current giving program as leading to major gifts, get ready to explore a
new and profitable area!

Reviving your pool of current donors

Before you begin targeting major gifts, make sure your donor list is current
and active. Your organization already has a record of who has given major
gifts to your organization in the past. Find this record and scour its content.
Who has given in the past and is still active in the organization today? Who
has given before but disappeared in recent years? Follow up with any currently inactive donors and try to find out why they stopped being active in
your organization. Maybe personal contact from you is just what the donor
needs to get reinvolved in your organization.

After you find the information on gifts made to your organization, make a list
of all the major gifts your organization has received in the last three years.
Then for each major gift, include information on what program the money
was targeted for (if any), the amount given, the terms of the gift (paid in one
year, over three years, and so on), and of course, the donor who gave the gift.
How have these gifts been used? What activity have these donors had since
they gave their gifts? With the proper attention, you can get these donors
to continue to be active in your organization. Research shows that if your
donors have given before — especially within the past 18 months — they
will be likely to give again. Cygnus Applied Research reports that most major
donors are interested in ensuring the sustainability of organizations they
already support as opposed to supporting organizations that are unfamiliar
to them.

Of course, unforeseen events and situations happen, and sometimes organizations fall out of favor with a donor for one reason or another. But being
new to the fundraising position in your organization gives you a great excuse
to reinitiate contact with all your donors. When you call a currently inactive
donor, say something like, "Mrs. Williams, I'm the new development person
at StreetReach. I can see that you were very active in 2006 and 2007, and your
involvement really helped our organization. I'm calling to introduce myself,
thank you for what you did with us in the past, and invite you back!"

Targeting your major gifts

As we discuss in Chapter 6, one of the first steps in effective fundraising is to know what your dollar goal is. Are you trying to raise $30,000 or $3 million this year? If you plan to renovate your building, calculate the renovation cost. If you need money for a certain music outreach program, determine exactly how much you need. Before you make a solid plan for the how, when, where, and why of major gifts, you need to know the how much — as in *how much* money you need to raise to reach your program goals.

After you know your dollar goal, you can create a giving pyramid to help you determine the kind of major gifts you're looking for and how many of them you need. (Check out Chapter 6 for how to create a giving pyramid.)

Keep in mind that your fundraising plan — and the giving pyramid — doesn't include only major gifts. You need to have several different major gift levels, such as $10,000, $5,000, and $2,500, as well as categories for lesser gifts. Not every donor gives the same level of gift, of course, and some, given a choice and gentle encouragement, may give a much higher amount than you expected!

Cultivating donors who have a lot to give

After you determine how many major gifts you need to receive to reach your fundraising goal, you need to begin thinking about which donors can help get you there. Where can you find major donors? The possibilities are endless! Here are just a few of the places where you can begin your search:

- On your board
- In the ranks of your volunteer corps
- On your donor list
- On the boards of other similar organizations
- In the community — people making waves
- In the community — people making headlines
- In the community — people making money

By far, your best tool for finding major donors is your donor list, which is why maintaining an up-to-date list and using it regularly is so important. For instance, as you update your donor list, you add new information you have learned about your donors and see ways to make better use of the information you already have. As you review your list regularly, slice and dice it by searching according to different criteria — age, interests, education, location — to look at it in a variety of ways. You may find donors "popping out at you" that you overlooked before.

The major donor profile

re what your major donors will
der the following common char-
t we find in our daily work:

- Major donors are usually already involved with your organization.

- Major donors are involved in a number of community activities in both for-profit and nonprofit worlds. (The best donor to solicit is one who has already given to something else.)

- Major donors often have high profiles in a community and feel they have a responsibility to give back.

- Major donors often have already raised their families (in other words, they're in their 50s and up) or haven't had children.

- Major donors often have at least some college education.

- Major donors may have volunteered when they were young.

- Major donors typically itemize their tax returns.

- Major donors are often involved in religious organizations.

Cultivating major donors in seven steps

The folks who are most likely to give major gifts are those who are closest to your organization — stakeholders, clients, and board members who obviously share the mission of your organization. (Read more about donor levels in Chapter 7.) They care deeply about the cause and the furthering of your mission, and, because their passion is in line with your own, they're going to be your highest-level donors.

But most major donors don't start out being major donors. Often they grow closer to your organization over time, perhaps starting out by making a $25 donation to your annual fund and then gradually moving closer to the heart of your organization, where they may give larger gifts to specific programs.

The donors who give at a low level today are your major givers of tomorrow, which means that *cultivation* — the art of enhancing and building the donor-agency relationship — is not only good practice, it's good business. Today's $25 donor may be tomorrow's $25,000 donor.

The process of involving a donor at ever-increasing levels of giving is a logical one and consists of the following steps:

1. **Identify the donors you feel are good prospects for major gifts.**

    • Review your donor list and giving records.

    • Talk to board members.

- Research *Marquis Who's Who in America* (www.marquiswhoswho.com) in your area of involvement.

- Use other research methods as needed (see Chapter 7 for more about donor research).

Make a sublist of your main list, showing only those prospects you want to follow up on as potential major givers. For example, you might use your donor management software to create a sublist of donors who have given to a specific program in the past or who have given at a particular giving level.

2. **Research the prospective donors.**

   As you do your homework on the individuals on your sublist, verify that their interests do, in fact, support the type of work your organization does. Get a sense of their giving interests, other philanthropic activities, likes and dislikes, preferences, and commitments.

3. **Based on what you know about the donor, design a strategy for cultivating the relationship with him or her.**

   What type of program and/or sponsorship opportunity may the donor be interested in? Would it be best to visit the donor in person, invite the donor out for a visit, or something else? How could a board member, volunteer, or supporter with a strong relationship to the donor support the cultivation strategy? The strategy you develop for each donor needs to be custom tailored to her needs, interests, and priorities.

4. **Build, or cultivate, the relationship with the donor.**

   Depending on the prospective donor, you may meet with her several times over a period of months or contact her via a number of means, such as a phone call, letter, or personal visit. Regardless of how you cultivate your donor-agency relationships, schedule true solicitation calls only when you feel your donors are receptive. Be sure to acknowledge the donor's past giving history and involvement through the process.

5. **Ask the prospective donor for the gift (a process we call "the Ask," which we explain in Chapter 10).**

   After you've cultivated the relationship with the prospective donor, you're in a position to ask for the major gift. Remember that you can't just jump from Step 1 to Step 5. Even if your donor gives major gifts hand over fist, you need to build your relationship with that donor before the gift is offered and continue to do so after you receive the gift.

A delayed gift doesn't necessarily mean no gift. In shifting economic times, your major givers are likely to be paying close attention to the stock market as they consider the gifts they plan to make. A delay may mean that your donor is waiting for a better time to donate stock, which may appreciate in the future.

express your thanks for the gift.

After you receive the major gift (assuming your solicitation is successful), expressing your thanks helps pave the way for a repeat gift at some point. Saying thank you graciously and remembering — and honoring — any promises you make to the donor allow you to cultivate the donor-agency relationship even further. But if you neglect to express your thanks or otherwise overlook the generosity of the gift, the donor may feel unappreciated, or worse, taken advantage of — and you won't see any repeat gifts from that donor in the months and years to come.

Recognize every gift in a unique way appropriate to the gift. You need to honor each donor so that she knows you truly appreciate the gift and the patronage. This equal recognition is especially important when your donors know each other and are likely to compare your recognition efforts. Remember, though, that people in the major giver category don't need another plaque. Something more personal, like a photo of the donor with a client or at the front door of the building she contributed to, will have more meaning and create a lasting memory.

7. **Account for how the gift is used.**

What you do with the gift is as important to the donor as what you do to get the gift. After you secure any gift — but especially a major gift — it's vitally important that you do with it what you said you would. The donor needs to see where her money goes, and you need to be willing to provide that information as soon as the donor requests it, if not before. Doing so goes a long way toward building the donor-agency relationship and may ensure that you get another gift.

Want to really impress your donors? Don't wait for them to ask about what's happening as a result of their gifts. Go to them and say, "I wanted to show you what your gifts are doing — look how happy these kids are!" Show the donors photos of the programs they've helped sponsor and let them see the fruits of their gifts. Donors love to see the outcomes of their philanthropy — and the sooner you can provide that information, the better.

Building a giving club

Although you may initially solicit major gifts for a particular program or campaign you want to fund, you eventually need to incorporate a major giving program as part of your regular fundraising strategy. Colleges and universities have perfected the art of major giving programs by creating *giving clubs,* which serve a number of fundraising-related purposes. First, they inform your donors about the benefits they receive at each of the different giving levels. Second, they help donors feel a part of something while building a sense of identity for your organization. Third, they make it easy for you to show donors how they can "upgrade" to a higher level of giving in subsequent years. For example, as part of your alma mater's giving club, when you give a large gift, your school may affix your name to the new library, to the endowed chair of a particular department, to a scholarship fund, or to any number of other long-lasting recognition opportunities.

As a member of your organization's fundraising team, you can begin a giving club by identifying the club levels you want to create, the names you want to assign to each level, and the benefits you want to offer the donors who give.

Table 9-1 lists four different giving club levels for a garden club association.

Table 9-1	An Example of a Giving Club		
Level I: *$500–$999,* *The Crocus Club* *Benefits*	*Level II:* *$1,000–$2,499,* *The Lily Club* *Benefits*	*Level III:* *$2,500–$4,999,* *The Iris Club* *Benefits*	*Level IV:* *$5,000 and above,* *The Rose Society* *Benefits*
Garden membership	All of the Crocus Club benefits, plus . . .	All of the Lily Club benefits, plus . . .	All of the Iris Club benefits, plus . . .
Tickets for two to an evening premiere	Dinner with the chamber orchestra at the garden	A tour of the Arlyle Garden Home (two tickets)	Breakfast with a master gardener
Free subscription to the *GardenWalk* newsletter	Gardening classes (six) with a master gardener	An evening for two in the garden with a horse-drawn carriage ride	A special birding event for Rose Society members
		Free admission to all garden events	An all-expenses-paid trip for two to our sister garden in St. Louis, Missouri

Recognizing Major Donors for Their Contributions

As we say repeatedly (and we can't really say it enough), giving isn't just an "I give, you get" transaction; it's an equitable trade that benefits everyone involved. Your organization receives something, to be sure, but you give something, as well. What you give your donors may be intangible — the good feeling that comes from helping a cause they believe in, for example. Or the recognition you offer them may involve something like a thank-you note, call, or visit to say, "Your gift was very important to us." In the following sections, we offer some ideas for acknowledging your donors' contributions.

Meeting your donors' expectations

What do major givers want to receive in return for their gifts? For one thing, they want personal contact with your organization. Personal relationships are especially important at the major giving level. Donors want to be sure you know who they are. They want to be recognized as higher-level participants than the donors who send in the $25 check once a year to your annual fund. The following list details some of the things major givers expect when they give a major gift:

- ✔ **Confidence in the board:** Your major givers are more interested in the makeup of your board than people who give at a lower level. They feel better about making sizeable contributions when they have confidence in the leadership and fiduciary responsibility of your organization, the chairman, the executive director, and other board members.

- ✔ **The efficiency of the management:** In addition to confidence in the board, major givers want some assurances that the organization is well run, efficient, and dedicated to fulfilling its mission. No one wants to donate a large sum of hard-earned money to an agency that may dry up and blow away next year.

- ✔ **The credibility of your advisory board:** Some organizations cultivate an honorary or advisory board to offer insight, perspective, and credibility to the board. Though these individuals don't do much in the way of leg-work, having their names on your letterhead can be impressive.

- ✔ **Recognition:** Some major givers — although not all — want recognition from your organization, from the community, and from their peers for their support of your organization. Part of your job as the fundraiser is finding the appropriate recognition that will be meaningful to your donors.

- ✔ **Personal contact:** We've already said this, but it's important enough to say again — your major givers want to hear from you. Notes, calls, and visits all say to a donor, "You're important to us and we want to keep you informed about what's going on." By giving at high levels, major givers make a significant commitment to you, and they most likely expect an equal commitment from your organization.

- ✔ **Financial advice:** Some major givers may want some professional assistance before their gifts are complete — from their lawyers, financial planners, or a foundation executive. Have someone on your staff or board who can speak knowledgeably about planned-giving instruments and tax issues complement, not replace, your major giver's own financial counsel.

Some community foundations are able to give donors tax and financial advice when they consider major gifts. Check your area to find out about workshops given by your local community foundation that may help train development staff and/or your board on tax and financial issues.

✓ **A way to extend the gift:** Often your major givers are business savvy and like the idea that their money goes even farther than a simple gift. For this reason, challenge grants are popular as major or lead gifts. (A *challenge grant* is a gift a giver gives to an organization that is contingent upon the organization raising a matching amount from other sources.) Your major givers may like the idea that the money they provide "starts something" and grows into two, three, or four times their initial gifts. (See Chapter 21 for more details about these gifts.)

✓ **Family honor:** Many families make major gifts not to secure recognition for themselves but to memorialize a family member who had an affinity for a particular group. Often these major gifts are made to endowment campaigns with the idea that the endowment then provides an investment so that the organization receives dividends to secure its existence in the future. In a recent creative recognition effort, a leading museum added a dinosaur exhibit, and the major donor contributing to the campaign named the dinosaurs for her grandchildren. Think outside the box when you look for naming opportunities — your major givers will love what you come up with if the connection is right.

✓ **Involvement in the community:** Giving a major gift may put a donor in a new social group or in a new light in a particular social group. For example, if a family is new to an area and has an affinity for a certain cause, giving a major gift may help establish the family in that area as an advocate of the arts, human services, or some other cause.

✓ **Immortality:** Many major givers have the desire — and the means — to do something significant, to leave the world a better place than they found it, to use their wealth to build a better future. If a donor's name appears on the new library at his local university, he doesn't have to worry too much about whether he has made his mark on the world. The feeling that you've changed the world for the better by being in it is something most people would like to experience at some point in their lives — your donors included.

Peer-to-peer contact is the best way to approach a major giver. For example, if Joe is the president of a local bank, prepare and send your board president, a company CEO, or a board member who is similar in professional and social standing. How exactly do you motivate the board member to do this kind of soliciting? Plan a board retreat that focuses on approaching major givers and helps board members get comfortable with their fundraising roles. For more on dealing with your board, see Chapter 5. For more about the nuts and bolts of asking for major gifts, see Chapter 10.

Providing donor recognition

Imagine that you're about to receive a major gift. Mr. Smith listened to your presentation, liked your ideas, and is receptive to your suggestion that he donate $20,000 over the next three years. Now you're back at your desk, soaking up your success. Enjoy the moment — for a moment. But then take the time to ask yourself, "Now what?" When you receive a major gift, or the promise of a major gift, you need to acknowledge the donor right away.

Providing recognition to your major giver is as important as all the steps you've taken leading up to the point of receiving the major gift. Remember that getting major gifts is about building relationships. So by receiving Mr. Smith's $20,000 gift, you've agreed to accept and be accountable for Mr. Smith's gift — and his involvement — over the next three years. In effect, you've said the following:

- "We value *you* — not just your money."
- "We'll use this donation wisely, as promised."
- "We'll be good stewards of this gift and be accountable to you for it."

In addition to keeping the promises you make to your donor, you need to recognize your major givers in other ways, such as the following:

- Write a handwritten thank-you note on very nice stationery.
- Follow up by calling your donor.
- Make visits or have lunch with your donor periodically.
- Get your donor involved in high-level donor affairs, such as preview parties, soirees, grand openings, open houses, and so on.
- Assign the donor to a board position or committee seat.
- Name a program, a building, a garden, or an evening after the donor.
- Invite your donor to focus groups where you discuss the future of the organization.
- Send invitations to your donor for special events, such as seeing the birth of a baby elephant, going backstage to meet a violin virtuoso, or traveling with a select group to see a renowned speaker.

Sometimes finding enough unique naming opportunities for which to recognize donors can be a challenge. One group we work with found a solution by naming items in their office area, such as the elevators, a meeting room, and so on, after particular donors. The only wrinkle here is figuring out what to do when the organization outgrows its current building and moves to a new office. If the office has no elevator, the development officer will have to come up with some creative alternatives to protect the agency's relationship with that donor.

Chapter 10

Asking for a Major Gift

*D*oes the title of this chapter put your stomach in knots and raise your blood pressure? If so, you're not alone. It's not unusual for people in fundraising, both experienced and new, to dread that oh-so-frightening one-on-one conversation with the donor when it's time for "the Ask." When you're going after a major gift, you eventually have to face the terrifying moment when you actually ask the donor for money. The stage is set. The spotlight is on you. Your tongue feels like it's the size of Nebraska, and you hope the donor doesn't notice that your hands are shaking. What's worse is that you're highly aware of the tumultuous economy and the impact it has had on almost everyone you know. Where on earth will you find the chutzpah to ask your donor for what your organization needs?

This chapter gives you a look at that terrifying moment and puts it in perspective with some basic management techniques for recognizing and responding to the challenges of asking for a major gift.

Pushing through the Fear by Focusing on the Greater Goal

The bad news is that sooner or later you have to push through your fear of asking people for money. The good news is that eventually "the Ask" gets easier, you get somewhat used to it, and being prepared, relaxed, and tuned in to your organization's mission really helps. In this section we address some common qualms and explore ways to make you more at ease as you do "the Ask."

Accepting that you have to talk about money

The fear of asking for money has numerous roots, many of which are completely understandable. First, money is still considered one of the big taboo subjects in society. You just don't start asking personal questions about money in polite company. It's none of your business how much one person makes as VP of his company or how much another has in her savings account . . . unless you happen to be raising funds for an organization that you (and potentially those two people) care deeply about.

No matter how you feel about asking for money, keep in mind that developing a fundraising system typically takes the work of many people for many months — it's not a one-man show — which means you're not the only one who has to face "the Ask." And by the time you get to the point when you're ready to ask a potential donor for a major gift, you'll have done considerable legwork and research on that donor and his relationship with your organization, which means you'll feel more comfortable and determined than you think when you finally reach the "Ask" (see Chapter 7 for more about researching your donors).

As you get ready to ask a donor for a major gift, keep in mind your organization's main goal (which is to further its mission in your community — not to get big bucks from rich folks). Remember also that you've laid the groundwork in your relationship with the donor up to this point, so chances are that he or she is anticipating the ask. Two tips to help you stay focused on the work at hand instead of getting blindsided by the money issue are:

- ✔ **Remember what's real.** Money is an exchange mechanism, and you're helping your donor participate in a charitable effort he cares about. Both your organization and the donor get something out of the donor's major gift.

- ✔ **Think about the other person.** Devote yourself to helping the other person give, not to taking his money. If the donor is concerned about something, help him allay those concerns. If he doesn't think it's the right time for him to give, help him explore why and try to find out whether other giving options are possible. If you focus on the giving rather than the getting, you can focus on the donor instead of just money.

We talk more about perceptions of money and how to deal with them in the later section "Checking Out Your Attitudes about Money."

Understanding that no doesn't equal failure

Another reason some people dread "the Ask" is because they have a fear of hearing no. For these people, perhaps no feels like a personal rejection or like the end of the line. Maybe no is one more nail in a fundraising campaign coffin.

Well, we're here to turn all those ideas on their heads. No only means what you make it mean — and we suggest that when and if you do hear a no, you think of it as *not yet* instead. If you continue respecting your donor, honoring your relationship, and listening to what your donor *does* want to do for your organization, that no will likely bring you one step closer to an eventual yes. Keep these tips in mind:

- **Go for a yes, but realize that you can live with a no.** Expect that the donor wants to make the donation, but remind yourself that a no isn't personal and has more to do with the circumstances and mindset of the donor than with anything you say or do.

- **Turn a no into a not yet.** The donor-agency relationship doesn't end with a single no. The relationship you've taken the time to build will continue whether or not the donor makes this particular gift. Keeping this idea in mind can help you remember what's important about what you're doing — building relationships and matching the right people with the right causes at the right time.

Throughout this chapter, you find out how to listen to noes with a different ear and to recognize new possible outcomes of hearing no. You also find out when to bargain down and when to regroup. We ask you now to change your attitude that no is a word to be feared and to consider how a no can lead to a yes.

Can't ask right now?

If you're tempted to delay asking a major donor for a gift — even though you've been working up to it for weeks — because of the pitching economy, reconsider. As we mention in Chapter 9, major donors are feeling the pinch like everybody else, but they also have plans in place to help them weather the economic flows successfully. Good times or bad, the major donor still has a giving plan in place and is still looking for organizations to support — your organization may as well be one of them.

Listen to your donor's signals, of course, but don't scrap your plan just because of the doomsayers on CNN. Go ahead and keep the appointment, work your plan, and hope for the best. Your donor will let you know if your request is outside the realm of possibility right now, and then you always have the option of bargaining down.

Remembering that you're a donor, too

A cardinal rule of fundraising is: You must be a giver yourself if you're going to ask others for major gifts for your organization. Before awarding grants, foundations want to know that the board is a 100 percent giving board. Being a fellow donor carries a lot of weight for you and your organization, and even if donors never know whether you give (few people actually ask), you'll be more comfortable knowing that you're asking another person to do something you're willing to do yourself.

Spending some time thinking about your own giving patterns can be a helpful way to prepare for meeting a major donor. John remembers his father coming home for dinner after volunteering at United Way. His father said, "I spent the whole day looking at budgets for nonprofit organizations. I never knew what all these different organizations did. And I decided maybe I ought to be a giver." Having had that experience in his early childhood, John recognized the value of giving from his father, and that experience became one that built his own habit of giving throughout his life.

Keep in mind that your giving doesn't have to be on the same level as the gift you're asking for, although it helps enormously with major gifts. For example, if one CEO approaches another and says, "I'd like you to join me in being a member of the Chamber Society," the message is that the asking CEO already gives at that high level and that the other CEO is being asked to donate at the same level. This comparison serves as a kind of endorsement for the prospective donor, and if the peer-to-peer relationship is such that the donor respects the asker, this endorsement sets up a natural yes.

So you can see that *being* a giver is an important part of requesting donations from a major giver, but should you ever divulge how much you give? Although the answer may vary from donor to donor, one subtle way to handle this issue is to have your organization's giving levels ready to show the donor. You can say, "My wife and I give at this level, and I was hoping you would do the same," while pointing out the appropriate category. That way no dollar amounts are named and the donor is invited to consider a specific amount. And, of course, you can always bargain down if you need to.

Checking Out Your Attitudes about Money

Before you can change your attitudes about money, you have to understand them. So what does money mean to you? Here's a little true-or-false quiz that can help you see which attitudes about money are floating around in your head. Some of these attitudes may actually be stopping you from confidently asking for major gifts before you even pick up the phone to set up a visit.

True or False: Money is an exchange mechanism

True. Money provides a means of exchanging one thing for another. The money exchange goes something like this: "I trade what I do for society with what other people do for society." Everyone has something valuable to give, and people today use money as the means of exchanging that valuable something. Although people have been debating alternatives to the current form of currency for some time, it beats carrying around a load of shells!

True or False: Money is the root of all evil

False. Money, being simply an exchange mechanism and not good or bad in itself, can't be the root of anything. (And besides, the real quote is "The love of money is the root of all evil.") *People* do bad things in the pursuit and protection of riches — you can't blame money.

Believing money is the root of all evil no doubt influences the way you expect your donor to respond — so no wonder you're afraid to ask! It's time to change your attitude about money and to begin to see it as a simple means of transferring things of value from one person to another — in your case, from one person to your worthwhile cause.

True or False: Money can't buy happiness

True. Money *can't* buy happiness. Many people use this common saying when they don't have quite as much money as they'd like and they feel that riches are just outside their grasp. "Oh well," they sigh. "Money can't buy happiness anyway." Although this saying is true, don't go to meet your donor with this outlook in your mind. If you do, you may be more likely to think something like, "Why is she giving to us, anyway? Is she trying to buy her way onto the board?" And these thoughts aren't the positive ones you want to fill your head with as you approach "the Ask."

Does it matter to you why your donor gives? It shouldn't. You don't want to accept a gift you know to be unethical or illegal, of course, but because donors give for so many different reasons — desire to help, self-aggrandizement, recognition, status, and so on — it's not your job to judge the giving that goes on. Focus on the good your organization does and resist the temptation to second-guess your donors' motives.

What do you think of the wealthy?

Just because you're on the asking end of the fundraising equation doesn't mean you're not wealthy yourself. In fact, peer-to-peer fundraising, as you find out later in this chapter, is the most effective means of approaching a major donor for a donation. But exploring what you think of people who have more money than you do helps you expose and weed out any negative thoughts you have (jealous or otherwise) that may get in the way of effective asking.

You can expose your hidden wealth prejudices by finishing the following statement with whatever comes to mind:

"People with a lot of money are _____."

How do you fill in that blank? You may come up with any number of words:

✔ Controlling

✔ Happy

✔ In a position to help others

✔ Lucky

✔ Miserly

✔ Open hearted

✔ Powerful

✔ Power hungry

✔ Successful

✔ Talented

✔ Unhappy

Think about whether your responses are largely positive or negative; if they're negative, change them. Perhaps you adopted your ideas as you were growing up (many of your money beliefs come from your early family experiences) or as you struggled over your own financial hurdles. But whatever the source of your feelings, recognize the ones that keep you from feeling strong, sure, and direct in your fundraising exchanges and get rid of them. Your fundraising abilities — and your relationships with major donors — will be better for it.

Sometimes donors may surprise you with candor and humor — and teach you something about fundraising at the same time. A prominent philanthropist was recently honored by a local chapter of fundraising executives as Philanthropist of the Year. When he got up to receive the award, he said, "I bet a lot of you people thought we just bought this award." He paused and looked around the room and then smiled. "And you'd be absolutely right," he said.

True or False: Money talks

False. Money is an exchange mechanism, so unless you fold the check up and make a little puppet out of it, it isn't going to talk.

But on some level, money truly can make things happen. In the 1980s, financial services company E. F. Hutton aired a commercial in which the narrator whispered, "When E. F. Hutton speaks, people listen." The idea, of course, is that money carries with it a certain amount of power, clout, or prestige. People with money get things done — and that idea still holds true today, even in a topsy-turvy economy.

As you consider your feelings and thoughts about money, we urge you to remember that money itself has no power. Individuals who have fortunes to manage may (and probably do) belong to certain clubs in town, frequent particular activities, and serve on selected boards. These people are real people — people with friends, people with problems, people with causes they care about and visions they'd like to see fulfilled. And these people, if their interests align with the mission of your organization, can be great potential donors — not because of the amount of power they wield, but because of the help, access, and perhaps endorsement they can bring to your mission. It's the people, not the money, who bring the power to your organization.

If you're worried about dealing with wealthier people, keep in mind that they respond well to businesslike reasons and sound arguments for spending their money on your cause. So prepare well for your pitch, make it professional, and don't waste their time beating around the bush.

Figuring Out Who Should Ask for Money

Long before you go on that donor visit during which you intend to solicit a donation, you need to figure out who does the asking for your organization. Few things look more unprofessional than a fundraising team, standing on that proverbial doorstep, unsure about who's doing what, which is why finding and preparing the right person to do the asking is key in securing major gifts. The right person ideally

- ✔ Has a peer-to-peer relationship with the prospective donor
- ✔ Is a giver himself
- ✔ Is comfortable with fundraising
- ✔ Understands that the donor expects to be asked to give
- ✔ Is a people person, able and willing to focus on building relationships with donors over time
- ✔ Is forthcoming, honest, and willing to help donors resolve any questions or concerns that may be keeping them from giving
- ✔ Is confident and secure, unshaken by a no that could be a yes down the road

Perhaps the single biggest consideration in choosing the person who does "the Ask" is the peer-to-peer relationship. If you're approaching the CEO of a corporation for a major gift, have your organization's CEO or a person on your board who's a peer in terms of social, economic, and professional status do "the Ask." Similarly, if you're approaching someone who has volunteered for the organization for a long time, send another volunteer — not a paid staff member — to do the asking. The similarity of the roles — whether those roles are professional, social, experiential, or professional — helps build a sense of trust between the donor and the fundraiser. People in unequal positions of power — a CEO and a paid staff member, for example — often have trouble reaching the comfort zone that people of like means or status share. And of course, whether the donor is asked by a peer or a staff member, an established relationship should already exist so the donor anticipates the coming question.

In the following sections, we explain how two people can work together to ask for a major gift, as well as what you should keep in mind if you're doing "the Ask" on your own.

Teaming up for dollars

Some people prefer to work in fundraising teams, which are often comprised of a paid staff member and a board member. The board member is traditionally the one doing "the Ask," and the staff member goes along for support and encouragement.

The problem with the two-person approach is that some donors may feel "ganged up on" if they're put in the minority. For this reason, you need to always be explicit about your intention to visit as a team: "Diana has a brief presentation she'd like to show you about our new waterworks. Would 2:30 be a convenient time for us to come by?"

But, on the flip side, two people can be helpful in fundraising calls because

- ✔ They represent two different views of your organization.
- ✔ They give the donor a feeling that many people support the work.
- ✔ They're more likely to cover all the key points, leaving nothing important out.
- ✔ If one person is having trouble establishing rapport with the donor, the other person may hit it off.
- ✔ The second person may bring additional ideas to the conversation.
- ✔ With two people listening to the donor, they're more likely to hear the donor's perspective and respond appropriately.

Practice makes perfect. Even though your board members may be CEOs and top-level community members, they can still use a brush up on fundraising skills. Before you begin an active campaign in which your board members are soliciting gifts (or accompanying you on donor visits), reserve time to do some role-playing. Be sure to reverse the role-play so the asker also gets to play the role of the donor. Have one member act as the potential donor and one member act as the fundraiser and then switch — don't make it too easy, and have fun!

In the real world, all kinds of interruptions and roadblocks happen during fundraising calls, and the better prepared you and your board members are for them, the better the outcomes will be. With this idea in mind, in one of our role-playing sessions, we had the "donor" keep answering an invisible phone on his invisible desk during the meeting. The "fundraiser" could barely get a sentence out without an interruption. In the meeting, we laughed, watching the "donor" frazzle the "fundraiser," but we knew how helpful this practice could be for our fundraisers.

Flying solo

If you choose to go on your fundraising calls alone, you have a number of factors working in your favor:

- ✔ You're the only one responsible for doing the preparation, which means nothing (hopefully) will fall through the cracks.
- ✔ You have a good chance (assuming a peer-to-peer relationship) of reaching a comfort zone with the donor on a one-to-one basis.
- ✔ You won't feel that anyone is looking over your shoulder.
- ✔ You can go with your instincts to direct the flow of the conversation.

But, on the other hand, the amount of responsibility you carry on a solo visit may be a bit heftier. For example:

- ✔ You have to be careful what you promise — no one checks and balances you but you.
- ✔ You can't ask an informed third party how well you did in the call.
- ✔ You rely on your own facts and figures, with no one to back you up (so you'd better know your stuff!).
- ✔ If the donor call doesn't go well, nobody can help you out of it but you.

Developing the Mechanics of Asking

After you investigate some of your attitudes about money and consider who's the best person in your organization to do the asking, you're ready to get down to the nuts and bolts of "the Ask." This section takes you through the actual process and gives you tools to use along the way.

Recognizing the equitable exchange

Picture this: You have a pair of concert tickets you can't use. You decide to call a few friends to see whether anyone else can use the tickets. You dial the phone happily, feeling that special "I have something great for you!" feeling. The first two friends you call say they have other plans for the night, but they're pleased that you thought of them; the third is thrilled and accepts the tickets gratefully. After the concert, she calls and tells you all about it (it was great, apparently), and she wants to take you to lunch to thank you for thinking of her. You didn't get to go to the concert, but you did get to be part of an exchange that made another person happy, which can leave you with a pretty good feeling.

Why does your role in fundraising have to be any different than the situation with the concert tickets? Granted, you aren't giving away concert tickets (unless, of course, you work for a symphony and are giving them to your high-level donors), but what you're offering your donor is as important and as valued as a nice gift.

Fundraising isn't just about getting money from people who have a surplus of it. It's about matching caring people with the organizations that support the areas they care about, whether those areas are music, art, human services, education, civic affairs, or health.

Using the tools of the trade

Until the advent of the Internet and digital everything, the standard tools of the trade in fundraising involved a lot of costly, slick, four-color print brochures and annual reports. You may still have some professional leave-behinds to give to your donor, but you may also take along a laptop with a PowerPoint presentation.

At the very least, you need to take the following items with you to any visit during which you plan to do "the Ask":

- ✔ A card or brochure showing your giving levels
- ✔ A presentation (if you're using your laptop), brochure, or report that tells the story of the difference you make (You can get more details about putting these materials together in Chapter 11.)
- ✔ Pledge cards

Taking a laptop to a presentation may be a hip and low-cost way to tell the story of your organization, but not all donors will like it. If you use the laptop to display the presentation, be sure to close the laptop and place it on the floor after you finish the presentation so that it isn't an obstacle or a distraction between you and the donor while you're chatting afterward. Also, be sure to rehearse your presentation in the office before you show it to your donor. Recovering from technical glitches and then moving to a successful ask is a huge challenge.

Knowing the donor

By the time you reach "the Ask," you should know the donor well. Consider the answers to the following questions as part of the preparation for your donor visit:

- ✔ How long has the donor been giving to your organization?
- ✔ Why does she care about your cause?
- ✔ How much has she given in the past?
- ✔ How did her past donations help the clients who receive your services?
- ✔ What are her key interests?
- ✔ Which of your programs are aligned with her key interests?
- ✔ Have you prepared to ask for a donation in one of those key areas?
- ✔ How much are you asking her to contribute?
- ✔ What do you expect her concerns to be?
- ✔ How will you address those concerns?
- ✔ What recognition opportunity will be meaningful for the donor?

We can't say this enough: The more you know before you ask, the better experience both you and your prospect will have, and the more likely your prospect will be to see the match between your mission and her interests. Check out Chapters 7 and 8 for more about getting to know your donor.

Focus group for donors: "Why do you give?"

When you prepare for a major giving campaign, consider having a donor focus group to help you discover why people give to your organization. You may already know the main reasons, but revisiting the question "Why do people give to your organization?" from time to time is worth your effort.

Get some of your active donors together — perhaps over a simple lunch. Ask, "Why do you give to our organization?" and keep track of the answers you get. Most likely, you'll get a wide variety of reasons and you just may discover a thing or two about your organization — and the public's view of your organization — that you didn't know.

Checking out each step of "the Ask"

You can break down almost every process — including the process of asking for a major gift — to a simple step-by-step procedure. The following steps can help you navigate the safe areas for conversation and comfort-building as you ask a potential donor for a major gift:

1. **Open:** 3–5 minutes

   You know about the introductions bit. As you're walking into the meeting, you and the donor both talk about the weather. You also mention how great the irises looked outside the conservatory this spring, which provides a segue into the next section of your conversation.

2. **Engage:** 5–20 minutes

   "Have you ever been out to see the gardens in full bloom?" you say.

   "No," says the donor.

   "Oh, this year we included 14 new varieties of hybrids," you continue, which enables you to spotlight a few of the things you did with the donor's contributions to the Flower Fund last year.

   The point of this step is to truly engage the donor, to understand where she's coming from, and to find out a bit more about her specific interests right now. The engage step enables you to see where her "hot buttons" are currently, even though you may already know what she cared about last year. For example, if she comments, "I'll never give to that group again if they're going to remodel their offices with my money!" — you know she's not interested in funding renovations. You also uncover any new key interests that may help you see further how your organization's mission and her interests match.

   The most important three words to remember during this stage of the visit are "Ask and listen!" Know what questions you want to ask ahead of time so you can get a good sense of what the donor wants to know more about, what her concerns may be, and how you can resolve those concerns. Be aware of your history with this donor, but also keep your mind — and ears — open to hear new connections that may arise. But most importantly, use this step to listen carefully. Watch her face; read her body language; wait for the signs that she's really excited about what she's talking about. From that sensitive listening, you can begin to get a sense of which type of gift would most engage this particular donor's imagination and interest.

3. **Tell your story:** 10–15 minutes

   Now you're in the groove. You've set the stage, found out about her primary interests, and discovered the angle that gives you the best chance of appealing to her philanthropic interests. You now explain the program or campaign you're here to talk about. You talk compellingly about the need (which the donor should empathize with), and explain how your program or organization serves that need in such a way that gets the donor interested in being involved. During this step, you rely on the information you brought with you, perhaps handing her brochures as you talk or showing her slides of the possibilities or programs you're discussing.

During this step, don't do all the talking; it's important to stay alert to clues from your donor that she has concerns or questions. Stop and answer any questions she has. Be forthcoming and consider each answer you give as a step toward bringing the donor into a better understanding of your organization.

4. **Ask for involvement:** 5–?? minutes

   In sales terms, this last stage is called *the close.* Fundraisers are often reluctant to use sales terminology (it isn't a sales job, after all), but the result is the same: You need to ask the donor for a donation. Sooner or later, it comes down to that important question.

   You move right from your presentation to the close. "I can see that you're interested in our visiting horticulturist program — I thought that you'd be one of the people most excited about this idea. We were hoping you would make a lead gift of $15,000 to start out this new program. And, with your permission, we would like to name the program after you and your husband, Joe, for all the important contributions you've made to the garden and to the community in the last 40 years. Is this amount something you're comfortable with?"

   You've brought it to a yes or no response. If you get a no, don't panic — you still have some things to do to try to turn that no into a yes (see the "Moving Beyond No" section for more details). If you get a yes, hand the donor an elegant pen with which to make out her check (or bring out that pledge card).

As hard as it may be to remember, this donor visit isn't about you or your organization. It's about your donor and how you can provide her the service of contributing to a cause she cares about, which means you need to fight the temptation to monopolize the conversation (something that's very easy to do, especially if you're feeling nervous). Instead, sit back and listen attentively. What is she really saying? What are her interests? How can you best serve her? You best represent your organization when you truly have the donor's best interests at heart.

Moving Beyond No

Suppose that the worst happens and the donor says no. Chances are your donor isn't going to say, "No! And get out!" but rather something a little less harsh, such as:

✔ "Not right now."

✔ "I'll think about it."

✔ "I need to talk to my financial advisor about it."

✔ "I don't think that's something I'm prepared to do right now."

The most important thing to remember at this point in "the Ask" is that, in fundraising, you will get all kinds of noes and partial noes, but you can't just give up at this point and say, "Oh, okay. Well, thanks for your time."

Instead, do a little investigating to discover the why behind the no. Here are some questions you can ask your donor:

✔ **"Are you concerned about whether this is a good use of your money?"** Perhaps the donor still has some unresolved concerns about your organization that you can clear up.

✔ **"We were hoping you'd feel comfortable giving in the $10,000 to $15,000 range, but it's most important that you give a gift you're happy with. Would you like to divide that over three years, or make a smaller gift? We'd be grateful to receive anything you're interested in donating to our organization."** Maybe the amount is too large for the donor to give in one gift. Don't be afraid to bargain down.

✔ **"Would another time be better?"** Perhaps now's the wrong time for the donor to give. If the donor offers a time that would be better for her, be sure to pencil in a time to meet again.

✔ **"What can I do to help you say yes?"** Whether you should ask this question depends on the personality and mindset of the donor. Some donors don't shy away from saying no directly and may say with a wry smile, "Nothing today — sorry." But others who are more hesitant to slam the door in your face may suggest something like, "Well, if I could be sure that the funds were going to go to. . . ." If a donor gives you that kind of response, you have something to work with in terms of furthering the relationship and getting closer to the point where he feels comfortable giving to your organization.

Is it ethical to mention other people in this donor's social group who have given to your organization? Doing so may be ethical, but whether or not it's a smart thing to do depends on the donor. Some people are put off by what they hear as "name dropping." Others are encouraged when they hear that people they respect have given to your programs — as a result, those names serve as a kind of endorsement for your organization. Listen carefully to your donor, and if you gauge an interest in knowing who else has given, mention someone he may recognize and notice his response.

Dealing with the less-than-perfect call

Not all your calls will go the way you want them to. You'll have an occasional meeting when somebody is put off by what you're doing. Remember one important rule: "Don't worry about it!" Then move on to your other prospects. With the number of people you're going to see and calls you're going to make, a few of the calls may not go well.

If you remember the big picture — what your goals are — and know that a certain percentage of calls aren't going to be perfect, you can deal with the ups and downs that come with the territory. You always have the continuing opportunity to build the relationship with the donor — even though the call flopped — and to get closer to that eventual yes.

Rating Your Yes-Ability

After you finish the call, do a quick assessment to see how you did. If you did "the Ask" on your own, think about your comfort level — and that of your donor — during the conversation. Take a look at your results. Where do things stand now? Did you get the gift? Did you get one step closer to the gift? Replay the conversation and notice where you did well and where you want to improve for next time.

If you have a partner for your fundraising call, you have a built-in evaluator. After you leave the donor, ask your partner, "How do you think we did?" Hopefully your partner will feel comfortable talking about the good — and not-so-good — parts of the visit. You can find out valuable information from the insights of another person who is at least partially objective. You may want to ask your partner the following questions:

- "Did we seem well prepared?"

- "Do you think we handled the question about last year's shortage the right way?"

- "Do you think the donor felt comfortable with spreading the gift over three years?"

- "Did you notice anything you think we should work on?"

- "What aspect of the visit do you think we did best?"

After you complete the call, you need to document the information in the donor's file. Write down the answers to the previous questions, as well as pertinent facts you need for fundraising calls in the future. Even if you received the Big Gift, you need to continue to build your relationship with that donor, as you see in the following section.

Even if the meeting didn't go as planned, still continue building the relationship with the donor over the coming months. You may want to change the venue — meet for coffee instead of going to the house, for example — or, if necessary, consider sending somebody else to call on the donor. You don't want to leave a bad taste in the donor's mouth about you or your organization, and replacing the difficult meeting with a better experience afterward creates a better memory all around.

Following Up after "the Ask"

Finally, the call is over. You're driving back to your office with the nice feeling of having a $15,000 check for your organization in your briefcase. Mrs. Donor was very gracious and pleased that you approached her to give the lead gift for your new program. She likes the idea of the program being named after her family, and she wants to serve on the committee to help organize the kickoff event.

What are your responsibilities toward Mrs. Donor now that she's given her gift? You'll be faced with this ethical question over and over again in fundraising.

Donors are not just money sources. They're people with interests and passions and troubles and fears. It's not unusual to meet a major donor late in his life who has lost a spouse, and he may want to spend time talking, remembering, and visiting. When that donor writes you a major check, you have an obligation to show the donor that your relationship isn't just about money. Here are just a few ways you can follow up with a donor after you receive a major gift:

- ✔ Send the all-important thank-you note.
- ✔ Make a follow-up phone call.
- ✔ Provide information on the new program as it develops.
- ✔ Send your organization's newsletter or e-newsletter.
- ✔ Send invitations to all high-level social events.
- ✔ Set up occasional lunches or visits.
- ✔ Send invitations to participate in focus groups and/or special engagements.
- ✔ Send invitations to get involved in other organizational events the donor may be interested in.

As we say repeatedly in this chapter, "the Ask" doesn't have to be a panic-inducing event. Even if you don't get the answer you want, you can make this process a positive contribution to building the relationship between you and the donor — which is likely to lead to a yes down the road.

Chapter 11

Writing Winning Grant Proposals

. . . .

In This Chapter

▶ Defining a grant and knowing where to find grant funders

▶ Getting ready for the grant proposal process

▶ Researching grantors and finding the right one for your cause

▶ Writing an effective grant proposal

▶ Following up on your proposal and realizing what no may mean

. . . .

*T*he idea of getting a grant to help fund new initiatives, underwrite existing programs, or pay for special capacity-building opportunities is certainly something that should be on every fundraiser's radar screen. That being said, however, grant funding is *not* a quick-fix kind of funding — it requires the research, dedication, and commitment to relationship building that you invest in your major donors.

In a down economy, grant funding fluctuates depending on the funds that different foundations have available. The Council on Foundations (www.cof.org) estimates that foundation endowments fell by 28 percent in 2008, a drop of $200 billion dollars in the United States alone. What this statistic means for your grant proposal is that, to gain serious consideration from a particular foundation, you need to be both realistic in your grant expectations (because the grants given may be smaller than you hoped) and focused on demonstrating how your organization's mission fits the foundation's giving initiatives. For example, in a booming economy, when foundations have ample giving capacity, the programs funded may fit the foundation but may not demonstrate the highest overall attunement to the foundation's goals. When funds get tight, however, only those programs that precisely match the foundation's goals survive the cuts.

Are you discouraged yet? Don't be — even in down economies, you can find funding from granting organizations all over the country. Just be sure to begin your grant search and proposal preparation with your feet on the ground. Your challenges will be in finding the right foundation to fund your program and articulating your mission as clearly and engagingly as possible so the foundation can clearly see you're working toward the same goals. You also need to think carefully through each step of the grant proposal process. And that's just what we help you do in this chapter.

Getting a Grip on Grants

At its most basic level, a *grant* is an award of money given to a charity or an individual. Nonprofit organizations receive grants for a variety of purposes: to start or run programs, to build buildings, and to build strategies. No matter what the purpose, all grants have a common theme — generally, a grant is freely given, which means you don't have to repay it.

One exception to the free-grant theme comes in the form of *program-related investments,* which are actually loans that further the missions of nonprofits. Foundations treat program-related investments like any business investment and expect to be paid according to the terms established between them and their grantees, sometimes with interest. For example, a large foundation may fund a community organization designed to provide low-income housing. As the housing organization is paid for the housing it provides, the organization repays the foundation from which it received funds to provide the housing in the first place. To make a program-related investment a businesslike arrangement, the foundation may charge interest (2 percent, for example, which is considerably below the standard rate). Charging interest isn't mandatory for program-related investments, but some foundations feel that paying interest — even if minimal — is part of the discipline of repayment.

Identifying Different Grant Givers

Grants can come from a variety of sources. When you begin your grant research, think about which of the following sources may be most likely to "catch the spark" of your organization's mission:

- ✔ **Government agencies:** These agencies comprise a large percentage of the sources available for grant seekers.

- ✔ **Private foundations:** These foundations award grants that are consistent with their own mission and interests. Check your local philanthropic library for sources that provide information on current private foundations in your area.

  Be sure to check the Foundation Center Web site (`http://foundation center.org`) for information related to private foundations.

- ✔ **Corporate foundations:** These foundations give grant awards to charitable organizations that seek funds in their areas of focus. The corporate foundation is often driven by employee interest and focuses on funding programs in areas where the corporation has a presence.

- ✔ **Family foundations:** These foundations are organized and managed by family members, a board of directors, or a trustee. They make grants in accordance with the mission of the family foundation.

✔ **Community foundations:** Community foundations, which make up the fastest growing group of foundations, are local foundations set up to make grants for community-serving programs and projects. This type of foundation is a special kind of foundation under the law, designed to be a place for people in the community to leave a lasting legacy. A community foundation's first obligation is to its donors and then to the good of the community. It uses monetary donations either for the designated purpose that the donor requests or for the general improvement of the community. These foundations are trusted recipients of people's legacies. The boards of community foundations tend to be staffed with people in the community who have a high moral sense.

Choosing the Right Project to Get Funded

What kinds of projects can you get funded through grants? Part of the answer to that question depends on the funder you approach. Different grant makers are open to different types of programs, which is one reason why you need to research your potential donors, including foundations, carefully before making that first contact. In the following sections, we list some general categories for which grant makers award grants.

Starting from the ground up: Seed money

Because everybody loves a great idea, getting *seed money* — the startup funding you need to launch a new program, extend your adult day-care program, or host this year's job fair — is probably the easiest type of funding to gain through grants.

As you begin to research and approach foundations, you may grow accustomed to seeing the phrase *no operating support,* which means don't even try to approach the foundation for funds to continue the good work you already do. Some foundations are exceptions to this rule, but most foundations don't want to fund your day-to-day operating expenses.

Why are foundations unwilling to support the ongoing good work they're willing to fund at its startup? We have a number of possible responses to that question, but the predominant one is that foundations like to "see" the good they do — their purpose is to help you start a new successful program that will sustain itself down the road. For example, if you start a new program with a foundation's grant funding, or if you create a new computer lab in your school with the grant award, the foundation can see exactly where its money went and get a positive sense of carrying out its own mission. Using grant funds to maintain an already-running program doesn't give the foundation the same do-good sense.

Are you starting a new organization? The amount of startup funding you're able to secure for operating expenses speaks volumes about your ability to create and sustain your mission. Do your best to have two years of operating funds before you open the door — doing so will be quite impressive to any grant maker you approach.

Expanding your reach: Program funds

Program funding may be slightly different from seed money in that you can often get a grant award to continue an existing program if you're trying new things with that program. Mother's Helper, for example, is a small nonprofit organization that helps teen mothers continue their education while learning about basic parenting skills. Mother's Helper plans to add a mentoring component to the program that will require additional volunteer solicitation and training, marketing costs, and so on. The development person who writes the grant proposal at Mother's Helper needs to address this new component in her proposal.

Foundations look for the possibility of replication in the programs they fund. In other words, if a foundation funds your program, it wants to know whether your program "has legs." Teach for America is one example of a nonprofit organization that replicated in a dramatic way, growing exponentially as it spread across the country. If the foundation you're approaching for a grant can fund one program and watch the good spread to many places, it's more likely to show an interest in your program and the possibilities it presents.

Grants: Just one piece of the fundraising puzzle

The hallmark of your fundraising program is its staying power, not its grant awards. Although your good ideas may touch many lives and improve conditions for your community, if you don't address the economic factors that enable your organization to sustain itself over time, your mission will always be dependent on that One Big Grant to keep it alive another year.

Staying power is one of the best reasons for seeing your various fundraising efforts as an interrelated whole. If your donor base is strong, your donor list is up-to-date, and you're continually cultivating major donors, and if you run a successful annual campaign every year, use your resources, and build relationships with individuals, corporations, and foundations, you can reap the income you need for operating expenses from the results of your healthy fundraising system. In that kind of fundraising system, grant awards can give you the working capital you need to be creative, to launch new programs, to try new things, and to build on the solid foundation of your other mission-related activities.

Building for the future: Capital campaigns

Capital campaigns fund new buildings, which makes *capital funding* another great way for funders to see the good their money does in a concrete way (pun intended). Capital campaigns enable funders (and donors and board members) to create something from nothing. From an idea, to a plan, to a model, to a reality, the capital campaign gives funders the opportunity to participate in an organization in a big way by creating the future of the organization and perhaps realizing an important naming opportunity for themselves.

Raising money for a building that's already built is tough to do. Recently, a museum erected a new structure. The building was exquisite and the city was pleased with its new structure, but, when the organization began raising money to help pay for the already-built building, the general response was, "Well, you obviously didn't need our money to build it!" Better to let people in on the opportunity to help with funding when the building is still a dream — then everyone can share in the excitement as the plans progress. You can attract a lot more investment and support — financial and otherwise — when you allow your donors to participate in the building process as it unfolds rather than when you go to them after the fact and ask them to pay for this really great building that you built without them. (For more info on capital campaigns, see Chapter 20.)

Laying the Groundwork for Grant Seeking

If you've never prepared a grant proposal, you have a wide-open — and exciting — field before you. If you (or your organization) have been applying for and receiving grants for many years, you have a track record you can review, revise, and reuse.

As you prepare to build a grant-seeking program either from the ground up or from an existing program, you need to consider several key ideas:

- ✔ Is your board ready to begin seeking grants?
- ✔ Do you have leadership in place to head up the grant-seeking effort?
- ✔ Have you thought through a strategy for grant submissions?
- ✔ Are you ready to administer grant monies and report back to the grantor on their use?

Although applying for grants haphazardly is possible — and sometimes, by a fluke, profitable — your efforts pay off better when you develop a strategy for your grant seeking. You find out how to create a grant-seeking strategy and how it fits in with the grant application process in the following sections.

Turning to your board for support

Some nonprofits have huge boards with multiple subcommittees, a full development staff, and an army of volunteers; other nonprofits have a small board, no paid staff, and few volunteers. If you're a one-person development shop (whether you're paid or unpaid), turn to your board to provide good leadership for your grant-seeking program (and your other fundraising functions, as well).

Even if you have few resources, your board leadership should be willing to help you (1) identify grant possibilities; (2) gather the information you need; (3) locate potential funders, opening doors when necessary; and (4) provide the input you need to complete the grant application and submit the proposal.

Having good leadership for your grant-seeking program is important for another reason, too: Any foundation thinking about funding your good work wants to see evidence that you have strong leadership from the board before it awards you any grant. Strong leadership often includes being able to report that 100 percent of your board gives financially to your organization.

Developing a grant proposal writing strategy

What should your grant-seeking strategy look like? Most importantly, the grant-seeking portion of your fundraising efforts needs to be only part of the strategic whole — not the sole object of your efforts. During different portions of your year (depending on the time and people resources you have available), you need to focus on different aspects of funding. You must continue to contact and cultivate donors throughout the year, no matter how many other fundraising activities are going on. Although seeking grants is an important part of fundraising, it can never replace face-to-face visits and donor contact.

As you begin to plan your grant-seeking strategy, remember to use all the resources at your disposal. You can ask for help from your board, hire an outside grant proposal writer, take a class in grant proposal writing, and even use portions of grant proposals your organization has previously submitted (be sure to go over any recycled content thoroughly, though, to make sure it fits your needs today). Track your grant research in a database so you have a ready file of good foundational fits for grant possibilities in the future.

The grant-seeking strategy you create is just a general road map for your fundraising plan. Throughout the year, you may hear about new grants being offered by ABC or XYZ Foundation, and you don't want to skip applying just because it doesn't fall into the grant-seeking schedule you created! You need to take advantage of any grant possibilities that come to your attention — especially when they look like a good fit for your organization. As a general rule, though, planning time to focus on building your grant program helps you concentrate your energies where they're most effective. And even though your actual grant-seeking program may look very different from the ideal one you draft at the start, having a plan gives you something to get the ball rolling.

Looking at the grant process, step by step

Your board is ready to apply for grants, and you have the leadership and strategy in place. What's next? First, you need to understand the basic process of applying for a grant, which involves the following steps:

1. **Identify a need for which you want grant funding.**

2. **Begin to develop the idea into grant proposal form.**

3. **Research grantors to see which ones support the type of issue you're addressing.** (See the "Finding the Right Funder" section later in this chapter for more on this step.)

4. **Get current application guidelines from the proposed funder.**

5. **Write the grant proposal following those guidelines, and assemble all support materials.**

6. **Submit the grant.**

7. **Respond to any further requirements the grantor may have.**

8. **Get the grant award!**

9. **Submit any follow-up reports required by the foundation explaining how the monies were spent.**

Hopefully, the grant process follows those steps. But you must remember that not every one of your grant proposals will be funded. Being denied funding doesn't mean that (1) the funder is mean, (2) your proposal is bad, or (3) your cause isn't worthy. Often, being denied funding simply means your proposal isn't the right fit for the funder's current focus. Or it's too late in the year to receive funding. Or the proposal didn't get to the right person . . . or any number of other things. So what do you do when you don't get the grant? Turn to the "Putting a Positive Spin on No" section for the details.

Finding the Right Funder

Where do you find all the foundations that are willing to fund your great programs? Well, you look for them — at the store, online, at the library, at the theater, and in your local coffee shop.

Sound implausible? It's not. We point you toward places you can look for grant opportunities in the following sections.

Starting your search for funders

As you begin to think about where to start your foundation research, remember the following tips:

- ✓ **Keep your eyes open.** You can find names of local and national foundations on everything from special event invitations to raffle tickets. You can then research those foundations to see whether your programs fit their funding initiatives.

- ✓ **Go to the library.** If you can get to your local Foundation Center library, great! If you can't, check out the Foundation Center online (www.foundationcenter.org). Either way, try to find foundations that make grants in your service area.

- ✓ **Check out your local donor's alliance group.** Every state has a donor's alliance group of some sort. Contact your local chamber of commerce to find out the name and number of the donor's group nearest you, and then get to know more about the funding experiences of other nonprofits that are part of the group.

- ✓ **Research related organizations.** Find out who else does what you do on the national and local levels. What kind of grant funding do they receive, and from whom do they receive it?

The best place to start looking for funders is right at your own desk, carefully reading a copy of the newspaper — especially your local business journal — and visiting fundraising Web sites. From newspapers and Web sites, you can pick up on which local foundations are making grants and what types of projects they're funding. And don't just check these sources now and then — you need to keep your eyes on the changing nonprofit environment every day. By reading your local business journal or visiting your chamber of commerce's Web site, you find out a lot about the exchange of money and influence in your city or town.

As you become aware of who funds what, you start to see names everywhere. For example, the John D. and Catherine T. MacArthur Foundation funds a number of public television programs. All you have to do is watch a local PBS station to hear the name of the foundation mentioned. Likewise, you hear about United Way agencies and the Bill & Melinda Gates Foundation funding programs all over the place. When you go to the zoo, you see names of high-level donors, including some foundations, etched on plaques, drinking fountains, and benches. When you go to the store, you may see Target or Walmart on information placards by the registers touting their corporate-giving programs. To find possible funders, all you have to do is open your eyes!

Zeroing in on your fundraising category

Imagine that you're on the game show *Jeopardy!* and the following conversation transpires:

> You say, "Categories for $100, Alex!"
>
> "Answer . . . Where one would look for grants for a local theater," says Alex.
>
> "What is Arts and Humanities?" you exclaim!
>
> "You got it!" says Alex.

When you begin using foundation and corporation reference books, you quickly realize that grants are awarded in different categories. This categorization helps foundations control the types of grant proposals they receive and helps you determine how likely a given foundation is to fund your particular proposal. You find the following nonprofit categories on grant application literature and foundation references:

- Arts and Humanities
- Civic and Public Affairs
- Education
- Health
- Religion
- Environment
- Science
- Social Services
- International

After you identify which category your organization belongs to (you may be able to be creative about fitting into more than one), you can search for the funders who grant awards in your category.

The preceding list isn't the only way to categorize organizations. The National Taxonomy of Exempt Entities (NTEE) has devised a categorization system that includes 26 different groups under 10 broad categories. You can find this taxonomy on the Urban Institute's National Center for Charitable Statistics Web site at nccs.urban.org/classification/NTEE.cfm.

Using local sources first

Although grant sources in your organization's category abound all over the globe — and they do — your best bet is to start with those sources closest to home. Sources right in your area are more likely to fund you simply because you're local. So how do you find the grant sources closest to your neck of the woods?

Start with the following local sources:

- ✔ Community foundations
- ✔ Local private foundations
- ✔ Organizations associated with the services you provide
- ✔ Local corporations and corporate foundations, especially those near the site where you provide service

A little bit of sleuthing can go a long way. Prepare to spend as much (or perhaps more) time educating yourself about your local funders as you do researching and writing your proposal. A good fit is half the battle: You can have the best-written, most exciting proposal in the world, but if you miss the deadline or submit it to a foundation that doesn't support your type of mission, you're going to come away empty handed.

Remember the importance of face-to-face meetings with major donors. Personal meetings can make a difference with foundations, as well. After you've researched a foundation and found a local funder that's a good possibility for your program, find out whether the director is open to an in-person meeting. (Often the funder publishes in its grant guidelines or in the foundation reference books whether it accepts a personal meeting as an inquiry method.) Relationship building is at the base of successful fundraising, and if you're willing to build a relationship with your local funder, you may enhance your chances of getting that grant — if not today, then in the future.

Working your way away from home

What happens when you exhaust your local fundraising options? Suppose that you received a grant for $10,000 from the XYZ Foundation to provide seed money for a job-training program your organization is starting for teens. Congratulations! After you celebrate, you realize that you're still $15,000 short of your goal. What's the next step in your grant-seeking plan? Use the XYZ grant to leverage other grants.

Resources for grant research

Use this short list of helpful funding references published by the Foundation Center as you begin your search for the right funder for your organization. But don't stop here — you can find many more out there!

✔ *The Foundation Directory 1 and 2* (online at `www.fconline.foundation center.org`)

✔ *National Guide to Funding in Health*

✔ *National Guide to Funding in Arts and Culture*

✔ *Guide to U.S. Foundations, Their Trustees, Officers and Donors*

Getting any grant at all — regardless of the size or the source — is a seal of approval for other funders. The fact that you've secured funding is an encouraging sign to those who may consider funding you in the future because it shows that someone already thinks your organization is worth investing in.

The next step after you receive one grant is to research foundations and corporations not found locally that are similar in mission to the foundation that has already awarded you a grant. Review your proposal, and revise it to mention the money you're getting from the local foundation. Then make a trip to your nearest library. Get your hands on a foundation reference book (see the list of resources in the "Resources for grant research" sidebar), and begin your search for foundations that are a good match for the program or project you seek to fund.

On the Foundation Center Web site (`www.foundationcenter.org`), you can search the Foundation Finder database to find good foundation matches. You pay a subscription fee, but depending on the types of grants you receive as a result, the price may be well worth paying.

Digging deeper to find the right grantor

Foundation and corporation reference books, as well as foundation Web sites, provide a wealth of information about the grant makers you want to investigate. But which pieces of information are important? What data should you pay the most attention to? As you dig deeper in your search for the right funder, find the following information about each corporation or foundation you're considering as a potential funder:

✔ **The types of programs the corporation or foundation funds:** Many foundations support a wide range of program areas in varying degrees. Read carefully through the program priorities of the foundations you're researching. This information helps you determine which candidates are most likely to fund your particular project and which ones are the long shots.

✔ **The average grant amount:** The reference books list both a grant range (from smallest to largest) and an average grant amount. If you're seeking $120,000, you know you're way off base when you're considering approaching a foundation with a $35,000 average award.

✔ **The number of grants awarded last year:** Obviously, the greater the number of grants awarded, the better your chances of winning a grant. Numbers can be deceiving in this regard, though, because the foundation probably also receives a greater number of proposals than smaller foundations, which means more competition for you. More important is how closely your program fits its mission and how clearly you make that connection.

✔ **The time of year, or specific date, when the organization accepts proposals:** Different foundations have different proposal time frames, usually connected to when the staff or board discusses grant possibilities. Submit your proposal in plenty of time to make the deadline.

✔ **The submission process the foundation or corporation wants you to follow:** Some funders want letters of inquiry (see the next section for an explanation of these letters); others want full proposals; still others invite personal visits. Some funders won't accept unsolicited proposals at all, so read each foundation's listings carefully! If you don't do exactly what the foundation requires you to do, even if it's just attaching some supporting document, you may lose out on the grant on a technicality.

Inquiring about Letters of Inquiry and Grant Guidelines

Most foundations today want to see a letter of inquiry before they invite you to submit a grant proposal. What is a letter of inquiry, and what should you put in it? A *letter of inquiry* is a letter (okay, that part was obvious!) you write to the foundation providing an overview of your project and requesting the grant application and guidelines.

The letter of inquiry gives the funder a quick way to determine whether your proposal is in line with their funding goals. In essence, the funder wants a brief summary of your project or program, a sense of the grant amount you're seeking, an understanding of the principal people in your organization, and a summary of how the program runs.

The grant guidelines, on the other hand, are for your benefit. They essentially tell you how to prepare a grant proposal just the way the funder likes it, which is important information to have as you write your proposal. Grant guidelines provide the following specifics:

- ✔ The mission and focus of the foundation
- ✔ Eligibility requirements for grant seekers
- ✔ The process for how the foundation evaluates proposals
- ✔ A summary of which types of projects receive funding and which ones don't
- ✔ Questions the funders want you to answer in your proposal
- ✔ Deadlines for proposal submission (including the schedule for grant awards)
- ✔ Contact and proposal submission information
- ✔ A list of the supporting materials the funder requires with your submission and in what format those materials need to be

Grant guidelines are an important road map for the grant proposal you're preparing. Some grant guidelines are available on the Web; others you may need to request by calling or writing the foundation. No matter how you get the grant guidelines, be sure to take them seriously.

Many organizations today accept, or, in some cases, require, online submission of grant applications. Check the foundation's Web site to determine its preference. Submitting online can sometimes be a lifesaver when you're up against a tight deadline.

Getting Down to Business: Writing the Proposal

After you do your research and identify one or many potential funders, the next step is to write the grant proposal. Before you start groaning, think of it this way: Grant proposal writing is the art of passing the spark of your mission on to those funders who may be willing and able to help in a big way.

As you create each element of the grant proposal, use the most compelling information from your case statement so that your proposal demonstrates the following ideas to the funder:

- ✔ Your organization has an effective solution to a real need that the funder cares about.
- ✔ You have thought through the program carefully.
- ✔ You have planned out the process to implement it.

✔ You have selected strong leadership for the program.

✔ You have been (and will continue to be) financially responsible with the program.

✔ You have a track record of accountability and will keep the funder informed of the program's progress.

Although the proposals you write may vary depending on what the funder wants to see, a complete grant proposal usually includes the following elements:

✔ Cover letter

✔ Executive summary

✔ Introduction

✔ Program needs statement

✔ Program goals, objectives, and evaluation

✔ Program budget and budget narrative

✔ Leadership, staffing, and location information

✔ History of the organization

✔ Addendums such as your 501(c)(3) letter and financial statements

How long should your grant proposal be? Only as long as it takes to convey the problem, the solution, and the facts the funders need to make their decision whether or not to fund you. Let the grant guidelines give you an idea of what length the funder expects. Some foundations ask for brief (even one page!) proposals. Others leave the length open ended. Because you want to keep the funder reading, keep the proposal streamlined and interesting. Don't restate on page 4 something you said on page 2. Tighten your words and lead the reviewer to the conclusion that you're describing a program he'd like to fund.

Ready to start writing? The following sections explain each of the elements your grant proposal package needs to include, in the most engaging, clear style you can muster.

Creating a comprehensive cover letter

Your *cover letter* introduces your organization and explains to the funder what's in the grant proposal package. The cover letter also includes any and all contact information you can provide for your organization, including e-mail addresses, your organization's address, and a Web site, if you have one.

Online resources for grant proposal writing

Check out the following Web sites for guidance as you prepare to write your grant proposal:

- ✔ The Foundation Center: www.foundation center.org

- ✔ Grants.gov: www.grants.gov

- ✔ Grant Station: www.grantstation.com

- ✔ Changing Our World, Inc., On Philanthropy: www.onphilanthropy.com

---

Providing an overview with the executive summary

The *executive summary* (also called the *abstract*) may be the single most important section in your proposal. It should be short — one to two paragraphs — but complete. The executive summary gives a complete overview of your proposal, telling the funder who you are, what need you're trying to fill, how your organization plans to respond to that need, how the funder can help you effect that response, and how much money you need to do so.

Because of the volume of proposals foundations receive, the foundation often divides them among board members or staff to review, and the executive summaries are the sections that speak to the overworked, time-crunched executives. Make your case clearly, compellingly, and concisely in your executive summary.

Ask a number of people both inside and outside your organization to read over your executive summary after you finish it. How could you improve it? Does it get to the point quickly enough? Does it say what you want to say? Use the reactions of your peers to streamline the summary so that it's as effective as possible when it gets to the funder.

Introducing your idea

The *introduction* should also be brief, explaining a little more specifically what's to come in the grant proposal. You can include a table of contents if you choose, although in shorter proposals, doing so is unnecessary. The introduction is a good place to tell the story of your organization or spotlight someone who has been helped by your services.

Stating your program's needs

Your *program needs statement* paints the picture of the cause that your organization exists to support. The content for this statement can come right out of your case statement, if that document is up-to-date. You may want to tweak the information a bit, including specific examples of people who have been helped by your organization or situations that need your help, which can help the funder "connect the dots" between the need you're describing and the real people you serve. When you explain your program's needs, you also tie together the program you're proposing and the potential funder's funding criteria. The more you can connect what you need with the funder's mission, the better your chance is of obtaining that grant.

Outlining program goals, objectives, and evaluations

The focus of this section is showing your funders how you plan to be responsible for the grant — through program goals, objectives, and evaluations. Here are the basic differences between these three concepts:

- ✔ **Goal:** Answers the question, "What do we want to accomplish?"

- ✔ **Objective:** Answers the question, "How will we accomplish that goal?"

- ✔ **Evaluation:** Answers the question, "How will we know that we've accomplished that goal?"

Foundations want to see what the outcomes are going to be before taking a chance on funding your organization. If you're awarded this grant, can you show how you will demonstrate success? Will you increase your capacity to serve the homeless by 25 percent? Graduate a greater number of high school students? Showing foundations how you plan to be successful — and how you will recognize success when you achieve it — is a key part of this section of your grant proposal.

Often foundations give you some kind of idea about what they'd like to see in a grant proposal from you. Be sure to write directly to any suggestions or questions you receive, and be able to demonstrate whether your program is replicable. Also include quantitative measures to show the results of your program's efforts.

Detailing the program budget and budget narrative

As you may expect, any funder thinking about giving you money wants to know specifically what you plan to do with it. Your *program budget* needs to show that you've thought out all the budget issues related to the project, that you've tried other sources (or plan to), and that you're willing to make investments yourself to make the program happen.

The *budget narrative* explains your budget numbers in broad but accurate terms. You don't need to walk the reviewer through every nickel and dime (nor should you include every nickel and dime in your balance sheet — rounding to the nearest dollar will do). But you do need to explain where your major expenditures will be, how you've planned for them, whom you've approached for funding, and what results you anticipate. Be as clear and forthcoming as you can be, but expect questions.

Foundations often ask for clarification on various points in your proposal. Instead of being alarmed when you get the call, be excited: The fact that the funder is taking the time to call you to clarify a few points on your proposal means the funder is interested enough in your idea to pursue it further.

Explaining your leadership, staffing, and location

You need to tell the foundation about the leadership you've selected to run the program or project. This information is very important to the funder because having good leadership is as important as having a well-thought-out budget plan, and the funder wants to know that you have the people to put your program into action. Include biographies and résumés of the key people — people in leadership roles and staff members — involved with the program, and be prepared to have them sit in on a site visit if the funder asks to meet with you face to face.

The location of the program or project gives the funder a good idea of what type of facility you have, which ties to the practicality and the thoroughness of your idea. For example, if you plan to increase teen participation in a particular program by 15 percent but you're already up against the fire marshal's limit for your small bungalow, the funder may question your plan. If, on the other hand, you have a nice facility with room to grow, the site will work to your advantage. Having an appropriate facility assures the funder that your program — and ultimately its money — will have a real impact on the need you so eloquently communicate.

Sharing your organization's history

Some grant proposal books may tell you to lead your proposal with the history of your organization, and you certainly can do so in any case if you believe your organization's history plays heavily to what you're trying to communicate in your proposal. In most cases, however, the reader skips over what you did yesterday to find out what you're doing today and planning to do tomorrow. History is important, but in a grant proposal, it's probably not the most important thing you want to communicate to your potential funder. Because you have only a few minutes of the reviewer's time, it's better to lead with the strong stuff and include the history at the end.

Your organization's history may include a long list of accomplishments and names of famous people who have aligned themselves with your mission, or it may be the simple story of a need and the people who address it. Make sure the examples of your accomplishments illustrate your ability to make a difference. Whatever your story is, remember to tell it with heart and spark.

Including the necessary extras

At the end of your proposal, you need to attach a copy of your 501(c)(3) letter from the IRS, at least one year of financial statements (certain funders may request more), and your organization's budget for the current year (not just the program or project budget that you included in the proposal). Check the funder's guidelines for any additional materials that you may need to include, such as sample marketing materials.

Following Up on Your Proposal

How long do you wait after you submit a proposal before you follow up with the funder? Until your fingernails are gone? Until you can't stand the suspense anymore?

Most funders give you an idea in their grant guidelines what to expect in terms of review time. If you're uncertain, call the funder and ask how long you should wait before checking back. You may get a "don't call us, we'll call you" response, but in most cases, the administrative assistant gives you a workable time frame. After the review time period ends, make a brief call or send a short letter to the funder to follow up on your proposal. Just make sure you stay current with your contacts, documenting your calls and the funder's responses. Most funders respond in a reasonable amount of time, and you'll most likely be contacted with questions and/or visit possibilities if a funder is actively interested.

Handling a site visit

Before giving a major grant, foundation representatives may want to visit your organization in action to see what you do. The experience of seeing the need and the work firsthand is very telling — and often inspiring.

When a foundation contacts you and wants to make arrangements for a site visit, don't panic. Simply do the following:

✔ **Relax.** The foundation isn't coming to "check up" on you or debunk your great proposal. Instead, the grantors are interested in seeing with their own eyes how

the work you do fits with their mission and goals.

✔ **Plan.** Think about what the grantors can participate in that would give them a taste for your mission. Think *hands-on experience* as opposed to *presentation.* Giving your grantors a chance to meet your clients, hang out with your teens, or hear your patrons talk about the difference your organization has made can have a bigger impact than showing them charts and figures over coffee.

And besides, who has time to sit around and worry about a submitted proposal? You have too many other fundraising duties to attend to! So, while you wait for a particular funder's response, move on to the next potential funder on your plan.

Putting a Positive Spin on No

If you hear the word *no* the first time you submit a grant proposal, don't lose hope. Remember that, in fundraising, each no takes you one step closer to a yes. Especially in times of economic hardship, the noes are likely to outnumber the yeses you receive. Some foundations may tell you they have "no money" for the program you want them to fund. You can use this bit of information to gauge interest and discover ways to make your proposal better by asking the funder this question: "Would you have been likely to fund this program if times were better?"

Ultimately, a no can mean any number of the following:

✔ The funder has already funded many programs similar to yours this year.

✔ The funder has other priorities right now. For example, you may have submitted a grant for your arts organization, but the funder is currently focusing on educational issues.

✔ The funder didn't understand your proposal.

✔ The timing isn't right, and the funder may want to wait until you're further along in the development of your program.

✔ The funder doesn't feel that your organization is at the right point in its growth to tackle the proposed undertaking.

✔ The funder isn't the right one for your organization.

No isn't the end of the world. Review your proposal to make sure it's as strong as you can make it, and try the next candidate on your funder list.

If you've at all intrigued the foundation and have established some kind of rapport, going back a second time makes a lot of sense. If you've established a personal conversation with a foundation representative, you can continue to build on that relationship for future submissions.

Seeing Your Grant as a Relationship

Finally, remember that similar to the relationships you care about and cultivate with major donors, the relationships you establish with foundations that may be good fits for your organization grow over time. Maintaining clear, respectful contact, sharing program changes and accomplishments, and keeping the lines of communication open for future possibilities may lead to funding down the road, even if the time isn't right today.

When you do get a yes from a foundation, your relationship moves to the next level. Now you likely have more back-and-forth communication as you fulfill the reporting requirements for the grant. For example, you may be asked to submit quarterly reports to keep the funder informed about your progress on the new program their grant is helping to fund. You may also have to set up and plan for site visits from foundation representatives during the years of your funding.

When a foundation chooses to fund your mission, the investment is a statement of belief and trust in your organization. Now it's up to you to do what you said you would do. Take the time to make sure your reports and other communication methods demonstrate, over time, that the foundation's decision to fund your organization was a good one.

Grant officers are very interested in programs that have the potential to go to scale. If you have a program that you feel can be extended to other locations, your grant officer may be willing to talk with you about other opportunities for funding and growth.

Part III
Telling Your Story and Building Your Brand

"The donors liked our proposal — particularly the in-depth assessment of our competition, which is who they decided to give to."

In this part . . .

*J*ust a few short years ago, you likely communicated with your donors in a fairly traditional way: You delivered your message in person, on the phone, by letter, or in your annual report and related brochures, and your donors responded accordingly. Each of these approaches had merit in its own right, but today — with the Internet, social media, PDF files, presentations, and more — the story you tell about your mission can leap off the page and come to life right before your donors' eyes.

This part of the book shows you how to bring your story to life and build brand identity, engagement, and inspiration along the way — as cost-effectively as possible — all while keeping an eye on what works (so you can do more of it).

Chapter 12

Connecting for Profits: Sharing Your Story by Print, Mail, and Phone

• •

In This Chapter

▶ Creating your communications plan

▶ Saving money by printing only what you need

▶ Knowing what to send and how to send it

▶ Soliciting your donors over the phone . . . effectively and carefully

• •

*T*hink back to the last time you were contacted by a nonprofit organization you'd never heard of. Which medium did they use? A four-color mailed brochure? A letter? A banner ad on a Web page? A phone call?

The organization contacted you to tell you its story — did it use the right medium to reel you in, or were you put off by the way the organization approached you?

Now think of an organization that you're familiar with. How does it communicate with you? By e-mail? Phone? Twitter? Letter? All of the above?

Just like the many groups that have tried to get your attention over the years, your organization has a need to be heard and remembered — for the work you do, the people you serve, and the hope you represent. Before new or experienced donors can truly understand and engage in what you do, they need to hear and connect with your story. Your organization's story brings your mission to life; it includes heart and passion; it testifies to your account-ability and stewardship; and it builds trust with your donor. This chapter is all about planning how to tell your story to maximize your communications dollar and share the inspiration as far and wide as possible.

In this chapter, we also talk about ways to share your story through print and direct mail and by phone. The other chapters in this part look more closely at other communication approaches, including writing grant proposals and growing your presence online and in the media. The bottom line when you share your story is donor engagement — when your donors are inspired about what you're doing, they naturally want to be part of your good work.

Thinking through Your Communications Strategy

Once upon a time (four or five years ago), much of nonprofit storytelling was done in print. Your annual report, case statement, and various brochures carried the weight of your story, introducing donors to the people, programs, and practical considerations of daily life at your organization. This storytelling came with a high price tag — having your materials professionally designed and printed in four colors was a costly enterprise.

Today you have many ways to tell the story of your organization. Your traditional publications can take on new, electronic life in the form of downloadable files, e-newsletters, even Webinars, YouTube videos, and Twitter blurbs. This frees you from the cost and commitment print requires, and enables you to respond quickly in a way your donors are likely to see. Creating a communications strategy that enables you to think through the different types of communications you want to send — and the format in which you want to send them — is an important part of controlling your communications budget and making sure you're getting the best return on your messaging investment. Knowing how to target just the right donor groups for specific communications is an important part of your overall plan because it helps you make sure you're sending the right pieces to the people most likely to respond to them.

Evaluating your communications costs

How much does your organization currently spend on communicating with donors? You may need to do a little research to come up with your preparation, printing, and postage costs from the previous fiscal year, but chances are you need the numbers for your budget anyway. Taking a look at the amount of money you spent to bring in additional dollars is a helpful way to determine which of your communications efforts pay for themselves and which ones don't. Use the worksheet in Table 12-1 to put your numbers together.

Table 12-1	Evaluating Communications Costs			
Method of Communication	*Cost to Produce**	*Number of People Reached***	*Estimated Cost Per Person*	*Success of the Approach*
Web site				
Annual report				
Direct mail:				
Mailing 1				
Mailing 2				
Mailing 3				
Telephone campaign(s)				
Newsletters				
E-mail				
Other				
Totals				

*Include staff time in the expenses. ** Estimate this based on the number of mail pieces you sent, less any returns you received.

Tracking your communications approaches in this way helps you think through the results you want for each category. You can also gather good data to show you how much the various methods cost you. Although the costs will vary among nonprofits and may be skewed depending on whether a simple e-mail message brings in a major gift (it's possible!), the information you gather will help you find out more about which communications methods are most cost-effective and produce the best result for your organization.

Here are a few suggestions of calculations you could do to connect your efforts to their results:

- ✔ Divide the total of your communications costs by the total number of people reached to determine a per-person communications cost.

- ✔ After a certain period of time (perhaps three or six months), you can divide the cost of a campaign by the number of new donors the method brought to your organization. This will help you determine how much this approach costs to bring in each new donor.

- ✔ Determine whether each approach provides you with a good return on your investment in terms of reaching, retaining, and engaging donors.

Considering your communications options

So what's the best way for you to tell your story? The logical answer is which-ever way grabs your donors' attention. Depending on the age and interests of your donors — and the type of story your organization wants to tell — you may use any or all of the following means to communicate with your donors:

✔ **Personal meetings:** Face to face is still a great way to communicate if you have both the time and a willing donor. Although the cost of meeting a donor in person may be low, you need to take some materials to leave behind (perhaps an annual report, a pledge card, or a brochure on the program you're introducing).

✔ **Print materials:** You can print your annual report, brochures, pledge cards, and other materials to distribute to donors and the general public.

✔ **Direct mail:** You can use print pieces to solicit for your annual fund and special projects, and you can distribute those pieces through the mail.

✔ **Telephone:** For some people, a phone call is the next best thing to meeting face to face — for others, it's an interruption and an annoyance. If a telephone campaign is part of your communications strategy, make sure you honor your state's do-not-call lists and follow the necessary steps to keep your donor's irritation factor low. (We discuss do-not-call lists in the "Knowing your no-call responsibilities" section later in this chapter.)

✔ **Social media:** Facebook, Twitter, LinkedIn, YouTube, and MySpace offer viable ways to connect with donors and keep them in touch with your mission. Chapter 14 shows you how to build your donor base using social networking.

✔ **E-mail lists:** Most organizations communicate with donors, prospects, board members, and constituents via e-mail. You can use e-mail to simply keep in touch with donors, to send out monthly e-newsletters, and much more. Chapter 15 is all about connecting with your donors through e-mail and e-newsletters.

✔ **Web site:** Use your Web site, which you most likely have already set up, to tell visitors about your mission, your programs and services, your board, and opportunities for involvement. Chapter 16 shows you how to maximize the use of your site.

✔ **Downloadable files:** You may make your annual report downloadable from your Web site. Additionally, you may offer volunteer forms, calendars, and other important donor-related documents on your site. Offering all these documents in one place allows your donors to find out what they want to know about your organization with minimal work involved.

> ✓ **Webinars and podcasts:** If you want to get really sophisticated (and save beaucoup travel bucks), consider having your meetings online using Webinars. A *Webinar* is a Web-based seminar that enables you to show presentations, chat as a group, and share your desktop with others in real time. You can also use podcasts to communicate your messages and opportunities to your donors. A *podcast* is an audio or video recording of a meeting, seminar, or lecture that you make available for people to download to their MP3 players or computers. See Chapter 19 for the ins and outs of Webinars.

Each of these communications methods may have a place in your overall fundraising strategy. Which of these methods fit your donors best? And how often do you plan to use these approaches? The answers to these questions — and others — help you lay the foundation of your communications approach.

Crafting a communications approach

The idea of drafting a comprehensive communications plan that includes all your communication goals and objectives for the year may seem daunting, but taking the time to plot your communications strategy for the year is more than just a good idea. Looking specifically at the approaches you use to reach donors can help you determine how to best reach your donors in a low-cost and far-reaching way.

Begin by looking at a yearly calendar and plotting your major communications initiatives — your annual report, your fall and spring annual fund letters, and your spring fundraising event, for example. Create a month-by-month list of all those regular initiatives and determine which communications approaches may work best for your various donor contacts. Where can you trade print for e-mail? Where can you post something online instead of mailing a packet to a donor? You may be surprised by the money you can save when you get creative about the ways you share your story with your donors. Keeping your particular donors and the types of communications you send in mind is important.

For example, in considering your annual report, you may ask the following questions:

> ✓ Will we make this report available in print, online, or both?

> ✓ Will we offer the annual report as a presentation?

> ✓ Will we offer a Webinar or online meeting to introduce the report to key donors?

> ✓ Will we use e-mail to get the report to donors?

The list! The list! Pull out your donor list!

After you decide *which* type of communication to use to tell your story, you need to select *who* will receive your well-planned communications. Your donor list, containing all the donors in your database, is a vital part of your communications approach and it's precisely where you need to start as you try to identify the who of your communications strategy.

Use your list to provide the names, e-mail addresses, and postal addresses for all the donors you contact in the various campaigns throughout the year. Your donor management software helps you collect information about donors, store ongoing information, produce targeted lists based on search criteria you enter (for example, all new donors in 2009), and produce subsets of the list that enable you to send communications to targeted groups. (We discuss donor management software and other ways to keep track of your donor information in Chapter 7.) For example, depending on what audience you want to reach, you may creatively slice and dice your list and send communications to

- ✔ Volunteers who helped with special events last year
- ✔ Directors of nonprofit organizations
- ✔ Donors who give through a specific corporate giving program
- ✔ Donors in a particular area of your city
- ✔ All donors with pets

By figuring out how to slice and dice your list, you can also be more intentional about the message you send out. For example, using your donor management software, you can create a list of all donors who haven't yet given this year and send them a special e-mail message you compose just for them.

What happens when you do a particularly successful communications campaign and one of your sister organizations wants to use your donor list? Is sharing your donor information with other organizations ethical? Will doing so make your donors unhappy? This situation is when the opt-in/opt-out question on your donor information form comes in handy (see Chapter 7). You can share the contact information for those donors who indicate it's okay to do so.

Printing Only What You Need

Although many on-a-shoestring nonprofits put printing designer-made annual reports, color brochures, and engraved letterheads at the very bottom of their priority lists, you can still publish less costly print pieces now and save printing the fancy stuff for a time when you can more easily afford it. After all, some print pieces play such an important role in your communications approach that you can't afford not to print them — even when you're on a tight budget. Here are the major must-have print pieces:

- ✔ **One- or two-color brochures:** Your basic brochures introduce your organization to people who are new to your organization. You might hand out brochures at special events, include them in press kits, or share them with your community foundation or other area agencies.

- ✔ **Pledge cards:** You will include pledge cards in your annual fund appeal letters and also have them on-hand for personal visits and special events.

- ✔ **Basic annual report:** Depending on the expectations of your donors, you may decide that you don't need to print your annual report — especially when you see the potential cost-savings. Many organizations decide to print a limited number of annual reports that interested donors can order by request, while making the report available as a downloadable file online. Because these are more high-profile than other print pieces, we devote a section to them later in this chapter.

Consider posting your printed materials on your Web site so that donors can download and print them easily. That way you leverage all the effort that went into the printed pieces, tell your story cost-effectively (by not having to print as many copies), and give donors the option to print them when and if they want to.

Do you even *need* print anymore?

Print materials can be costly and labor-intensive to produce — and with the rising cost of postage, they're getting increasingly expensive to send. With so many possibilities available for sharing information online and electronically, in PDF format, do you really need print at all?

During times of economic cutbacks, evaluating the investment you make in print and determining whether you're getting your money's worth in donor return is a good idea. That being said, however, offering your donor something in print can speak volumes for you long after your meeting is over, which is a benefit you can't ignore. No matter how convincing your presentation to a major prospect may be, your words may fade quickly from your donor's mind if you don't have something to leave behind. Leaving behind a folder with the annual report, the current newsletter, and a program brochure or two gives your donor something to review — and remember — after you've left.

Print pieces also offer several other benefits. For example, they can

- ✔ Be your communication (through the mail) to donors you can't visit face to face

- ✔ Keep donors informed and involved with your programs

- ✔ Reach new donors

- ✔ Build your organization's identity when distributed in the community

- ✔ Be included in your corporate and foundation grant-proposal packages

- ✔ Reinforce the stability and credibility of your organization

Saving money on printing

Printing doesn't have to eat up a large portion of your total fundraising budget. Here are just a few ideas on how you can save money on your printing (we're sure you can think of others, as well):

- ✔ **Print only what you really need.** Although you may want to send a personalized letter about your organization's current projects to every donor on your list, perhaps sending a simple, conversational e-mail message will do the trick. That way you may not need a full-color brochure describing those projects in detail. Or if your heart is set on the print brochure, consider going with a single-color or two-color piece to reduce the printing costs.

- ✔ **Use a full-service copy shop.** You can print at a full-service copy shop rather than a print shop and still have nice print pieces.

- ✔ **Do it yourself.** Computers, graphic design software, and laser printers have made print pieces easier and less costly than ever to produce in small volume right in your own office. Buy brochure stock at your local office supply store, and then print on that stock, using your laser printer. Use document templates in software products such as Microsoft Word or Publisher to easily generate self-mailing flyers, brochures, or business cards.

- ✔ **Try to get your printing donated.** You may be able to align with another organization, such as a local library, that can do your printing as an in-kind contribution. Or maybe one of your board members is a business owner and can donate some printing services. Ask around, and be creative. Many large organizations and companies in your area have their own printing resources and may be willing to share their resources to help your cause.

Showing progress with an annual report

Every business entity — from Fortune 500 corporations to the tiniest non-profits — has an annual report, but today's annual reports are changing a lot from those of years past. Traditionally, annual reports were slick, four-color, expensive print projects. But because of the advancements in technology and the easier and more flexible ways to share and download files today, printing annual reports isn't mandatory for many organizations. Thus, you can produce a terrific report with great content, beautiful images, and a professional layout, but save the exorbitant cost of high-quality printing and make the report available as a downloadable PDF from your Web site. Some organizations also offer their annual reports as PowerPoint presentations or YouTube video clips.

No matter how you distribute your annual report (as a PDF or as a printed piece), it still serves the same purpose — to tell both the inspiring story and the story of accountability your organization wants to share. Your annual report does the following:

- ✔ Informs donors (and the community at large) about what you've been doing with the money you've received (referred to as accountability)
- ✔ Connects leaders of the organization with the public through letters or articles included in the report
- ✔ Reviews the accomplishments of the past year
- ✔ Thanks the people who helped you reach your yearly goals
- ✔ Announces goals for next year to tell donors your plans for using their donated dollars in the year to come

No hard-and-fast rule indicates exactly what elements you must include in your annual report, but your stakeholders expect to see

- ✔ Something from the board president
- ✔ Articles focusing on successes during the year
- ✔ Your mission statement
- ✔ Financial information
- ✔ A thank-you list of donors by amount or giving group
- ✔ A list of goals for the next year

A carefully timed year-end annual report helps remind donors of all the good they did in the current year and encourages them to build on their gifts in the coming year. Many organizations print only a few annual reports to provide to those donors who still want the printed version but make their annual reports available online for everyone else who's interested. In this way, you can share your story in an attractive and compelling way with an unlimited number of people. And the flexibility and cost-savings that the electronic format offers makes it very appealing to any money-conscious fundraiser.

Taking the Direct (Mail) Approach

Direct mail has long been one of the most popular means of keeping donors in touch with the happenings at organizations. With a simple piece of mail, you can invite new donors to join your organization, tell existing donors what a difference their gifts are making, provide important information about the fiscal responsibility of your agency, and persuade donors to participate in giving clubs, planned-giving programs, and endowment campaigns.

Your overall goal with direct mail should be to draw donors closer toward the heart of your organization, with the end goal of continually upgrading them in their giving patterns until they reach the level of major givers, when possible. Direct mail casts a big net, and if you're lucky, it may bring in some donors with whom you can cultivate a relationship over the years.

The problem with direct mail is that the *open rate* — the percentage that's actually opened by recipients — of appeals is very small, which means you run the risk of wasting a lot of money on printing and postage unless you're certain your mailing list will bring a good rate of return.

Direct mail can certainly be effective in some situations. In the following sections, we tell you when a direct mail campaign may be worth the time and money, and we explain when using e-mail may be a more effective (and money-saving) alternative to a direct mail appeal. Finally, we give you some hints on what to include in your mailing.

When direct mail works: Asking current donors to give again

You may want to consider using direct mail for a donor renewal campaign. *Donor renewal* refers to the process of contacting existing donors — members of your organization or people who donated to it last year — to get them to renew their membership or commitment. Direct mail pieces are likely to be a bit more effective with previous donors than with new prospects because

- ✔ The donors know what they're getting (they were members last year).
- ✔ The donors are already in alignment with your mission.
- ✔ The donors already have a relationship with your organization.

When you offer a donor the convenience of renewing her membership through the mail, if she has had a positive experience with your organization in the past, she's likely to renew. Direct mail campaigns also make you look businesslike and efficient, something donors like to see when they're investing in your organization.

Even though you may be trying to reduce communications costs, putting a return envelope in your donor's hands at least once a year is a good idea. Donors may collect solicitation letters for a while before deciding where they want to send their donations; giving them a return envelope serves as a good reminder and makes it as easy as possible for them to give to your organization. If your donors don't respond right away, don't worry — the gift may arrive down the road somewhere, and the envelope helps increase the likelihood that it will.

The big question is this: Do you need to use direct mail — that is, real printed letters in real printed envelopes — to get that renewal you're seeking? Perhaps an e-mail would work as well, at a fraction of the cost.

When the most direct mail is e-mail

If our mailboxes are any indication, direct mail is still alive and well and on the radar screens of most nonprofit organizations. Times are changing, however, and the tightening of budgets is causing many organizations to look carefully for ways to trim expenses from their operating budgets, which is where e-mail comes in.

E-mail can be an inexpensive and effective way to reach your donors for several reasons:

- Your donor management software likely has an e-mail feature built in that enables you to sort your list and track the messages sent.

- Most of your donors are probably comfortable with e-mail and can read it at their convenience.

- Today's e-mail messages can carry images and branding, which enables you to include your logo, program photos, and more.

- Some software enables you to track e-mail open rates so you know how many donors are actually reading your message.

- E-mail enables your donor to take action immediately — by clicking a link to give electronically, sending you a return e-mail message, or going to your Web site.

 Composing an effective e-mail message is similar to writing a great direct mail letter. Be personable. Be real. Give the donor the facts, but make your call to action clear by adding a link that says *Click here to make your donation now,* for example. Invite feedback by providing a return e-mail address or adding a link recipients can click to ask a question or pass along an idea or comment.

Chapter 15 has more details about how to build e-mail campaigns and create and send e-mail newsletters to your donors. It's easier — and more cost-effective — than you may think.

 If using e-mail for direct appeals is new for your organization, test the approach with a select group of donors first. After they receive the message, ask them to send you their thoughts. Was your message clear in the e-mail? Did your recipients know what to do with it? Would they prefer e-mail or direct mail in the future? Be sure to use the feedback you receive and thank the donors somewhere publicly — on your Web site, perhaps — for the time they took to share their ideas with you.

Figuring out what to send

When you're ready to put your direct mail piece together (whether you're using traditional postal delivery or e-mail), what do you need to include? Here are the basics of what you need to include with most mailings:

- **The letter:** Write your letter of purpose in a friendly and earnest tone — telling specific stories of people your mission has helped. Some additional tips for the letter include:

  - Spend time crafting your opening sentence and the P.S. to make sure they convey the main ideas of your campaign and your organization because many people read only these elements.

  - Think carefully about who signs the letter. Someone well known or high up in the organization brings the most credibility. For example, former President Jimmy Carter and his wife write direct mail appeals for Habitat for Humanity. If you have a high-profile spokesperson, make the most of that person; even if you don't have one, think of people in your area who would enhance the credibility of the pieces you send out.

    The most effective approach in direct mail is to create the letter so that it looks as though it was sent from a person the donor knows. If the donor recognizes the name and knows the person who sent the letter, she's likely to at least open the letter as a courtesy to the person who sent it.

  - Think in terms of emotional appeal, but provide facts, too. A reader may turn away from your cause if you hit her with too much emotion too quickly. Tell the story of the need by giving the facts on how her donation can help your organization meet that need. In a challenging economy, you have the opportunity to tell the very real story of how the demand for your services is creating a greater need.

  - Keep the letter brief; to one page, if possible. Use attachments if you need to supply more details.

  - Call for action in the letter, giving the donor a specific amount to respond to (say, for example, "Your gift of $75 will help feed a family of four for three months!").

- **The pledge form:** The pledge form is the actual response form the donor fills out and returns to your organization along with her pledge or donation. Be sure to include room for the donor to correct changed contact information. Remember to also include your organization's name and bulk mail number on the pledge cards if you want donors to send them to you via return mail. (A bulk mail number enables you to send a large mailing by using the number — which shows you have paid for a bulk mail account — instead of stamping individual envelopes.) To save money on the return postage, you can get a bulk mail permit by going to your local post office, requesting a bulk mail application, and paying a small fee.

> A number of nonprofits that rely heavily on direct mail techniques use their bulk mail permit on the envelope but add a note, saying something like, "Your first-class stamp here will help us feed another family!" (when the organization raises funds to feed families). Doing so can save the organization mailing costs and give the donor yet another easy way to make a difference.

 Before you print and send your direct mail piece, pass a sample around the office and ask for feedback. Is it upbeat? Does it give the reader a good sense of the organization? Is the call to action clear? Make sure your mail piece hits the mark before you commit the funds to send it on its way.

To Call or Not to Call

Telephone solicitors have a bad reputation — and for good reason. Unwanted phone calls seem even more intrusive than spam or junk mail or magazine salespeople who knock on your front door at dinnertime. For this reason, many fundraisers have a bad taste in their mouths when they think about turning telephone solicitors loose on their donor lists. However, armed with a few good tips and some careful planning, your callers can make your telephone campaign effective. (If you want more information about dialing for dollars than what we provide in the following sections, check out *Telephone Sales For Dummies* by Dirk Zeller [Wiley].)

Making your callers the good guys

Before you can find success in your telephone campaign, you need to make sure you have the best people doing the calling. Who will make the calls? Here are a few ideas:

- ✔ **Start with your board.** Anyone interested?
- ✔ **Ask your volunteer corps.** If you have a group of positive, like-minded people, you may have a swirl of interest. If you have a collection of busy professionals, you may get a lot of people looking at the ceiling. Persuade reluctant volunteers with (1) how much good they can do for the organization, (2) how they will benefit socially by helping in a group for only a few hours on a special weekend, and (3) a promise of a reward, such as a discount on their membership renewal or an invitation to a thank-you dinner after the campaign is over.
- ✔ **Go to the people you serve.** If your nonprofit is a school or university, consider asking parents, alumni, or the students themselves to do the calling.

Calling donors and getting their data all at once

If you plan on making a significant splash in the world of telephone soliciting, you may be interested to know that the high-end telephone industry is merging audio and data capabilities like you wouldn't believe.

With some telemarketing technology, when you make a call, a computer logs the phone number; then instantly, before anyone even says "Hello," all the pertinent data about the donor and her history is displayed on your computer screen, including where she lives, how much she's given, where she works, and what

her dog's name is. (Okay, maybe not the dog's name, but you get the idea.)

If you plan to do a considerable amount of telephoning over the long-term, look into purchasing (or getting donated) sophisticated phone and data systems to help you capture, use, and maintain all the data that's available through your donor list and telephone system. These systems may be luxury items in a down economy — or perhaps completely unnecessary if you phone donors only once a year when you're soliciting funds for a special event.

After you pick the people you want to call your donors, make sure they know what to do to make each call an opportunity. Most importantly, they need to do the following:

- ✔ Respect people's privacy and call before or after traditional dinnertime.
- ✔ Call only those individuals you identify as being interested in your mission and likely to want to help.
- ✔ Acknowledge the donor's gifts and services in prior years.
- ✔ Be attentive to people's responses and engage them without being pushy.
- ✔ Care about issues people raise and attempt to address those issues or refer the call to someone in your organization who can.

The purpose of your calling campaign doesn't always have to be to ask for money. When you use your phone program to update your donor list, ask people's opinion about a new program you're thinking of launching, or simply say "Thanks" to a significant donor, you go a long way toward building your donor-agency relationship. No-strings-attached calls like these examples say to your donors, "We value you for more than just your money."

Knowing your no-call responsibilities

The last several years have seen much legislation and discussion about telemarketing. Make sure to check the latest regulations before you start a telephone campaign — we address the current scoop here. Some states have their own statutes, which may be more stringent than the federal laws. Be sure you find out about your state laws as you plan your phone campaign.

The FCC maintains a National Do Not Call Registry; however, you may not realize that it doesn't cover all types of calls. This registry prohibits only calls made to sell goods or services through interstate phone calls. It doesn't prohibit calls from political organizations, charities, or telephone surveyors.

What if you sell products to raise funds? You may still be able to call if you've done business with the person you're calling in the last 18 months. Having done business in that time period makes your relationship with that person an *existing business relationship,* in which, presumably, the recipient of the call has shown an interest in your products by buying them in the past. However, if someone asks you not to call, even if you have an existing business relationship, that's it — you can't call that person again.

One final note: Beyond your legal obligations, in the interest of your donor relationship, if you get the message that someone doesn't want to receive calls, take that person off your call list and find another way to communicate with her — perhaps e-mail would be a better option.

Telemarketing to cellphones is illegal. FCC regulations prohibit telemarketers from using automated dialers to call cellphone numbers.

Working the phones with a positive attitude

If you think a phone campaign is the way to go, here are seven principles to help you (and your callers) stay on the straight and narrow, honor your donors' choices, and maybe even bring in some much-needed donations:

- ✔ **Respect the donor.** Listen, listen, listen, and provide just the information your donor needs — and then get off the phone. Tell your story, invite the donor's gift, and respect the donor's time.

- ✔ **Be friendly.** Anticipate a good response, and smile as you dial. Remember why you're proud of your organization, and choose two or three things to share with the person you're calling. Even if the recipient is less than enthusiastic, remember that your voice and demeanor leave the person listening with a sense of your organization.

- ✔ **Prepare a script and know it well.** Know your call script inside and out before you call, and think through different types of call recipients — welcoming, surly, resistant, curious, and so on. Know what to do when the donor asks you a question not on the script. Consider the resources you need before you call, and know what to do when you can't answer a call recipient's question (refer the recipient to another person in your organization, for example).

As you prepare your script, make sure you include the following elements:

- The name of your organization

- A brief statement of your mission

- The fact that you're participating in a campaign to raise funds for a specific program and a description of what that program is

- An example sentence for you to use to ask the renewing member (or current member) if he would like to upgrade his gift

✔ **Believe in your cause.** Chances are that believing in your cause comes naturally, but you may want to reread your mission statement before you call. Think of a few real stories you can share about people who have been helped by the programs and services you offer.

✔ **Smile throughout the call.** Even if you're a bit nervous when you make the call, try to relax and smile. The recipient can hear the smile in your voice, and your message carries better.

✔ **Get the name right.** Mispronouncing the person's name in a phone call doesn't do much for your chances of getting a donation. The mispronounced name tells the listener, "This person doesn't really know me," and that creates instant resistance to your message.

✔ **Don't take a no personally.** Try to hear a no from a donor as a not yet, which may eventually lead to a yes. When you're on the phone with someone, hearing no without taking it personally may be difficult because of the personal contact, but be pleasant about the recipient's response. Remember that your response after the no is still a relationship-building moment for your donor — the way you respond makes a big difference in the way he perceives what you do.

Even when a prospective donor tells you no, recognize that you have made an impact and a personal connection for your organization. That connection helps build awareness for your agency, which may result in a donation down the road. That's why it's especially important to be friendly, professional, and accommodating. Though the person may not give today, he may be impressed by your group, which is an important part of your ongoing storytelling effort.

Chapter 13

Projecting Your Image in the Media

In This Chapter

▶ Using radio, television, print, and the Internet to get your news out

▶ Dealing with damage control on media disasters

Y ou're not camera shy, are you? Don't worry — many people are at least a little bashful, at first. But being willing and able to pursue media exposure for your organization is both smart for your fundraising program and advantageous for building the overall credibility of your cause. Arming yourself with some basic how-tos for handling, and even enjoying, media relations can give you the confidence you need to see media for what it is: a golden microphone to address masses of people.

Although working with media takes a little time and some careful and creative thought, your use of the media can go a long way toward building an awareness of and a reputation for your organization. Having an outgoing personality helps, but it's not a prerequisite. All you have to do is master a few media basics and you can communicate your cause clearly and with passion.

In this chapter, we take you through a number of media channels, helping you investigate ways to get positive attention for your nonprofit organization through radio, television, print media, and the Internet. (In this chapter, we touch on using the Internet to create awareness; we cover how to use social networking, e-mail, Web sites, and blogs in more detail in Chapters 14 through 17.)

Getting the Media Exposure You Want

Many fundraisers work day in and day out without giving a lot of thought to media coverage. If media attention happens, great (assuming it's positive, of course!), but who has time to go looking for it? When you consider the amount of time you spend researching donors, narrowing down your donor list, and educating people about your mission and your programs, however, you realize that spending just a little time planning some media exposure can pay back many times over in terms of public awareness and interest.

Here we give you an overview of how you can work with the media to promote your organization, and we offer some ideas on how to improve your chances at getting your organization's story in the media.

Realizing what the media can do for you

Not every mention of your organization has to be the lead story in the morning newspaper or on the evening news. Rather, you can use the media to let the public know about everyday events and activities your group is doing. The following list includes some other ways you can use media exposure to promote your organization:

- ✔ Prepare news releases, requests for volunteers, and event announcements to run free on the radio or on local news calendars in the form of public service announcements. (Check out the "Working in Sound Bites: Public Service Announcements" section for more details.)

- ✔ Do a television or radio interview, talking about a new survey released by your organization.

- ✔ Make your organization the subject of a feature article in your local newspaper or magazine that ties in to concerns in your community.

- ✔ Create a Facebook group for your organization or event.

- ✔ Create a Twitter feed that shares ongoing program news, announcements, and links.

- ✔ Post video clips of your programs and events on YouTube, and then post the links to your Facebook and Twitter pages.

- ✔ Create a blog to build visibility in your area of work; link to other groups, funders, and organizations that seek to meet the same need.

- ✔ Create and post podcasts as a way of sharing success stories, inviting others to get involved, or spotlighting critical issues in your service area.

- ✔ Participate in an online chat on a Web site that deals with issues in your organization's area of work.

Think of media exposure as a way to educate your community about your organization. When you run a 30-second radio spot, for example, you tell the listeners who you are, what you do, why they should care, and how they can help.

In a short television interview, perhaps on your local afternoon news program, you can

✔ Inform viewers about your organization, perhaps for the first time.

✔ Offer viewers a visual of what your organization is all about, perhaps through a video of a recent event at your facility or video clips of your organization's volunteers working with those you serve.

✔ Provide viewers with contact information so they can get in touch with you if they want to (through an on-screen display of your organization's name, phone number, and logo, for example).

✔ Allow viewers to put a face with a name.

✔ Interest viewers in your organization's current work or upcoming events.

In a print article in your local paper, you can

✔ Relate how your organization is currently addressing real needs in your community.

✔ Convey a sense of the spark of your mission.

✔ Educate readers about various programs you're currently working on.

✔ Include contact information encouraging readers to donate time, goods, or money.

✔ Showcase a success story to build confidence and trust in your work.

With Web and social media exposure, you can

✔ Establish your social networking presence.

✔ Raise awareness about a community need and your organization's relevance.

✔ Show visitors who you are and what you do (through words, video, and photos).

✔ Gather an audience by enabling visitors to become friends, fans, or followers.

✔ Share upcoming events or program announcements.

✔ Provide links that are helpful for visitors.

Getting the most of your media time

One of the challenges in getting media exposure is that you have very little time in which to relay some really important information. Take a look at these media forms in terms of the amount of time each one offers you:

✔ **Radio:** A typical PSA (public service announcement) gives you only 30 to 60 seconds of airtime.

✔ **Television:** Even a lengthy news interview may be only two minutes of actual airtime; and when you clip out newscaster lead-ins and voice-overs, you may have only one minute of real footage from your organization or your interview. More typically, you have less than 30 seconds.

✔ **Online:** When you're leading a chat, you have a longer period of time to get your main points across to your audience (up to an hour, in some cases); but the medium requires tight control — a group chat can be like carrying on 20 individual conversations at once. Moderated discussion forums and your own Web site allow you to post information and leave it there indefinitely for people to see. An online broadcast or Webcast can give you greater flexibility, but viewers tend to watch only the first few minutes of live or prerecorded content. Facebook, Twitter, and blogs offer as much content exposure as you want for as long as you want because these channels belong to you. For that reason, however, they may not carry as much credibility with potential visitors as third-party "objective" media groups may offer.

✔ **Print:** Print is a medium in which the time allotted is virtually unlimited. You may have an hour interview with a reporter, which translates into a (hopefully) good story that the reader can read again and again if she chooses. If the article appears on the newspaper's Web site, you can link to it from your own site for even greater exposure. Make sure to keep copies of print articles to make available in your fundraising packets, as well.

Making the first contact

For many nonprofits, the road to media exposure begins with a simple *press release,* which is an announcement of an event or other newsworthy item you send to press outlets — newspapers, Web sites, and TV and radio stations — in your local area. Just a few years ago, you mailed or faxed press releases to media outlets, but today the approach of choice is e-mail. In your press release, be sure to include the name of someone at your organization whom the media and/or your audience can contact about the information in the release — and make doubly sure that you've got the right address for the media recipient.

The press release approach is likely to work better if you've taken the time to develop good relationships with media leaders in your community (see the next section for details).

Just as you do with donors and grantors, find out what interests your local media and consider how you can help your needs and theirs fit together. Media people get inundated with press releases and bids for inclusion on their Web and print pages. Give them interesting information in a professional format and you'll get into their good graces — eventually. *Human-interest stories* — stories about people's successes, challenges, and needs that draw empathy and sympathy — are widely used in all media, and most nonprofits have these stories by the dozens.

Coming up with story ideas for the media

Does your local feature reporter yawn when he sees you coming? Have the radio stations stopped running your PSAs (public service announcements)? How do you get your media contacts to wake up and take notice of the good work your organization is doing?

The following tips can help you come up with stories and other media ideas that the media will *want* to run:

- ✔ **Show your role in responding to a community crisis.** For example, if a measles outbreak has occurred in your area, your Vaccines-for-Every-Child program fits right into the media hoopla. Offer to do a live interview or write an article in which you offer more details about both the crisis and your response to it. Remember the old PR line, "A good crisis is a terrible thing to waste." Get a local celebrity whose area of expertise relates to the crisis to talk about it for you. In the best-case scenario, this person is one of your board members.

- ✔ **Plan an event that links with another current-events story in the news.** For example, if you run a literacy program, plan a Read-a-Thon to occur just before school starts to fund your new reading program, and plan a Graduate Celebration at year's end to reward people who have achieved their goals through your program. These types of success stories make a nice topper to the sometimes hard-to-take evening news.

- ✔ **Look for happy media opportunities.** Suppose that someone's favorite feline climbed to the top of the tallest tree at your recent Humane Society pet show, and your board president, who also just happens to be the fire chief, climbed a ladder and got her down. Grab your camera, or better yet, alert the media, if they're close. You just might get to be the "good news" at the end of the show.

Don't create such opportunities where none exist — experienced news people can smell a plant-the-cat-in-the-tree hoax a mile away, and it can damage your relationship and your credibility with the press. Besides, you don't want to endanger a pussycat or your board president for your 15 seconds of fame.

✔ **Don't wait for the media to call you.** If you have a good idea, be willing to talk about it. Don't alienate your media contacts by barraging them with inane ideas, but when you have an interesting idea that lends itself to a good radio, television, or print story, knock on the necessary doors.

✔ **Refresh your content.** If you've been describing your organization the same way for two years in every press release, or if the paragraph at the end of your releases describing the history of your group has read the same for five years, rewrite it to jazz it up.

Working in Sound Bites: Public Service Announcements

If you aren't currently using any media at all, you may be pleased to find out that you have one completely free media avenue open to you right this very minute — and that avenue is *public service announcements (PSAs)*. PSAs are radio, television, and sometimes print advertisements that enable you to get the news out about what your nonprofit organization is doing. Are you hosting a chili cook-off next month? Preparing to release your latest community development report? Let your city know about it through a PSA.

Government regulations of the public's airwaves require that television and radio producers offer free public service announcements to local nonprofit organizations. Although many newspapers offer such announcements as part of their civic responsibility, no federal regulation requires them to do so.

Check with your local station about rules for PSAs, but be aware that most stations require you to schedule recording time in advance. Be sure to mention your organization's name, your nonprofit status, your mission, who you serve, important information about your event, and the way the public can contact you. Mention your Web address several times, and check with the station director to request a copy of the PSA so you can make it available for playback or download on your Web site.

When you talk to the folks at the radio station, request that your PSA be aired during prime listening time (6:00 a.m. to 7:00 p.m.). Often PSAs get pushed to the off-peak hours (7:00 p.m. to 6:00 a.m.) because the paying clients fill the commercial air slots during prime time, but it's worth asking for prime time. Also, don't hesitate to ask whether the station offers special deals for nonprofits buying airtime; many do.

If you're recording for radio for the first time, here's a tip: Smile as you talk. When you smile as you read, the sound of your smile carries in your voice — no kidding! Listeners will find your voice more pleasant and personable and may just end up smiling, too.

Looking Good on Television

Come on; tell the truth — you've always wanted to be on television, right? With the seemingly endless range of cable channels, the ever-lengthening morning and nightly news programs, and the dozens of talk shows (stay away from the ones that tend to have fistfights), television presents you with countless opportunities for wide exposure. In the following sections, we give you some advice for making the most of your television opportunities.

Seeking airtime on the small screen

Television opportunities aren't part of the daily fare for most nonprofits, but there's nothing stopping you from pitching your own possibilities. You could suggest TV coverage to your local station for your upcoming special event where a popular personality is appearing; follow a nightly news story with a related successful initiative you've launched; or work on a televised fund-raising campaign for your public television station. (Hey, don't laugh — you could sit at a desk for an hour answering the phone with your nametag and organization name in front of you. The message to viewers is "we help other organizations, too," which says a lot about the character of your agency.)

Preparing for a television interview

Suppose that your organization's idea has captured the attention of a local TV news producer, and now she'd like to send a reporter out to talk to you about the ranch you run for at-risk teens. Now what?

First, say, "Sure! Come on out!" in the most confident voice you can muster. Next, spend some time thinking about what you're going to say and do during the interview. Consider the following questions as you prepare for your television interview:

> ✔ **Who is the best person to talk to the reporter?** Whether the person doing the talking is the founder, the board president, the executive director, or you, make sure that person is (1) personable, (2) articulate, and (3) passionate about your organization's mission and the work you're currently doing.

✔ **What do you want to say most?** You only have a few minutes on tape. Get clear in your mind what you most want to say, and then, even if the reporter asks questions that take you in a different direction, steer the conversation back to what you really want to say about your organization.

Think success stories. Although the temptation to focus on the need may be great, remember that you want to show viewers that good things are happening at your organization and inspire them to want to be part of the good that's going on.

✔ **What do you want viewers to see during the interview?** Think through the eyes of the camera. Where do you want to shoot the interview? What does the place look like? How can you help viewers get a sense of your mission? The biggest impact comes from the picture of work actually being done, not from people talking about the work that's being done somewhere off-camera. If you have footage of your organization at work, provide it to the producer to cut away to during your interview.

✔ **What do you wear?** Dress for success. On video, busy patterns in your clothing can be distracting patterns. Avoid patterns, stripes, and bright white clothing. Your best bet is something simple and subdued. And here's a little tip: Blues work great on video.

After you make your way through these questions and feel relatively prepared for your television interview, make sure you practice, practice, practice (do we need to say it again?). Before you go on the air, try a mock interview with a friend or colleague, especially if you know somebody with public speaking or media experience. Check out *Public Speaking For Dummies,* 2nd Edition, by Malcolm Kushner (Wiley), to get more ideas on how to make a flawless presentation.

Remembering on-air cues

When you're sitting in the hot seat and see the big open eye of the camera on you (or the oversized microphones hanging above your head), keep your wits about you and remember to do the following:

✔ **Relax.** Relaxing is the name of the game. If you practice what you want to say until you know it inside and out, you can relax and be yourself during the interview. Remember you're representing good work — that in itself, not your performance, is what carries the day.

✔ **Make a good first impression.** Start your interview smiling, whether you're sitting behind a camera or sitting in a recording studio, as in the case of a radio interview. When the camera's red light blinks on, don't do a Fred Flintstone and stare blank-eyed and slack-jawed into the lens. As the producer counts down, take a deep breath and release it, sending with your exhale any negative thoughts and tensions about the interview.

Then smile and answer the questions one at a time, as they come, in the best way you know how — after all, that's all you can do.

✔ **Keep it short.** Whether you're being interviewed or contributing to a panel discussion, keep your comments brief and packed with meaning. Say what you want to say, say it smart, say it concisely, and be as clear as possible. Your audience (and interviewers) will thank you for it.

✔ **Give your audience something to remember.** Whether your audience members are in your industry or just listening casually out there in audience-land, try to leave them with something concrete they can try — a new idea to consider or a new tool to use.

✔ **Don't just tell them; show them.** If you have control over any part of the story — for example, if the television crew is sending a camera person out to your facility to film the interviews on-premises — use every opportunity to show viewers what you do instead of simply telling them.

✔ **Provide your Web address.** Chances are the show's producer will already be on top of this tip, but, if no one asks you, ask the reporter or producer whether your organization's Web address can be posted along the bottom of the screen during the interview. Most news channels also make links available on their Web site for a limited period of time.

✔ **Take the interview with you.** Before the reporter leaves, ask whether the video will be made available on the station's Web site. Find out whether your organization can embed the video on your own Web site or on social media sites. Every little bit of exposure helps.

Even in an on-camera interview, you aren't talking to a camera; you're talking to a person. When you're doing a call-in show, you're still talking to real people on the other end of the phone line. Remember that the person you're talking to is the most important person in the world at that time.

 Give each interviewer your undivided attention, and focus carefully on the subject at hand. The media feeling just falls away, and the interview becomes part of what you're so good at: the relationship building that's so much a part of the fabric of fundraising.

Taking Advantage of Print Opportunities

Suppose that getting into print is your objective. Depending on your background and the type of organization you work with, finding print opportunities may be easier than getting a slice of that coveted airtime you need for a television interview. What kind of print opportunities do you have in your area? Your local media may include daily, weekly, or county newspapers; community foundation newsletters; chamber of commerce publications; business journals; and more.

And what are all these print sources looking for? Something quotable, something unique, something people will talk about and repeat today and tomorrow, something people will come back for more of. (See the "Making yourself quotable" section for more details on how to give print sources exactly what they're looking for.)

Community foundation newsletters are a great place to break into print and get the word out about your organization. These newsletters often include features about nonprofit groups in the local area. Keeping people up to date is an important part of their objective, and they offer broad circulation and credibility because the information they publish is all related to nonprofit organizations.

A key to making good use of print coverage is to use every bit of news as another reason to get in print. If you run a playwriting competition, announce that you're accepting entries and have selected judges; then publicize the pending final deadline for entries, the judges' choices, the awards ceremony, and so on. Build excitement about longer programs and keep the public engaged.

Making yourself quotable

Editors love a good quote, and there's nothing wrong with writing a few favorites up before an interview so you have them ready. After you identify what you want to say, write a few statements that relate to that idea. Remember the elevator pitch for your mission statement? It's that simple, heart-felt statement that tells people what you do in a few short words. Your quote is a good place to put that idea into play.

A good quote sounds right, is short enough to remember, touches the heart, and includes a call to action.

In other words, your quote should almost burst with meaning and impact. A good quote will resonate with the person who hears it and reinforce what you want her to remember about your organization — your mission, your compassion, your impact.

Fixing mistakes in print

What happens when the reporter gets something wrong? He forgets to add that you're a 501(c)(3) organization, or he publishes your fundraising goal for your new campaign as $1 million when it's really only $250,000. Worst of all, he misspells the name of your biggest donor, the one who recently gave you a donation large enough to purchase art supplies for your kids for the next three years.

First, keep your cool. Next, write down the errors in the article and call the reporter or send him an e-mail message. Go over the items with him (calmly), and ask him to print a correction in the same spot in the next issue. He probably has to talk the situation over with his managing editor (in fact, you may need to talk it over with his managing editor, as well), but most newspapers are willing to correct errors that you call to their attention. And — here's a bit of good news — the correction gets your name in print again.

Choose your battles wisely. Don't be ready to duke it out over every misspelling or piece of erroneous reporting related to an upcoming event. However, if the article compromises your mission, tarnishes your reputation, or in some other way creates a negative public awareness, by all means, take your case to the editor. You want to maintain a long-term relationship with the publication, but be willing to contest false or misleading statements in print.

Leveraging Online Coverage

Today the Web is rivaling print and even television as a suitable news outlet. Newspapers are feeling the pinch, in fact, and more and more organizations are offering premium news stories on the Web as exclusive stories (instead of in print as they once did). Part of maximizing your exposure in the media definitely includes thinking through Web-based outlets for your stories and updates, which is where this section and Chapters 14 through 17 come in.

For more about creating and building social media channels — including Facebook, Twitter, LinkedIn, and YouTube — see Chapter 14.

Begin by using your favorite search engine to look for sites that talk about the following topics: philanthropy, charitable giving, fundraising, and nonprofit organizations. Search for Web sites that relate to your mission: If you help homeless teens, search with terms such as *teens, homeless,* and *runaways.* Check out the promising sites to find out

- ✔ What they have to offer in terms of information or resources
- ✔ Whether they allow nonprofits to put their own links on the site
- ✔ Whom to contact if you want to contribute an article idea or story

The following sections explain how to get stories about your nonprofit posted on other Web sites.

Posting your story everywhere

As part of your effort to gain an online presence for your organization, you can approach the editors of online versions of print publications about possibilities for feature articles. Sites such as www.msnbc.com, www.usatoday.com, or your local newspaper may be open to your ideas. Visit these sites and review their policies on article submissions.

Though the Web has global reach, don't overlook interest in your cause right in your own community. Your hometown may also offer sites that give nonprofits free exposure on the Web. The information the nonprofits provide on these sites may be nothing fancy, of course; but you can add your organization's name and mission to a page along with a link to your organization's own Web site (see Chapter 16 for more about maintaining a Web site for your organization).

Filling a need for news with news feeds and blogs

Most Web sites today don't have time to write all their own content. Instead, they use *news feeds* or *RSS feeds* (Really Simple Syndication) to pull stories from other sources and display them, or links to them, on their sites. The Christian Science Monitor and CNN are just two sites that offer news feeds, but RSS is everywhere. Some news feeds aggregate stories from many sources. The point of doing so is to multiply your exposure by getting your story placed on a site that provides news feeds of its stories to others. There are various Web 2.0 tools you can use to add RSS feeds to your site — talk to your Web designer to find out which tool would be best for your organization's site.

Blogs are another source of online information that your potential donors may read. A *blog* is simply a collection of frequently updated stories, comments, and links. Blogs are often opinionated and full of personality; in some cases, groups of people blog together toward a common goal. In fact, a number of nonprofit organizations use blogs "from the field" to share stories with various staff members around the globe. This kind of storytelling can be very effective in fundraising (flip to Chapter 17 to find out more about blogging).

Crisis Control: When Media Attention Is Unwanted

Not to end this chapter on a somber note, but we have to give you a few tips on what to do when you get media exposure you don't want. Sometimes negative things happen that the public has a right to know about, and it's the media's job to report them. For example, a board member gets investigated for some illegal activity, a volunteer dispute breaks out, or an inebriated MC hosts a special event.

Because public perception of your organization can have such a substantial impact on your fundraising, it's important to respond to this type of coverage in a direct and candid way. Choose a person with authority in your organization who isn't directly involved in the crisis to speak about the situation. Make sure that the message expresses stability, responsibility, and the wish that the good work of your organization will continue even during this troubled time. Suggest that the person reflect on the organization's mission before speaking to the press — this will help refocus the message on the ideas and approach of the organization and not the particular trouble that is currently impacting the organization's reputation in the public eye. Taking the high road now and staying focused on your long-range goal (reaching the people you serve) will increase your standing in the long-term, so weather the storm with class.

Getting the crisis under control fast

When a disaster does happen and the media comes running, you need to think quickly on your feet about what to say to protect both the reputation of your organization and the trust you've built with your community. Here we give you some tips to help you quickly handle a media crisis:

- ✔ **Don't be defensive.** Denial is not only pointless; it can also be downright dangerous when you're talking about reputations, as the current political environment in the United States has shown time and time again. Instead of defending your organization, shifting the blame, or claiming innocence, evaluate the situation as quickly as possible, and face the issue head-on. (It's okay to tell the media, "We don't know yet, but we're finding out," until you know what happened.)

- ✔ **If you goofed, admit it and apologize.** You may think admission is a logical outcome of not being defensive, but, in actuality, admission is something else entirely. Whether it's a public or private gaff, don't just refuse to be defensive; be determined to tell the truth. For instance, if you dropped the ball and applied $10,000 in restricted funds to your scholarship program, admit it. (Of course, if it's a private issue, don't go seeking media exposure to reveal your mess.) Remember that candor, with compassion, is helpful even when you're delivering bad news — and it builds trust along the way. Apologizing for something that has impacted the organization, your donors, or the people you serve is not only smart crisis management — it's the right thing to do.

- ✔ **Do something about the problem.** If the crisis has hurt or harmed — or maybe just annoyed — somebody and the media picks up the story, start by saying, "Our organization doesn't exist to create situations like this. We're here to help at-risk teens master the skills they need to be successful in life. We're not yet sure how this happened, but we're going to make very sure it doesn't happen again. Now, here's what we're going to do about it. . . ." Then be sure to provide specifics on how you'll approach this situation in the future. The bad press turns into an awareness-building story that can help people find out about your organization and about how it responds to a problem.

✔ **Don't ignore the situation — now or in the long-term.** Be sure to address continuing questions about the problem with an honest face and straight talk. This reaction is important, both for the continuing pride of your organization (seeing how you and your board weather this storm gives added strength to your staff and volunteers) and for the rebuilding of your relationship with the community. Be prepared to answer questions and respond to the issue for as long as it takes. "No comment" may work in some public arenas for some organizations, but if you care about building a reputation for your nonprofit based on trust and good stewardship, being as open and above-board as possible is the best approach.

When trust has been broken, a quick fix and a claim of redemption don't guarantee anyone's belief; be prepared to use this situation as a positive building block — and a significant learning experience — for the organization you want to be in the future.

Drafting a disaster control plan

Although nobody wants to anticipate crises and consider ways to limit the damage done as a result, having a disaster control plan in place is a good idea — both for you, as the fundraiser, and for your board, as the protectors of your organization. In one of your board meetings, put "Media Crisis" on your agenda and get the board talking about the following questions:

✔ **What kinds of disasters could we be faced with?**

✔ **What's the worst that could happen?** You may want to role-play a few of these uncomfortable scenarios. Or perhaps simply write out a few examples that would be realistic for your organization.

✔ **How would we react if the worst happened?** Come up with a specific series of steps that detail who takes charge, how you investigate, what team contacts the media outlets in your area, and what recovery mechanisms you use to begin rebuilding your reputation.

After you draft a plan, write it up and make sure each board member has a copy. Make it part of your board packet and future board trainings. A disaster isn't something anyone likes to think about, but the potential of one happening is there — as they say, better to be safe than sorry.

Chapter 14

Social Networking: What's the Connection for Your Organization?

*R*eady for a great new idea in online fundraising? If you haven't yet ventured into the "friending" world of social media yourself, you may be surprised to hear that social media is offering an exciting new frontier for nonprofit organizations. Blossoming as the brainchild of Generation Y, social media combines the best of individual expression (blogging and more) with Web 2.0 tools, offering individuals and organizations a brilliant way to create custom audiences that are engaged, interactive, and having fun together.

Sounds like a great environment for a happy donor, doesn't it?

This chapter gives you a glimpse of the quickly evolving offerings available in the social media realm. Here, you find out more about what social media is, which features are most helpful to you, and how you can use the tools to reach and mobilize your donors.

Even though social media may be the next great frontier in fundraising (or at least *friendraising*), if you're running a one-person department trying to fund your organization, you have to be judicious about the way you spend your time. You may want to test the waters with a social media tool that doesn't take a lot of time — like Twitter — and try it consistently for a month. See whether it strikes a chord with your donors. Test the tool and see whether it catches on. If it does, great — you know the tool is worth the time you invest. If it doesn't, focus your attention on something that's sure to bring the results you want.

Wondering about Web 2.0? Lucky for you, all you need to know to understand this chapter is that the second wave of Web technologies called *Web 2.0* introduced blogging, wiki generation, and social networking capabilities. In other words, the development of Web 2.0 made social media possible.

Getting Started with Social Media

Before you can understand how you and your organization can take advantage of social media in a fundraising sense, you need to know a bit about social media, find out who's using it, and discover how building community in this way can benefit your organization. Lucky for you, we address all three topics in the following sections.

Surveying the basics of social media

The world is abuzz with tweets and friends. Sound like a note you intercepted from your sixth grader? Well, it isn't. It's becoming the talk of grown-ups everywhere. This new conversation is unfolding — with or without you — on computers reaching around the world. With the help of super-popular sites like Facebook, Twitter, LinkedIn, MySpace, and more, friends and friends of friends are becoming fans of organizations like yours, sending updates and Web links to others they know, and posting comments, photos, and opinions about their favorite causes worldwide.

Social media, put simply, is about the relationships and links made through social interaction online. A number of different types of sites offer individuals and groups the ability to express themselves, create groups of friends and fans, invite comments and crosslinking, and much more. Some of the most popular social media sites include the following:

- ✔ **For connecting with friends, family, events, and causes:** Facebook (www.facebook.com), LinkedIn (www.linkedin.com), MySpace (www.myspace.com), and Ning (www.ning.com)

- ✔ **For microblogging (presence technology):** Twitter (www.twitter.com)

- ✔ **For sharing photos:** Flickr (www.flickr.com), Photobucket (www.photobucket.com), and Picasa (www.picasa.com)

- ✔ **For sharing events:** Meetup (www.meetup.com)

- ✔ **For wiki creation:** Wikipedia (www.wikipedia.org)

- ✔ **For social news:** Digg (www.digg.com)

- ✔ **For sharing opinions:** Epinions (www.epinions.com)

> ✔ **For video sharing:** YouTube (www.youtube.com)
>
> ✔ **For asking and answering questions:** Yahoo! Answers (www.answers.yahoo.com)

Note: A *wiki* is a collaborative, open, Web-based, document-creation tool that enables an unlimited number of authors to create, modify, expand, and edit one another's work.

The idea of creating a kind of "presence" with technology can be a powerful benefit for your organization because it builds connections, and, as you know, connections are the heart of your donor base. When you share what you're doing on Twitter, post your organization's stories on Facebook, or connect with others on LinkedIn, you're inviting your donors into your organization's life. Doing so enables people to feel like they're connecting with you in real time, which builds trust (and your donor-organization relationship).

Identifying who uses social media and what they can do for you

The potential size of the audience currently using social media technologies may be a difficult concept to grasp. Millions and millions of users — all over the world at this very moment — are trading photos, chatting, and posting links to interesting Web sites. And in case you're thinking social media is just for the younger crowd, think again — the number of social media users between the ages of 39 and 64 is growing at twice the rate of the 18-and-younger group.

Although many of the activities Web 2.0 users enjoy are free, statistics show that online users are indeed spending money. In 2007, online advertising in the United States alone reached $14.6 billion dollars, and online holiday purchasing reached an all-time high in 2008 — in spite of the economic downturn. Ever-increasing Web traffic shows that people spend a lot of their time and attention online, and reports let savvy Web watchers pinpoint interests, trends, and the next big thing in online sales.

A report on social media and cause-related marketing released by the Cone group (www.coneinc.com/content2601) says that even though 4 out of 5 social media users interact with companies and causes online, fewer than one in five (18 percent) has made a donation using social media tools. The report cites lack of trust *(Will my donation really go where they say it will go?)* as one of the key reasons why donors aren't yet giving in higher numbers.

So what do these statistics mean to you as a fundraiser wanting to harness the power of the social Web? They illustrate that you have an almost-unlimited audience coming to social networking sites because they want to connect in a fun, interesting, and personalized way and get involved with the ideas and communities they connect with.

The power of choice is something that Web 2.0 users and your donors have in common. According to the 2009 book *Socialnomics: How Social Media Transforms the Way We Live and Do Business* by Erik Qualman (Wiley), 78 percent of consumers trust peer recommendations, while only 14 percent trust advertisements for the same products. For you, this stat means that personal stories — and the testimonials of clients you've served — will be far more powerful than your own marketing copy or block advertisements.

And the fact that friends of friends become fans of your organization will carry more weight with social media users than the high-profile board members on your board. Your interactions online — the tweets you post, the links and notes you add to Facebook, the questions you ask on LinkedIn — will do a lot to either bring your friends and fans closer to your organization . . . or not. So be friendly, be timely, and give your social media friends something to talk about.

 Want to know more about how your organization can take advantage of social media technologies? Check out the books *Groundswell: Winning in a World Transformed by Social Technologies,* by Charlene Li and Josh Bernoff (Harvard Business School Press), and *Socialnomics: How Social Media Transforms the Way We Live and Do Business* by Erik Qualman (Wiley).

Building a Community of People Who Care

People have always been social animals, and today they have more things to share — and a farther reach — than they've ever had before. Social media technologies now enable people to connect in real time, on their own terms, creating the communities of friends and families they choose. They can connect with the causes they care about and share those causes with others in their social networks; in turn, those friends share causes with others in their networks — thus, you see the power of social media.

The following sections introduce you to three popular social media networks. We encourage you to spend some time online exploring these sites and getting a better feel for how they work.

Feeling all a-Twitter

Twitter is a free microblogging tool (think "little blog") that enables users to share whatever is on their minds at any given time. Twitter essentially asks its users, "What are you doing?" and gives them 140 characters with which to respond. The brief responses people leave on Twitter are perfect for text messages or Web displays, and they can — and typically do — include links to other sites for more information.

Tweeting to bring people closer to the action

How exactly do organizations use Twitter? Well, the idea is to personify your organization and keep the people who follow your Twitter feed close to the action. So, on your organization's Twitter feed, you may post a tweet on any of the following:

- ✔ A new program you're introducing
- ✔ A link to a story on your Web site about an event you hosted
- ✔ A call to volunteers for your next social action night
- ✔ An announcement of an exciting award
- ✔ A link to a new research study in your area of service

Twitter has swept like wildfire across the Web 2.0 world, engaging users in conversations that bounce back and forth across continents. Countries have used Twitter to stage coups; environmental groups have used Twitter to create an instant "flash mob" in a public demonstration against global warming (read the article at www.sltrib.com/news/ci_13065009).

Of course Twitter was in the news when politicians were tweeting during President Obama's 2009 speech on the state of the economy; and Twitter is now being used by many newscasters, celebrities, marketing professionals, and everyday folks all over the world. The idea that you can share what you think, what you do, and what interests you — anywhere, anytime — has created a fascinating in-the-moment reporting culture that keeps an on-going, worldwide conversation alive and well.

You can get up-to-the-minute alerts about the advocacy actions you care about in more than 60 social areas, ranging from Africa and AIDS actions to youth advocacy, with Twitter Action Pack: www.socialactions.com/labs/twitter-action-pack.

Twitter users engage each other in real-time conversation by replying directly and posting comments in their Twitter feed responses to each other. Additionally, Twitter users can tweet about a specific topic by using what's known as a *hash tag,* which identifies the topic of a post so others can find it easily. For example, the hash tag *#cop15* enables a user to search for all the tweets related to the COP 15 summit on global climate in Copenhagen in December 2009.

Getting a feel for tweeting

With the 140-character messages you post on Twitter, you have a chance to microblog what's going on with your organization today. In real time, you can give subscribers the feeling of participating in your agency's work as well as a link back to your site. Here are just a few examples of what you can tweet:

✔ Getting ready to announce our 2009 Volunteer of the Year award! Check out our Web site later today!

✔ This WSJ article on energy efficiency quotes one of our staff members.

✔ We're planning our dog wash for next Saturday afternoon — sign up on the Web site!

Note: Your tweets aren't just informational — you also want people who follow your Twitter feed to come back to your site. So don't forget to link any reference to your Web site or other relevant sites you mention in your tweets.

The 140-character limitation can be a hindrance when you've got a really long Web address. You can shorten the Web address by using a utility called TinyURL, which is available online at `http://tinyurl.com`. Simply go to the site, paste your long Web address in the text box, and click the Make Tiny URL! button. You can then copy and paste the shorter URL (short for *Uniform Resource Locator*, which means "Web address") into your tweet and send it normally.

Putting Twitter to use for your organization

So how will you use Twitter as part of your organization's fundraising initiative? Twitter gives organizations that work in any kind of advocacy a great opportunity to become part of the real conversation in their particular industry areas. To help spread the word about your twitter feed (and to attract potential donors and advocates to your cause), post invitations and links to follow you on Twitter on your Web site, e-newsletters, and e-mail messages.

Not sure what to tweet? Send an e-mail message to your staff members asking them what they're working on today. By choosing what to tweet from different aspects of your organization, you broaden the sense of work your organization does and help users see into the daily life of your group.

Connecting constituents with LinkedIn

LinkedIn is a global social network that focuses on networking opportunities for professionals in more than 170 industries in 200 countries. LinkedIn includes executives from all Fortune 500 companies and estimates that half of the network's 47 million members live outside the United States.

The idea driving the success of LinkedIn is the same one that forms the basis of any thriving community — that shared knowledge and experience benefit every person in a community (whether it be a company, a nonprofit organization, or a neighborhood). In addition to the one-to-one connections via personal networks, LinkedIn includes a groups feature that enables individuals, organizations, and businesses to build communities that share articles, discussions, polls, presentations, and more.

So how might you use LinkedIn to build awareness of your organization? Here are just a few ideas:

- ✔ Create an organizational profile and connect with all your staff, board members, committee members, and volunteers.

- ✔ Post information about your programs and services, as well as your needs and news.

- ✔ Add a group that discusses key ideas and developments in your area of service.

- ✔ Join other groups that serve members in your demographics.

- ✔ Post articles and answer questions about your industry area. (Doing so builds your brand and demonstrates your organization's expertise in your service area.)

Like other social networks, LinkedIn is free to join, but it also offers premium services — such as member research and targeting — for a fee.

Sharing the love on Facebook

Facebook is the premier social networking site in the world at the moment, recently passing the 300-million-member mark, and its basic services are free to use.

Facebook users create profiles giving their demographics — their age, location, employment, education, marital status, and more — and then they begin identifying people they want to "friend" (which has become a verb, by the way) as they build their personal networks. Facebook users post photos, add links, upload videos, tell others what they're reading, rate their favorite music, and chat in real time with each other. In addition to the dozens of applications available within Facebook, developers have created literally thousands of add-in applications that offer just about every type of extra available in the world of social networking.

Fun is the motivating force on Facebook, and users often send each other gifts, take quizzes (like "Which Hobbit are you?"), play games, and watch and rate videos. In addition to the lighter side of Facebook, friends and families mobilize to join causes they care about — which, as you may have guessed, is where you come in.

Facebook enables organizations to create their own pages and build fan bases. Similar to a personal account, the organizational page is free and includes all the social media features available on other pages. People can click a small icon to become "fans" of your organization. Whenever you post an update — by adding new content in the form of a new link, photo, video, or event to your profile page — your new content becomes visible to all your fans by way of their personal news feeds pages. These automatic news flashes help keep your organization in the minds of your public — and build on your "friendly" brand at the same time.

So what can you do in the way of fundraising with a Facebook page? Here are some ideas to get you started:

- ✔ Post your mission, Web site, and programs.
- ✔ Add photos of your staff or facilities, as well as photos of your programs in action if that's appropriate.
- ✔ Add videos of staff members or recent programs.
- ✔ Create an events page to publicize upcoming events.
- ✔ Answer questions from fans and donors.
- ✔ Add a Causes module to raise funds online.
- ✔ Send updates to all your fans.

Be sure to get permission — in writing — before posting the photographs of any of your staff members, constituents, or volunteers. You can find standard model release forms online at the American Society of Media Photographers Web site, `http://asmp.org`.

Remember that fundraising is all about making connections. Posting information about your organization on Facebook and other social media networks allows you to connect with a wide array of people across the globe that you simply can't reach any other way.

In addition to the basic updating features Facebook gives to organizations, it also offers you the ability to target specific groups of your users. (This service requires an upgrade on your account, though, which incurs a cost.)

If you choose to expand into the for-fee realm, you can also send messages to all Facebook users and create advertisements that display along the right side of Facebook users' pages. The ads that appear on users' pages are targeted to the specific demographic information in the users' profiles, so your chances of getting your animal rights' organization in front of animal lovers are pretty good.

More than 1.5 million pieces of content (links, stories, blog posts, notes, photos, and so on) are shared on Facebook every single day. If you post a great story on your Web site and then add it as a note on your Facebook page, your fans may just share it with others, who may share it with others . . . and so on and so forth as your message spreads across the Web.

Understanding What Your Social Media Users Want

The three popular social media sites that we profile earlier in this chapter — Twitter, LinkedIn, and Facebook — offer different goals, tools, and audiences. And although all social media enthusiasts have something in common — the desire to connect with others online — before you start networking away, you need to determine which social media network offers you the best chances of reaching your particular donor group. Keep in mind these general guidelines as to the main audiences each network attracts:

- ✔ Twitter appeals to high-tech audiences who are always connected via computer or cellphone. They love news, trade the latest stories, and share social commentary and advocacy ideas.

- ✔ LinkedIn is directed toward the professional crowd. LinkedIn focuses on business and organizational networking, developing expertise in industry areas, and showcasing projects, programs, and more.

- ✔ Facebook is all about building relationships, having fun, and spreading the word. The overall energy is creative and engaging. Although Facebook originally started for the college-age crowd, the average Facebook user joining today is older. Still, fun, friendliness, and high energy are the order of the day on Facebook.

Regardless of which group they belong to, users of social media have similar attitudes and goals when they connect with your organization. Read on for some insights that can help you make the most of these relationships.

Visibility and voice: Here we are!

Users of social media are drawn to online networks because they want to belong to a community — and they want to be able to choose the groups and individuals with whom they connect.

When your organization gets started in social media, remember that your potential donors want to be able to share what they care about, so ask questions, post polls, and offer ways for your fans and friends to get involved on your social media pages.

When users post comments on your social media page or send you messages, be sure to answer promptly. Long delays (days or weeks) indicate a rarely tended site in social media, and, in the quick-moving social universe, your silence usually leads your fans to forget you fast.

Engagement and opportunity: Let me help

Social media users are interested in connecting for fun and profit, but many people are also looking for ways to add purpose and meaning to what they do. Thus, this group of online users is a prime audience for your causes and announcements. You can use your social network to post the following:

- Calls for volunteers
- Notices about new volunteer trainings
- Invitations to public events
- Notices about volunteer awards
- Calendar items for your upcoming volunteer opportunities
- Open committee positions
- Links to stories about needs in your industry area

The freedom to choose: I want it my way

Web 2.0 tools enable users to pick and choose the kinds of gadgets and widgets they want in their social media toolboxes. And social networking technologies enable users to choose whom they want to befriend and whom they want to ignore.

Similarly, social media users can choose the groups they join, the links they share, the photos they post, and the level to which others can see the content they add. You can invite these users to join your Facebook fan page, follow you on Twitter, or join your network on LinkedIn, but the choice to follow you online is ultimately the donors'.

Be sure to give your potential donors all the choices you can when it comes to managing your social media interactions. Let them opt in to your group when they're ready, invite them to participate in the way that fits them best, and don't be surprised when your donors show considerable autonomy and independence. If they share your story and further your links — and build goodwill for your organization in the process — they're doing more for your organization than you can do alone.

Taking the Plunge into Social Media

So you've decided to give the social media scene a whirl, and you've signed up your organization for Facebook and Twitter accounts. Now what?

First, let all your current supporters know you've got a presence on these sites. Publicize it on your Web page and in your e-mails or e-newsletters. They'll friend you, their friends will see the connection and perhaps join your network, and then you'll be on your way to building a larger circle of supporters.

The next thing to do is incorporate these outlets into your overall communication strategy. The following sections show you how you can communicate a message across various platforms, evaluate whether your social media efforts are paying off, and ensure the security of your online users' information so that they'll continue to connect with you and your cause.

Making sure your messages work together

As the social media field expands, both tools and users are becoming more savvy. Today you can publish a new blog post and have it appear automatically on your Facebook page. Similarly, you can connect your Twitter account to Facebook so that your Facebook status updates go to Twitter and your Twitter updates post as notes on Facebook.

Are you confused yet?

The key is to think through what you communicate in terms of holistic messaging and then to choose the channel you want to use to deliver the message. For example, if you're announcing a new scholarship program your organization is offering, you may communicate your message in the following ways:

- ✔ Send a press release to media sources.

- ✔ Post an announcement on your Web site. (Check out Chapter 16 for more on connecting with donors via your Web site.)

- ✔ Send an e-mail message announcing the program to donors who may be interested. (Go to Chapter 15 to find out more about getting the most out of e-mail.)

- ✔ Create a brochure that explains the details of the program.

- ✔ Post a note on your Facebook page.

- ✔ Tweet about the new program with a link back to your Web site announcement.

- ✔ Add a post on LinkedIn, inviting network members to ask questions or post comments.

It's okay to pick and choose the outlets you want to use for the messages you send. If you feel that a particular message won't be right for a certain social media audience, feel free to skip that post. Flexibility — not rigidity — is the name of the game.

Tracking and evaluating results

Especially when you're just getting started in social media, keep track of everything you can for the various tools you select. Watch the patterns of growth from week to week. At least monthly, take inventory of the following numbers:

- ✔ Number of fans on your Facebook page

- ✔ Number of times you've posted links, photos, videos, or updates

- ✔ Number of LinkedIn members in your network and/or group

- ✔ Number of links you've added, posts you've created, or questions you've asked or answered

- ✔ Number of subscribers following you on Twitter

- ✔ Number of updates you've posted on Twitter

- ✔ Number of direct replies and conversations you've had

 ✔ Number of people who have been drawn to your Web site through your various social media sites

 ✔ Number of donors who are now communicating directly with you because of your social media sites

After you tally up the numbers, identify one or two items you'd like to explore more fully in the coming month.

Don't forget to share your successes with your board! Knowing that your group is an active part of the social media movement is a source of pride — and relevancy — for everyone in your organization.

Creating credibility and security in social media

When social media was in its infancy, not long ago, many people were wary of the new technologies. Can social media be trusted? Are the organizations online trustworthy? How do donors know that the causes they support are authentic?

With the growth of social media, your organization will likely seem hip and in tune with the times when you launch your new tools. However, it's important to address any security concerns your donors may have.

In some ways, the social media networks themselves have taken steps to ensure authenticity among their users. For example, the Facebook Causes module requires that nonprofits be 501(c)(3) organizations listed with GuideStar.org, the database from which Facebook pulls all its Causes data.

Of course, you need to take your own steps to assure your donors that you're a legitimate organization that uses its time, energy, and donations to do good. On all your online sites, be sure to spell out for your donors who you are, what you do, and how they can find out more about you. If you plan to use your social media accounts to accept donations (as opposed to sending people back to your organization's Web site for online donations), use an entity like Facebook Causes that's set up to ensure a secure environment.

More than 30 million Facebook members currently use the Facebook Causes application to donate to their favorite nonprofit organizations all over the world. The Causes application is a Verified Application that passes Facebook's muster for trustworthy applications. After your organization is set up on Causes, your Facebook fans and friends can add the Causes application to their Facebook pages and choose your organization as the beneficiary of the donations they collect. Donations collected through Facebook Causes are processed by Network for Good, and payments are sent to the nonprofit on the 15th of each month. To find out more about Facebook Causes, visit www.facebook.com/causes.

The Big Dilemma: To Ask or Not to Ask?

As you use social media in your fundraising efforts, you'll eventually come up against the big question: Should you use social media to ask for donations?

We debated this topic, at first wondering whether making a real "Ask" on Facebook would be a violation of social media etiquette or an unwanted disruption in the give-and-take community that social media groups are creating (check out Chapter 10 for more on "the Ask"). The Facebook Causes application enables organizations to raise funds in a fairly low-visibility way, but is this application enough to get a return on investment for the time and effort you put into establishing and maintaining your social media presence?

We concluded that you can find the best answer for these questions within your own organization, donor base, and comfort level. Before you go looking for the answer, however, you may want to consider the possibility that your feeling about asking for donations on social media may have everything to do with your own money attitude.

To illustrate this point, here's a real-life story: John has served for many years on the board of The Garden, a church community that offers an alternative style of worship. The pastor and music director didn't want to ask the small congregation for funds, so week after week they sat buckets by the doors for a freewill offering. After some time, the community's leaders realized that these small donations weren't going to keep the church doors open, but they still didn't want to ask for money — they had both had previous church experiences in which fundraising was a point of pain. One day in the wake of 9/11, two firefighters visited the church and asked for permission to pass around a boot to collect funds for the spouses and children of firefighters who died in the Twin Towers. That Sunday, for the first time ever, the music director stood in front of the church and made an eloquent appeal for donations on behalf of the firefighters' families. That day the leaders' belief about asking for donations changed, and since that time, the church has grown and matured and is now working on building an endowment.

The moral here is listen to your heart and mind, talk to your board, and hear what your donors have to say. If you decide to go for the gold in social media, have fun with it — do a 12-hour fundraising drive and post every donation (with thanks and dedications) on your Twitter feed; create your own informal fundraising auction with Facebook gifts; design your own online event that makes the most of all the social technologies at your disposal.

Just remember that when everything's said and done — no matter how much flash and fun your social media sites may offer — fundraising is still all about the relationships you build online, offline, and in the hearts and minds of everyone affiliated with your cause.

Chapter 15

Getting the Most from E-Mail and E-Newsletters

In This Chapter

▶ Looking at the benefits of e-mail

▶ Creating effective e-mail campaigns

▶ Avoiding common e-mail mistakes

▶ Creating an e-newsletter that catches donors' interest

*I*f you haven't yet jumped with both feet into e-mail communications, you're missing a great — and inexpensive — way to get the word out about your organization and stay in touch with your donors. Just a few years ago, people primarily used e-mail for person-to-person contact, but today organizations are using e-mail for a whole variety of contacts — from general communications to newsletters to event announcements to fundraising approaches.

In this chapter, we show you the benefits of using e-mail to communicate with your donors. We also offer suggestions on what topics lend themselves to quick e-mails, who should receive your messages, and how to steer clear of e-mistakes. Finally, we take a close look at e-newsletters and the benefits they can offer your organization.

Making the Case for E-Mail

Of all the various approaches to donor contact, e-mail comes with the lowest cost and the smallest time commitment from you. With e-mail, you can send — with the click of a mouse — a friendly, engaging, well-written message to the thousands of donors you want to invite to contribute to your annual fund. And you can do so for free. Here are some of our favorite reasons for making the switch from print to e-mail for the bulk of your outgoing communications:

✔ **E-mail can be personable.** E-mail offers you an immediate way to reach your donors in the way they're most likely to receive it. You can personalize e-mail messages so that they include donors' names, favorite projects, and other relevant information — all of which goes toward building trust with your donors.

Depending on the age of your board members, some of them may feel e-mail communication is too impersonal for fundraising. Although this is true when you reach the more interactive level of relationship building with major donors, a well-written e-mail message targeted to a specific audience can attract many small donors with little effort.

✔ **E-mail saves time.** The time you take to write the e-mail message is the biggest segment of time you have to invest in this type of communication. Instead of writing a dozen different letters for countless different donors or audiences or creating a direct mail appeal and spending the morning at the printer while you print, fold, stuff, and stamp the envelopes, you can create just one e-mail and send it an infinite number of times.

✔ **E-mail is direct.** Direct mail pieces take time, money, and effort to put together, and then, after you finally get them ready to send, you have to wait for the pieces to be delivered. Statistics also show that a very slim percentage of direct mail brings any kind of suitable return. Because e-mail messages can be produced quickly, sent immediately, and received almost instantly, they're actually more *direct* than direct mail.

✔ **E-mail is low-cost.** Chances are you can send e-mail directly from the fundraising or donor management software you now use to keep track of your donors and their contributions. If your software doesn't have this capacity, you can piece it together on your own by using a spreadsheet and your favorite e-mail utility, or you can subscribe to an e-mail service like Exact Target (`email.exacttarget.com`), which enables you to create, send, and manage all e-mail communication sent from your organization.

✔ **E-mail is customizable.** Five or ten years ago, e-mail was pretty utilitarian; you could send or receive basic text with perhaps a link or two, but that was about it. Today e-mail can be customized any number of ways. You can add photos, formats, background images, and more. You can even include your organization's logo and a Donate Now! button that takes donors to your Web site, where they can donate online with their credit cards.

Some e-mail programs block images in an effort to protect users from unwanted spam, so make sure the text of your message introduces your organization and lets recipients know that you're legitimate.

✔ **E-mail is trackable.** A big plus to using e-mail over direct mail is that you can easily determine who opens your e-mail messages, what your recipients like about your messages, and which links they click on to find out more about you — a lot of information for a single electronic transaction. E-mail management programs allow you to keep an eye on the results of your e-mail campaigns so you can find out what your donors respond to, which can help you fine-tune your communications so you can do even better the next time.

Being Smart about E-Mail Campaigns

The average e-mail user today receives approximately 100 messages a day, many of which are spam, a few of which are from family, and a small number of which may be related to bills or purchases. How many messages do you receive from nonprofit organizations? Chances are you get newsletters you've signed up for and receive e-mail messages with program updates from the groups you follow regularly.

How can you be successful in grabbing a bit of your donor's attention when so many groups are vying for it? The short answer is simple:

✔ Send your e-mail to the right people.

✔ Ask for what you need and what you think your donors can give.

✔ Make the message personal for the donor.

The following sections cover each of these points in more detail to help you make the most of your e-mail messages.

Figuring out who should receive your e-mails

The more strategically you can target the recipients of your e-mail messages, the better. For example, choosing just the right group to receive information about the new naming opportunities for the campus library is one way to make sure your e-mail campaign is successful. But how do you pick out just the right people from your huge list of donors? You need to do a little slicing and dicing of your donor list.

If you don't know how to slice and dice your list to create small groups of targeted donors, contact your software vendor and ask someone to walk you through the process. (Depending on the complexity of your software, you may be able to figure out how to do so yourself by searching online for tutorials or reading the program's help system.)

When you slice and dice your list, you create a series of smaller lists that each focus on a specific group. For example, you may create donor subgroups from your overall list that look something like the following:

- Donors under 30 years of age

- Major givers ($5,000 and above)

- Donors who have given to specific programs

- Donors who receive your planned-giving newsletter

- Donors who have served on one of your organization's committees in the past

- Donors who are candidates for endowment or capital campaigns

- Donors from different zip codes

- Donors who don't have e-mail

- Donors with specific interests

Use these donor sublists to pinpoint the donors you want to include in particular e-mail campaigns. For example, if you're starting an e-mail campaign to raise funds for your new literacy program, focus on sending your e-mail messages to the donors who have previously shown interest in education and literacy.

Hopefully, you've been gathering e-mail addresses for your donors for some time, but even if you have, continue to be vigilant in collecting new addresses. Request e-mail addresses on items like tickets, sign-in sheets, order forms, and volunteer applications. You can never have too many e-mail addresses!

Knowing what to say

Your e-mail campaign should be as well thought out as any direct mail campaign you send to donors. Though it may seem easy to click the Send button after you have a list of people to e-mail, you can't simply dash off an e-mail in three or four minutes. You need to consider the e-mail's content, strategize its purpose, and plan to follow up on this particular e-mail. Plus, you don't want to make a careless, high-cost e-mail mistake, a topic we cover in the "Avoiding E-Mail Mistakes" section later in this chapter.

Consider your e-mail's purpose and desired results before you sit down at the keyboard. Some organizations use e-mail to solicit donations, others use it to maintain donor relationships, and still others use it to find and interact with volunteers. The possibilities of e-mail are really endless, but whatever your reason is for starting an e-mail campaign, understand what you want to get out of it before you even start composing your first e-mail.

The benefits of opt-in lists

One alternative to using a list of donors you already know is to buy or build *opt-in lists* for your e-mail campaigns. People on opt-in lists have asked for information from your organization. Not only do these people make up a richer potential mine of donor dollars, but they're also less likely to be annoyed when you communicate with them.

You can come by opt-in lists by doing the following:

✔ **Set up an opt-in function on your Web site.** When people register on your Web site, they may indicate that they're open to receiving information from you.

✔ **Share opt-in lists with other organizations.** You may have a relationship with another organization in which its members have agreed to receive communications from related organizations; as a result, the organization shares its addresses with you.

✔ **Buy an opt-in list from another group or opt-in list vendor to ensure that you have e-mail addresses that will go to live recipients.**

Regardless of how people on opt-in lists came to be on those lists, they've somehow indicated that they're open to receiving communications from you, which makes them prime recipients for your e-mail campaigns.

Using e-mail to get a donation

The most obvious use of e-mail for a nonprofit organization is to try to raise money. You can make it easy for people to donate to your organization and encourage them to do so by incorporating some of the following techniques in your e-mail campaign:

✔ **Include a link in your e-mail.** Providing a link in your e-mail gives recipients an easy way to go to your Web site or to an e-mail form to reply to your message. You can even include a secure link to a page where recipients can make a payment right on the spot, either through your site or through a third-party payment vendor such as PayPal.

✔ **Attach to the e-mail message a printable form that people can print out and mail in with a check.** Consider using a format such as PDF, which anybody using Adobe Acrobat Reader (www.adobe.com/products/acrobat/main.html) can open. Be aware, however, that some e-mail spam filters remove e-mail attachments, and users are counseled not to open attachments on e-mails sent from senders they don't recognize. For this reason, you may want to send attachments only to those donors you contact regularly or those on your opt-in list.

✔ **Use graphic images in your e-mail to drive your message home.** Show a picture of your new building, include an image of a group of distressed teens whom you've helped with your programs, or add a graph showing the positive results of your efforts over the past year. Remember, however, that some e-mail filters block images, so be sure to fully describe the image in the surrounding text.

> ✔ **Consider asking your e-mail recipients to forward the donor mailing to other people they think may be interested.** E-mail is easy to forward, and it's a free way to expand your message to other potential donors you don't even know yet.

You can also set up an automated confirmation that sends an instant e-mail receipt to any donor who donates online. The receipt serves as a tax record for the donor, but, more importantly, it can include an instant thank-you that makes your donors feel appreciated.

Using e-mail to build your donor relationship

E-mail may be a fast and easy way to communicate with your donors, but you need to know when enough is enough. Don't constantly hit people with e-mail requests for money. Consider alternating fundraising messages with useful or interesting information about your group or your cause to help build your donor relationships; for example:

> ✔ Let donors in on upcoming events or changes in your organization.

> ✔ Note milestones in donors' giving levels and thank them for helping.

> ✔ Provide a case study of a specific way your organization's efforts (and those of the donors) helped a person or group.

> ✔ Share a scanned thank-you note from someone your organization helped (a child your organization saved from homelessness or abuse, for example).

> ✔ Invite donors to share their thoughts about an upcoming program.

> ✔ Recognize donors and volunteers who helped bring success to a specific program or event.

> ✔ Acknowledge a special gift or all the people who gave in a particular month.

Using e-mail to find volunteers

When you're trying to find ways to use e-mail in your organization, don't forget about your volunteers — you know, that important group of souls who give to you in the form of time, passion, and perhaps even money. Sending an e-mail thanking your volunteers for their efforts, informing them of achievements, and singling out people for their contributions is easy and inexpensive to do.

If you have a big initiative coming up that needs a lot of volunteers, try sending a sign-up e-mail to past volunteers and people who have expressed an interest in volunteering for your organization. You may be surprised by the response you get!

Writing an e-mail that gets the results you're looking for

No matter which donor group you're sending to or what your overall message is, a well-written e-mail typically includes the following:

- **A clear and concise subject line:** Many people decide whether to read an e-mail simply by looking at the subject line. Use something like "Find out how you can save a child from abuse." Be specific, and be compelling — and make sure your subject line somehow says who you are so your message doesn't get caught in spam filters.

- **An identifier that says who you and your organization are upfront:** People want to know who's talking to them before they're receptive to the message. State your name, position, and organization at the beginning of your message so your recipients don't have any time to wonder whether the e-mail's legitimate.

- **A focused message:** People usually read e-mails on their computer screens; they don't print them out and read them on paper. Keep your message crisp, straightforward, and organized to keep your reader reading.

- **An explanation of any attachments:** Don't bury an important part of your message in an attachment people may or may not read. Also, be sure to assure your recipients that what your attachments contain is legitimate — otherwise, they may be afraid to open them because they may contain viruses.

One final note about how to write your e-mails: E-mail isn't a formal type of communication. Busy people, who want their information fast and to the point, read it on the fly. Don't put people off by having an overly practiced or wordy style. Be sincere about your message, don't stray from its main point, and make your reader feel comfortable with your communication.

Don't forget to track the results of all your e-mail campaigns. Assign a campaign code of some sort to each e-mail so you can attribute questions or donations coming in as a result of a particular e-mail to a specific campaign. In doing so, you can identify which campaigns are most successful and improve your content for future mailings. You can buy e-mail campaign management software, such as e-Campaign from LmhSoft (www.lmhsoft.com), or download the free Email Marketing Director from Arial Software (www.arial software.com) to help you keep track of your e-mail campaign's results. For a monthly fee, e-mail services, such as Vertical Response (www.vertical response.com) and Exact Target (email.exacttarget.com), also help you design your e-mail messages with templates and design tools.

Avoiding E-Mail Mistakes

In the same way that a telephone call can be either good or evil in the recipient's eyes (a call from Uncle Charlie — how nice; another telemarketer at dinner — what an annoyance!), an e-mail can be either a welcome communication or a complete nuisance. So before you send a mass e-mail, think about what you want to say, whom you want to contact, and how your recipients may perceive your communication. The following sections help you avoid the pitfalls of e-mail.

Don't use e-mail to spam

Spamming is the practice of sending out a lot — we're talking hundreds or thousands — of unsolicited e-mails in a hit-or-miss approach to connect with potential donors. Folks who receive spam at the very least delete it; at the most, they determine never to do anything to help an organization that encroaches on their privacy and inundates them with unwanted messages.

The alternative to spamming is sending e-mails only to people whom you identify using a donor list of your own or an opt-in list. (We discuss opt-in lists in the sidebar "The benefits of opt-in lists.")

Don't be a sloppy e-mailer

E-mail may be a quick and easy way to dash off an informal note to a colleague, but when you use e-mail to communicate with a donor, you can't afford to make your communication sloppy or full of mistakes. Sending a badly phrased or unclear e-mail is a waste of your recipient's time — and a ding to your professional reputation. What's worse, sending e-mail full of misspellings and grammatical errors sends a message about the caliber of your organization.

Never treat donor e-mail — whether it's going to a single person or hundreds of potential donors — with any less care than you do your organization's brochure, annual report, or paper-based mailings.

Here are some e-mail tips to keep in mind as you get ready to write an e-mail to one or more donors:

- ✔ Spell check, spell check, spell check.
- ✔ Ask someone else to read important messages before you click Send.
- ✔ Save a copy of your e-mail content so you can reuse it later.

Understanding the Power of E-Newsletters

Similar to the explosion of nonprofit Web sites in operation today, e-newsletters are now all the rage. Organizations have discovered that it's possible (and affordable!) to create high-quality newsletters with photos, fonts, colors, and more and make them available to donors in electronic format. This electronic option, which is typically informational rather than promotional, saves nonprofits a huge amount of money in print production costs and staff time.

Include a sign-up option on your Web site so interested people can sign up to receive your e-newsletter regularly — weekly, biweekly, monthly, or quarterly. You also need to provide a mechanism for people to unsubscribe if they want to do so.

The following sections help you figure out what to include in your newsletter, how to put it together, and how to distribute it.

Catering to your donors' interests

Be sure that your e-newsletter is interesting to your donors. Provide information about your group's activities, but also give your donors information on general trends in your area of service, information about what other groups are doing, events of interest, and so on.

For example, if you're an animal rights' group, don't just tell your subscribers again and again about your group and its mission — if you do, your donors will get bored fast. Sure, include information about your group, but also include pictures of pets available for adoption at the local animal shelter, information on the pet parade coming up at Halloween in a nearby city, grooming tips for housebound cats, and a recipe for healthy dog biscuits. Your donors' interests include your group and its activities, but they're more likely to enjoy your newsletter if you address their broader interests, as well.

Creating your e-newsletter

You can create your own e-newsletter in your favorite word processor or desktop publishing program and then save it as a PDF that you can e-mail to donors. Alternately, you can use an e-newsletter service like Constant Contact (www.constantcontact.com) or Exact Target (www.exact target.com), both of which provide easy-to-use Web-based interfaces into which you can enter your content. You create the newsletter in HTML format, and the service tracks the results of your e-newsletter campaign.

Regardless of how you create your e-newsletter, follow these tips to design an effective one:

- ✔ **Create an informative header.** Include information such as the newsletter name, your organization name and logo, the date, subscription details (such as how new readers can subscribe to the newsletter), and contact information.

- ✔ **Use a typeface that's easy on the eyes.** Verdana, for example, was specifically designed for Web documents because it's easy to read on-screen.

- ✔ **Use headlines effectively.** Grab the reader's attention with your headlines, but also make it clear what the article is about. Effective headlines save people time, and people value their time and expect you to do the same.

- ✔ **Add graphics and color for interest.** Whether you incorporate a visually appealing border, photograph, or chart, use a mix of visuals and colors to make your e-newsletter more attractive and interesting.

- ✔ **Provide links to other resources.** Links can take people to your Web site where they can find out more about your organization's mission, to other Web sites where they can look further into the topic of the article, or to a donation payment form, which they can use to make an online donation or to send a donation in the mail.

Even though you don't print it out, an e-newsletter is still a newsletter. Rules about using a compelling lead paragraph to put the important information right upfront and answering key questions like who, what, when, where, and why still apply in writing your article content just as they do in any form of journalism.

Adding multimedia pizzazz

More organizations are including links to videos or are embedding video, audio, or animation content in their e-mail or e-newsletter communications. People tend to listen to or watch multimedia content with great interest because sound and images can sell an idea where words fall short. Do you have a short video of your clients receiving help from some of your volunteers or an arts performance that your group sponsors? Can you provide an animation explaining the scientific ins and outs of how your group is working to improve the ecosystem? If so, put a link to your video in your e-newsletter and count how many people click on it!

Keep in mind that, generally speaking, people who watch or listen to such messages tend to be more likely to take action or donate.

Automating e-newsletter delivery

Delivering an e-newsletter is as easy as sending e-mail. But to effectively use an e-newsletter as a promotional tool, you need to get a bit more sophisticated in your delivery methods. In other words, don't just attach your newsletter as a PDF to an e-mail and forward it to a hundred different people.

The same software packages and online services that help you design e-newsletters also typically provide tools to set up and manage delivery of your e-newsletters. These management tools may include the following:

- ✔ Options for subscribing and unsubscribing

- ✔ Ability to personalize the e-newsletter, which allows you to include a greeting to the recipient by name in the body of your newsletter

- ✔ Delivery set up that may allow you to send as many as 20,000 messages an hour

- ✔ Verification of e-mail addresses, which is useful because sometimes people subscribe with phony e-mail addresses

- ✔ Management of e-mail lists with import and export features, which allow you to import subscriber lists you keep in external programs like Microsoft Excel

- ✔ Tracking features that show how many people opened or clicked on links in your newsletter

Some useful e-newsletter tools and services include Exact Target (www.exacttarget.com), eNewsletterPro (www.eNewsletterpro.com), and eNewsBuilder (www.enewsbuilder.com).

Trying to build your subscriber list? Add a link to your newsletter subscription form at the bottom of each and every e-mail message you send. For wider exposure, get your e-newsletter posted in e-newsletter directories such as EzineSearch (www.ezinesearch.com).

Keep 'em coming back

Always include a link to your organization's Web site, or even several links to different areas of your site related to certain stories, in your e-newsletter. After all, bringing people to your Web site allows you to tell more stories, point them to donation forms, offer volunteer sign-up forms, or provide more information on your services or activities.

Remember to publicize other ways donors can stay in touch with you and keep in sync with new developments in your organization. If you have a Facebook page, a Twitter feed, or a LinkedIn group, be sure to feature those links and logos prominently in your e-newsletter. Doing so lets donors know they have additional choices for staying in touch with you, and it builds your social media audience while continuing to get the word out about your organization. (See Chapter 14 for more about these social networking groups.)

Chapter 16

Ramping Up Your Web Site

Suppose that this afternoon a friend told you about a great new organization with a mission that sounds exciting. You want to find out more. What's the first thing you do?

Look for the organization on the Web, right? Most people have figured out that the fastest way to get basic information about anything and anyone is to do a quick Internet search. The results you receive will vary because of the vast number of sites out there that may in some way fit the phrase you entered for the search, but you're likely to find at least one or two links worth exploring in that first page of results.

When your organization shows up in other people's search results, a door to a world full of potential donors is opened — and, if your Web site is set up to accept donations — those donors may even make contributions right there on your site. Lucky for you, the Web offers a low-cost way to gain visibility with people who care about the work you do. This chapter is all about what today's Web offers nonprofit organizations who want to build visibility for their cause, attract supporters, and — hopefully — raise funds online.

Seeing How a Web Site Helps with Fundraising

Today every nonprofit organization needs a Web site. The Web today is similar to the phone book of yesterday; people look up your organization online to make sure you're legitimate. Some potential donors hear about your cause from a friend or see your Web address on one of your publications. Others hear about you through word of mouth and use a search engine to find you. Still others may benefit from your services, hear about an upcoming fundraising event, or discover your Facebook page. No matter how potential donors hear about you, if they're curious enough to want to find out more about you, your Web site is the first place they'll go.

Here are some of the ways the Web is being used in fundraising today:

- According to a study done by the Center on Philanthropy, 3 percent of all donations in 2007 were given online.

- The average gift for online donations is still small (between $50 and $250), but online donors often give to other campaigns, as well.

- Nonprofit organizations use orchestrated online efforts — through Web donations, fundraising e-mail newsletters, and social media causes — to offer donors a variety of ways to give.

Depending on the audience you serve and what you feel they expect from your site, you may not have to design a site that has a lot of bells and whistles. What are the basics your site visitors want to see? For starters, include your organization's history, mission, board members, address, staff, services and programs, and contact information. Sprinkle the site liberally with photos that show what great work you do and how you impact people's lives. You should also include information that clearly spells out how visitors can donate and whether you accept online donations, or provide an e-mail address that donors can use to request more information. For more information about setting up your site to accept online donations, see the section "Collecting Donations Online" later in this chapter.

Putting Your Web Site to Work for Your Organization

Your Web site can be as simple or as flashy as you want to make it. You can update it once a day or once a week. It can give a complete picture of your organization or it can provide just the basics. The important thing is to get something out on the Web that tells people around the world that you exist and gives them what they need to know in order to get a good picture of the type of impact you make in the world.

We're guessing that your organization probably already has a Web site, so, in the following sections, we help you evaluate your site so you know whether you're getting the most benefit from it. We also tell you how your Web site can show the public that you're serious about your mission.

If you don't yet have a Web site, you don't have to pay exorbitant Web site development fees to create a professional-looking site. Check with your board members, volunteer corps, or staff members to find someone with Web expertise who can assist you. If no one with Web experience steps forward, consider researching free site hosts like Microsoft Office Online. This free Web-hosting tool enables you to develop a low- or no-cost site that shares your organization's story in a professional, engaging way. Or pick up *Creating Web Pages For Dummies,* 9th Edition, by Bud E. Smith (Wiley) to try your hand at Web design.

Whether you design your own page or not, you have to pay someone to host it. Hosting services provide lots of useful tools to get your site up and running, and the cost isn't always too high. Visit www.web-page-hosting-review.com to get an overview of some of the many services out there.

Evaluating your Web site

If you haven't taken a look at your organization's Web site lately, now's the time to do so. Like it or not, your Web site is likely making a first impression with potential donors all over the world. Is your site making a positive first impression or a negative one? Is your mission clear? A great nonprofit Web site does the following:

- ✔ Introduces the organization clearly and concisely
- ✔ Is visually inviting and easy to navigate
- ✔ Includes real stories of real people
- ✔ Is updated regularly with fresh content
- ✔ Lists board members and states the organization's mission
- ✔ May include video or audio clips of clients or staff
- ✔ Offers visitors the ability to sign up for free e-newsletters
- ✔ Lets visitors download information such as brochures, annual reports, newsletters, and more
- ✔ Includes links to your pages on social media networks like Facebook, Twitter, and LinkedIn

Use Table 16-1 to help you identify ways you can improve your current site. Answer the questions in the table and take note of any updates you can make to your site to increase its overall effectiveness.

Table 16-1	Rate Your Web Site	
Web Consideration	**Yes or No**	**Ideas for How You Can Improve Your Site**
Has your site been updated within a month?		
Does your site include stories of people served by your organization?		
Do you post photos on your Web site?		
Do you list your board on your site?		
Do you offer donors the ability to donate online?		
Can donors sign up for an e-newsletter on your site?		
Do you provide a way for visitors to volunteer?		
Do you include links to social media tools on your site?		
Are your annual report and Form 990 available on your site?		
Do you provide existing volunteers resources on your site (for example, service schedules and opportunities for upcoming events)?		
Do you have an organizational wish list for in-kind donations and services?		

Building credibility for your organization

Having a Web site is a big step toward establishing your organization's credibility. When potential donors can find you online, you're well on your way to building your organization's legitimacy in your donors' eyes.

The Web is a big place, and most donors know that appearances can be deceiving. Small, kitchen-table nonprofits can look as big as national organizations online when they have talented Web designers at the helm.

How can you let your potential donors know that you're a reputable organization? Here are a few tried-and-true ideas:

- ✔ List your mission, history, and board where visitors can find the information easily.

- ✔ Provide visitors with an e-mail address they can send questions and comments to (and be sure to respond to messages quickly).

- ✔ Display your organization's physical address on every page of your Web site (putting it at the bottom of the page is fine).

- ✔ Make your Form 990s and annual report available as downloadable PDFs.

- ✔ Use a secure transaction site (like PayPal or DonateNow) to take online donations.

People are somewhat cautious about online scams and their personal privacy (as they should be). Be willing to go the distance and then some to show your online donors that you mean what you say. Down the road, your efforts will mean better-informed, more-committed constituents and a well-developed, useful, thriving Web site.

Adding Content and Keeping It Fresh

In times of economic challenge, your Web space (which includes your Web site and all your content in social media networks) becomes valuable real estate because it provides a low- or no-cost way for you to share your stories with the world. When you refresh your Web content regularly, sharing touching success stories, requests for volunteers, board involvement, and news about your organization, you show the world that you're thriving and continuing to do good work, no matter what the financial landscape may be.

Updating your Web content regularly not only gives your visitors something new to look at when they visit your site, but also increases your chances of appearing at the top of the results list when visitors search for your organization using popular search engines. We give you some suggestions for how to keep your content fresh in the following sections.

Putting your contact information front and center

Don't hide your light under a basket. Many people who come to your site may be looking for your contact information. Don't make them go through pages of content and scroll down just to find a simple phone number. Put your phone number, address, and e-mail address on every page of your site. Include a Contact Us page that puts all your contact information in one easy-to-find place, including a way to e-mail individual staff members directly.

Remember to include your organization's name and logo on every page to help reinforce your organization's brand. For more about branding your organization, see Chapter 17.

Including information that saves time

One of the great benefits your Web site offers when times are tight is a place where donors can find and download for free items that would otherwise cost your organization money and time to gather and mail. In addition to posting documents such as newsletters and brochures that volunteers would ordinarily stuff and mail, you can post your events calendar, hours, directions to your location, or anything else that people ask frequently. Doing so allows your volunteers to focus their time and effort on other tasks that may be more directly connected to fulfilling your organization's mission, such as reading to young children, building homes for the homeless, or going door to door to collect canned foods for your annual food drive.

Writing content yourself

If you have the time and energy to write fresh, new content on a regular basis, more power to you. But writing online content can be time consuming, especially when you need to refresh it regularly.

Try to spread the work around and post articles written by you, other staff members, board members, or volunteers. Even though you may have to edit materials for quality, organize a writing effort that involves many people to keep new ideas and perspectives at the forefront — and to keep you from becoming swamped with an endless need for new content.

Using existing materials

You can also keep your online content fresh by thinking creatively about ways to use the materials you already created for other purposes. You can simply modify these materials slightly for the Web. For example, you may want to take a look at the content in the following items and try to adapt them for Web use:

- Brochures
- Case studies of people served by your group

- Fundraising direct mail pieces
- Grant proposals describing exciting new projects
- Newspaper articles about your activities
- Posters for upcoming events
- Press releases
- Print newsletters
- Reprinted letters of gratitude from constituents (with their permission, of course)
- Your mission statement

The point is to use these materials you've created to keep your Web site interesting. Here are just a few ideas for how you can modify already-created materials for the Web:

- Add photos, videos, or audio clips.
- Use Web-friendly fonts and offer printable and downloadable versions.
- Keep stories brief and to the point. (As a general rule, people don't read lengthy documents on their computer screens.)

Linking to content on other Web sites

Another way to add interest to your Web site is by adding content from other sites. One option for doing so is adding a news feed to your site (a kind of subset of a news feed is called an *RSS feed,* which stands for Really Simple Syndication). Essentially, to add a news feed to your site, you use code provided by another site to place a feed of their content onto your site. News organizations like *The Washington Post* and *The New York Times* provide RSS feeds for their content. To keep your site interesting and relevant to potential donors and volunteers, you can include an RSS feed that relates to your particular industry area to provide site visitors with recent news about the area that impacts the people you serve.

You can also put links to other sites on your site. Doing so provides site visitors with a way to move from your site to another site to read its content and then to return to your site to keep browsing your content. Although your site visitors obtain the content from somebody else's site, they get to that other site through your site, which is a benefit visitors will associate with your site.

Search engines track links, so the greater number of links you include on your site, the more likely it is to get picked up by major search engines. So go ahead — link away!

Considering the value of online media

On today's Web it's easier than ever to add YouTube videos, podcasts, streaming content, Webinars, and more. All these items can run on your Web page, and you can add them almost as easily as you add links to other Web pages.

If you plan to venture into adding media to your site, make sure you consider the following questions:

- **What kinds of media will your visitors enjoy?** Video clips can be fun and engaging — and can tell a great story — but they can also annoy some visitors. Will you provide an opt-out option so people who don't want to watch your ten-minute video can skip it?

- **How computer savvy are your visitors?** Not all site visitors have state-of-the-art computer systems with the processing power (or the Internet bandwidth) to run high-end videos, large podcasts, or sophisticated animations. Instead of frustrating your visitors who have slower systems, think about how you can create a Web experience that will satisfy the greatest number of visitors.

- **Is your media original?** Most public sites like YouTube and Facebook today want you to guarantee either that the content you're uploading is original or that you have the necessary permissions to post the content. In other words, the videos and podcasts you post should be your own work or work that has been done expressly for your organization. Additionally, if any of the people you serve are in the videos, photos, or podcasts you want to upload, be sure you have their written permission before posting their likeness on the Web.

 A Webinar is a relatively new offering that can provide an exciting mix of instruction and inspiration, including chats, presentations, videos, and more. Find out more about hosting Webinars in Chapter 19.

Attracting Visitors to Your Site

The most obvious way to let people know about your Web site is to print it on each and every scrap of material that leaves your office. Here are just some of the places you can note your Web site address:

- Banners for events
- Brochures
- Bumper stickers

- ✔ Business cards
- ✔ E-mail newsletters
- ✔ Envelopes
- ✔ Grant applications
- ✔ Letters
- ✔ Press releases
- ✔ Public service announcements
- ✔ Signature line of your e-mail messages
- ✔ Social media sites
- ✔ Thank-you notes
- ✔ Volunteer nametags

One easy way to help people remember your site is to choose a Web address that's as close to your organization's name as possible. For example, the Web address for Indy Great Pyrenees Rescue is `www.igpr.org`. The Web address for the Jazz Institute of Chicago is `www.jazzinchicago.org`. When folks are guessing what your site may be, they often simply type a logical address in their browser to try to find you, so the more straightforward your Web address is, the better.

Sometimes people aren't looking for your organization or its Web site when they happen to stumble onto you by other means online. Isn't the Internet great? In the following sections, we tell you how to increase your chances of having this kind of situation happen.

Showing up in search engine results

Search engines such as Yahoo!, Google, Bing, and ChaCha help people find Web sites. The search engines regularly "crawl" the Web searching out new sites to include in their ever-growing indexes. Use the following tips to help your Web site show up in search result lists:

- ✔ **Submit your Web address to as many search engines as you can.** Go to `www.google.com/support/webmasters/bin/answer.py?answer=70897` to find out more about how Google finds and indexes sites for the Google search engine.

- ✔ **Think carefully about the keywords that are linked to your organization in a typical search.** If you're an animal rights group, for example, list yourself under the obvious *animals, dogs,* and *cats,* but don't forget *animal rights, animal advocacy, pets,* and *animal protection.*

> ✔ **Research submission services to find out whether you want to hire a service to submit your information to many search engines at once.** Sites such as www.morevisibility.com and www.wpromote.com are examples of these services.
>
> ✔ **Get included in lists of nonprofits on nonprofit information sites like www.charitywatch.org.** When people search those sites for your name, you want it to pop up.

Getting linked by other sites

If you're working with a Web designer to design your site, don't forget to have him or her also create an easily distributable link to your site. You can bring your site lots of traffic just by giving other sites the code they can place on their sites to allow people to jump to your site easily. Some sites post an icon or your logo for the link; others include a text link (your name highlighted in blue) that people can click to go to your site. Either way, site visitors have an easy way to go from one site to your site in seconds!

Here are some ideas of people or organizations you can ask to link to your site:

✔ Organizations with similar causes in other regions of the country or world

✔ Organizations or people who run sites that are central points for information about your type of cause

✔ Local organizations or corporations that you work with on a regular basis

✔ Media outlets such as local newspapers that offer nonprofits links on their sites

✔ Friends and fans who have connected with you through social media, such as Facebook, Twitter, LinkedIn, and blogs

 If you modify your site address in some fashion, don't forget to share the new address with other sites or provide a way for them to be forwarded from the old link to your new site. Otherwise, people trying to get to your site will hit a dead end and may give up trying to find you on the spot.

Collecting Donations Online

More and more nonprofit organizations today are offering their donors the ability to donate online. Although the typical online donor gives less than an offline donor, the good news is that many donors give both ways — with smaller increments online and larger amounts through the mail or in person.

When you offer your donors the ability to give online, you provide them with a convenient way to support you that they can access 24 hours a day. You also give people who are moved by the work you're doing the chance to donate anytime they're on your site without having to call anyone to make a pledge.

With so many benefits, why wouldn't you want to offer an online donation feature? Just make sure you post the fact that you accept online donations all over your site so visitors can easily find and use the feature.

Be sure to note on all your print materials that you accept donations online, and don't forget to include your Web site address, too. Even if you're sending a paper donation form to a potential donor, note your Web donation information on it, as well. Some people find it easier to make an online donation than to write a check, address and stamp an envelope, and put the letter in the mail — and making donating easy is one of your main fundraising goals.

When you set up a system to accept online payments, you need to design an interactive electronic form that users can easily fill out, navigate, and submit. You also need to allow for a selection of different payment types.

Be sure to make the donation form you post online printable for those donors who start to give online and then change their minds and decide to print the form and mail a check instead.

If your organization is already set up to accept credit card donations in person, you're pretty much set to accept credit card payments submitted online, too. Depending on how your Web site is set up to receive the payment information, you can elect to receive the electronic form in your office and then manually process the payment along with all your other credit card payments. Talk to your Web designer for more information on how credit card payments can be submitted and received from your Web site.

If you aren't set up to accept credit cards, you have to complete a few steps to get ready to accept online payments. First, you need to get a merchant ID from your state so that you can then set up a merchant account to receive credit card payments; then you have to complete the setup process with the credit card companies you want to accept payments from. Sites such as WorldPay (www.rbsworldpay.com) explain what you need to do to set yourself up to accept online credit card payments. Finally, you can use a payment service such as PayPal (www.paypal.com) to accept payments from people's bank accounts with bankcard payments.

Don't want to go through the hassle of setting up a merchant account to receive online payments? Consider using a third-party charity donation site to gather online donations for you. Sites such as Network for Good (www.networkforgood.org) charge a monthly subscription fee and offer services that handle all the donation submissions and processing for you.

As you prepare to raise funds online, do research in your home state to find out about any fundraising regulations that may apply. Some states require registration and will want to know how much you raise online and from where you raise it. Online fundraising is a quickly growing area, so be sure you have someone on your fundraising team who can help you navigate the legal issues if you plan to raise funds in cyberspace.

Chapter 17

Extending Your Brand Online

*H*ow is your organization known in your community? In your industry? In the world? When people think of your organization, what do you want them to feel? When they see your logo, what do you want them to remember about you?

The answers to these questions point to something important your organization builds with every single donor contact: your brand. This chapter helps you think through the brand you're creating as you communicate with your donors using various online approaches. Of course, your brand doesn't begin and end in the online realm — your brand is the intrinsic value and meaning your organization has in the minds and hearts of your donors. Your brand reaches right to the center of what your donors believe is true about you.

In this chapter, we help you understand what it takes to create a good brand, and then we show you how to use the Internet to extend the reach of your brand so you're reaching as many people as possible with the message you want to convey.

Knowing Your Branding Basics

Branding is a well-established phenomenon that dates back to the early days of advertising, but recently it's become more and more a part of the non-profit world. *Branding* describes the way a product, organization, company, or other entity is known and valued in the public eye. Your *brand identity* lets you know how many people recognize your brand on sight.

What do you think of when you read the names *Goodwill Industries, Red Cross,* or *United Way?* Unfortunately, not all your thoughts may be positive, thanks to challenges some of these organizations have faced in recent years. But when you consider what you know about the organizations — what they stand for, what services you think they provide, how they help others — you're considering what you know about their brands.

Your donors have similar thoughts about you. When they receive an e-mail message from you or they visit your Web site, they have a certain belief about who you are and what you do. As donors, they internalize your brand to some degree — and as a good, communication-savvy fundraiser, you want to build on the positive impact of your brand and make sure increasing numbers of people know about it.

Especially in times of economic challenge, your brand is a vitally important part of your organization's identity. How do people perceive your brand today? Your answer to that question may help you jumpstart interest in areas that had previously fallen flat. For example, John serves on the board of the Indianapolis Museum of Art, and, after testing its brand, the museum found that the general public regarded the art museum as an elitist organization. As a result, the organization and its board began working to change that perception. Their new ad campaign, "It's your art," built on the idea that the museum is accessible, open, and welcoming to all people interested in art.

Although you can find the term *branding* used in many ways in both the for-profit and nonprofit realms, we use it in this book to refer to the way your public knows you — both through personal experience and through the public sense of who and what you are. Luckily, the question of how you're perceived isn't answered only in the minds of your beholders; the messages you offer and the ways in which you communicate with your donors both directly and indirectly, online and in person, help you reinforce the brand you want to build long-term.

Assessing Your Brand

So if you're a small organization, how do you find out what the public's perception of you is? When you want to assess the brand your organization is developing, the best place to begin is with a good question:

> When you hear your organization's name (or see the logo), what occurs to you?

You can ask this question to donors, focus groups, people receiving your services, other organizations, or random passersby. You can send people around with clipboards, canvassing neighborhoods in your area. You can do a telephone campaign with the sole purpose of gauging public awareness.

You can hire a group to test your brand and give you a report on public perception (yes, this option is a little pricey, but it's likely to give you good info to start with).

You can also begin your brand assessment closer to home — with yourself and your board. Asking yourself and your board questions like the following can get you started in the right direction:

- ✔ How have we been mentioned in the news in the last six months?
- ✔ What are we hearing from long-time donors?
- ✔ Why do new donors say they've decided to support us?
- ✔ Which organizations in our community have contacted us in the last year for possible partnering opportunities?
- ✔ How do we feel we're regarded in our town?

These questions can keep you busy for an afternoon — or longer — and can get you thinking outside your walls to the larger public picture. In your brand assessment, be sure to include important bits of data like how many people visit your Web site during the month, how many people subscribe to your e-newsletter, and what your fan base looks like on Facebook.

Whether you use a third party to help you evaluate your organization's brand or you do it yourself (with your board and key staff members), pull all your data together in a brainstorming session and seek to get a sense of how your organization is currently perceived. The next challenge is to determine whether your results are pointing in the right direction, and, if they're not, how you can do a brand makeover with your communications efforts. The following sections explain what you can do if your organization is in need of a brand makeover.

Tweaking your brand

Suppose that after putting together a series of focus groups, an online survey, and a number of discussions with tried-and-true loyal volunteers, you determine that the public doesn't quite understand your organization's mission. Perhaps your organization is perceived to be a group that serves the elderly in your community when you really serve all families of any age. You have some tweaking to do to make sure that your services and programs are heard by the right people. Where do you begin?

First, evaluate your existing messaging and try to determine where you can expand stories, images, and more to show the piece of the puzzle that's missing from the public's perception — in the case of our example, the younger people in your community. Return to your e-mail messages, annual report, newsletters, brochures, Web content, and more. Anything that speaks to your organization's identity requires your full attention to determine where and how you can include the missing group more obviously.

Next, develop a new campaign designed to raise awareness specifically for the audience group that's previously been overlooked. Similar to the way the Indianapolis Museum of Art included the whole community — not just the elite population — in the "It's your art" campaign (see the "Knowing Your Branding Basics" section for specifics), develop a message that speaks directly to the mistaken view reflected back by your brand analysis. This helps you focus on the group of donors that may have missed your messaging in the past — which can translate to a boost in fundraising for your organization.

Finally, be consistent in your expanded messaging and be sure your improved branding efforts are reflected not only in print pieces and e-mail but also in the various ways you reach out online (which just happen to be the branding channels we cover in this chapter).

Developing brand strategies

Throughout Part III of this book, we talk about various ways to tell your story and build your organization's perception in the public eye. We cover sharing your story in social media outlets; working with television, radio, and more; improving your Web site; and sending e-mail and e-newsletters. Each of these avenues enables you to tell your story and invite donor engagement (and, hopefully, gifts).

The rest of this chapter focuses on additional ways you can help spread the news about your organization using online channels. The following sections offer additional online options for building your brand.

The most important way to communicate with your donor is the way in which he or she is most likely to hear what you have to say. Depending on the age and interest of your donors, and the focus of your mission and programs, different strategies work best for different groups. When in doubt about which communication outlet will work best with your particular set of donors, ask a few of your long-time supporters which outlets they prefer and which ones have provided them with the most useful information about your organization over the years. They'll be pleased you asked for their insight, and you'll gain the perspective of people who really know what you do and who you are.

Blogging Your Way to Funds

Chances are you're already aware of blogs. Maybe you even have one. Although blogging began as a kind of opinionated personal journalism, blogging started a new era of publishing that gave the voice of some authority to personal experience and perspective. Today individuals and organizations have blogs on which they share commentary, responses, links to other sites, photos, and even personal diaries.

As an individual fundraiser, you can either create your own blog or blog as the voice of your organization (be sure to check with your board and executive director about doing so before you set up your blog). Visit sites such as www.weblogtoolscollection.com or www.blogger.com to find simple tools for creating blogs. After you've created your blog, get it listed in blog directories like www.blogcatalog.com for maximum exposure. Or spend some time visiting blogs that relate to your area of interest, and post a few of your own comments, sharing the mission and passion (and Web site address, of course!) of your organization with others.

As you set up your blog, you may want to add an *RSS feed* to your blog so readers can easily know what's happening with your organization. *RSS* stands for *Really Simple Syndication* and it enables readers who subscribe to your RSS feed to automatically receive any fresh content you put on the blog. RSS feeds make receiving your updates easy for your blog readers and help you know your stories are being heard. For more about RSS feeds, see Chapter 16, and also consult *Syndicating Web Sites with RSS Feeds For Dummies,* by Ellen Finklestein (Wiley).

Figuring the cost of blogs

Blogs don't cost a whole lot to produce, except the cost of your time to post content, monitor the blog discussion, and respond to blog comments. For example, Blogger (www.blogger.com), which is Google's blogger service, is absolutely free. Setting up a blog on that site can take as little as a few minutes.

Going, giving, gone!

Following in the successful wake of eBay, online charity auctions are a recent phenomenon. These auctions offer cool ways to raise money for a particular cause or event. MissionFish (www.missionfish.com) is one good example of an online charity auction. You can trade on eBay through the MissionFish site. eBay sellers select a charity to sponsor, and then a portion of any of their sales goes to that charity. Donors can go to www.mission fish.com to see a list of eBay sellers associated with giving. You can easily sign up on this site to get your nonprofit registered with MissionFish. You just need to provide information about your 501(c)(3) status, a mission statement, a voided check, your e-mail address, and an electronic version of your logo. Best of all, registration is free.

Perhaps the greatest cost is in marketing your blog. But consider that you can piggyback your blog marketing onto every other marketing vehicle you use (your brochures or Web site, for example), and you can include the blog link in the signature line of every e-mail message you write for free.

Building your brand with an effective blog

Writing a blog is a little different from writing a brochure or a fundraising proposal. The idea here is to keep people intrigued and participating — and to continue to reinforce your brand in the process. Here's what you need to do to create a blog that helps you build your brand (and keeps readers interested at the same time!):

- ✔ Write about stories that showcase key ways your organization lives out its mission with real people.
- ✔ Post questions that get people thinking and contributing their own ideas.
- ✔ Offer statistics about your cause that may be new to your audience.
- ✔ Keep your posts positive. Be a voice of truth and hope in your industry, and reinforce the brand idea that your organization is an expert in a particular area and is working to be relevant to the needs of your community.

Publishing Online to Boost Your Branding and Credibility

If you've ever written a press release, you know the value of just getting your organization's name in print. The Internet contains a huge amount of content, and some sites may welcome articles or other pieces of news about your group. Not only will you gain positive exposure by getting published online, but you also build credibility for yourself and your organization by being quoted as an expert in your area of service.

Another great thing about publishing online is that information seldom sits still on one site. Other sites or search engines pick up links to articles; people forward articles to others via e-mail. Putting an article or press release out on the Web is like dropping a pebble in a pond: The ripples can continue for quite a while. The following sections can help you get published on the Web.

Getting published

To get content published online, you can follow several approaches:

✔ Visit sites that are somehow related to your target donor groups' interests, and send e-mails to the Webmasters of those sites, using the links on their Contact Us pages.

✔ Check out online versions of magazines or newspapers related to your potential donors' interests to see whether they include information on how to submit stories to them somewhere on their Web sites. For example, if you work for a musical performing arts organization, you may check into sites that cover musical interests, local music performances, or music schools.

✔ Submit questions or comments that may get published to related online publications with letters-to-the-editor kinds of features.

Some sites publish content that is then picked up for use on other sites. You can submit some of your own content to these sites — along with info about your organization, of course — to help build your visibility online. Try using these sites, called *content directories*, such as How To Advice (www.howto advice.com), to submit online content that gets exposure on many sites. Some sites also provide templates and articles explaining how you can write and submit content to their sites.

Creating good online content

You're more likely to get your submissions published if their content is what the publishing sites are looking for. Here are a few tips to help you create content that works well on the Web:

✔ **Pay attention to submission guidelines.** If the guidelines say no more than 300 words, don't submit an article with 350.

✔ **Format the article correctly.** Some sites want submissions in HTML, while others want plain text. Receiving articles in the proper format saves sites time and effort in making your content look presentable online.

✔ **Make the title mean something.** You want to grab attention right away, so make your title mean something to readers. After all, the title of your article may be the only thing that appears in a link a visitor clicks to view the entire article.

✔ **Use a good text editor, and check spelling and grammar.** Use the spell-checker in your favorite word-processing program before you send your content to an editor. You want your organization to look as good as possible, so make sure you double-check your spelling and grammar. After all, you want your readers to see that you care about your cause and your mission.

Joining Online Communities: Discussion Groups

A *discussion group* is an online community that discusses an area of common interest. Hundreds of thousands of discussion groups are available online, with topics ranging from schnauzers to special events.

Discussion groups have been a part of the Web for a relatively long time, but their power to connect with others and stimulate conversation about topics continues today. In many places online today, however, the old term *discussion forum* has become *discussion group.* Regardless of what they're called, these community-gathering spots where people post messages are reminiscent of bulletin boards you find in your office break room or local library. Discussion group conversations can go on for months or even years and involve hundreds of people.

You can use discussion groups to connect to the fundraising community for advice, or you can use them to gain exposure for your organization. Always be sure to include your organization's name, blog address, and social media connections in your signature line. And be aware that the content of your post — a relatively simple communication — is building your brand with every word you write.

The following sections offer some good places to start if you're seeking a discussion group to join. We also offer some tips about topics to address and avoid.

Checking out nonprofit discussion groups

As you begin your search for the right discussion group to join, take note of the many nonprofit-related choices out there. You can post comments on the discussion groups of fundraising-related sites to receive helpful advice and tips, or you can post on general nonprofit sites just to get your organization's name and mission out there for people to see. So how does the discussion group work? When you post a message, it becomes available in a discussion area to both the site's members and its visitors. People read your message and can respond with a comment. When you get multiple replies to your message, you end up with what's called a *discussion thread.*

More nonprofit-related discussion groups are springing up all the time. Here's a representative sampling for you to check out:

✔ **CharityChannel.com:** Click on the Forum link on the CharityChannel.com home page (`www.charitychannel.com`) to access discussion groups on topics such as annual funds and development.

✔ **Soc.org.nonprofit:** You can join the soc.org.nonprofit discussion group (one of the oldest nonprofit discussion groups out there) either by using a newsreader program to subscribe to the USENET group called soc.org.nonprofit or by sending an e-mail to `nonprofit-request@rain.org` with the word *Subscribe* in the subject field.

✔ **About.com:** Although this Web site provides information about many topics, you can go to `www.nonprofit.about.com` and click the Community Forum in the Discuss area of the page to find out more about nonprofit-related discussion groups you can join.

✔ **Idealist.org:** This site offers almost 2,000 idealist groups in 127 countries, boasting more than 20,000 members. You're sure to find a conversation you'll enjoy here. Go to `www.idealist.org` and click Groups to get started.

Promoting yourself through discussion groups

To get exposure for your organization among the donor population, try posting comments on sites related to your cause rather than on fundraising sites. Focusing on cause-related sites may be more useful because people who give money to your type of cause look for sites related to your cause, while other professional fundraisers visit fundraising sites. For example, if your organization deals with battered women, go to sites that provide advice or services to those people. If your organization helps take care of rescued animals, go to large chain pet store sites, sites that advise people on what breed of puppy is right for them, or pet food company sites and see if they have discussion groups you can join.

When you post comments in discussion groups, don't post a self-serving appeal for funds — doing so isn't good etiquette (see the nearby "Discussion group etiquette" sidebar for more info). Instead, try to provide information or respond to others' questions in a way that's useful and simply include a quick mention of your organization and your Web site address in your message. Over time, you establish a presence in these discussion groups, and people recognize that your group cares enough to help others out. In turn, they may wander over to your Web site and help you out with a donation. Remember, taking part in discussion groups is community building, not advertising! Discussion group involvement can be time consuming, but it can pay off in the end.

Discussion group etiquette

When posting to a discussion group, always make the subject of your post meaningful so others can easily figure out what your topic is and decide whether they want to become involved. Check your post for errors and clarity. Error-ridden postings are not only hard to read, but may also reflect badly on your organization. Be careful what you say: If you're responding to a negative comment about your organization, don't let your emotions take charge. Be thoughtful, informative, and gracious in your reply. Remember that your comments in discussion groups reflect on your organization as well as on you. Anyone can copy an irate posting and send it around the world via e-mail or some other vehicle. Do you really want something said in the heat of the moment to represent your cause and your organization?

Instant messaging and chat groups are different from discussion groups in that the conversations are held in real time (called *synchronous* communication in techie circles). In a discussion group, you post a message one day, and somebody reads it sometime later (called *asynchronous* communication). With instant messaging and chat groups, you send a message to somebody who gets it almost immediately and responds.

Partnering Online through Affinity Programs

An *affinity program* is an arrangement with a for-profit organization that agrees to donate a certain percentage of income to your charitable cause. For example, have you ever gotten a call from a magazine telling you that if you buy a subscription, they'll give $1 to some worthwhile cause? Or, does your local superstore offer a program whereby you can donate to local schools as you check out? If so, you've already encountered affinity programs in action. If your organization has a large membership or works with a large donor base, affinity partnerships may be particularly attractive to vendors because your large constituency enables them to expand their reach into new areas.

You may be surprised to find out just how many different affinity programs are out there. For example, Igive.com (www.igive.com) offers an affinity program that provides a penny for every search you do on its site and a percentage of each purchase you make there to the nonprofit organization of your choice. Other affinity programs offer credit cards that pay out a percentage to a sponsored nonprofit.

Notice that an *affiliate* program is different from an affinity program. With an affiliate program, you put a link to another Web site on your own site. When people click the link to go to the other site, you get a small commission. Affiliate programs can be profitable, but be sure that the affiliate sites are of good quality and that they relate to your areas of interest. Otherwise, your constituency will click on them and be offended, or just plain bored, with the result.

Keep in mind that the affinity groups you partner with want to make money off the goodwill your name generates, but they offer you an additional fundraising venue that can be profitable. Consider the character of an affinity group carefully before getting involved with its program. With affinity programs, you're stepping into the world of commerce, and you certainly don't want a badly or shadily run business hurting your organization's brand or reputation.

Because affinity groups are involved in e-commerce, the income you get from involvement in them can be subject to unrelated business income tax. Check with your lawyer or accountant before signing up with an affinity program.

Connecting with People through Association and Special-Interest Sites

Just as in the real world, people find people (and organizations) in different places online. Where you get noticed has a lot to do with the way people interpret your mission. If your site appears on a national organization in your particular service area, for example, this adds to the credibility of your nonprofit. If you show up on a hip, cool site frequented by college students, you may be seen as a youth-friendly organization. You may find that simply placing links to your site on other sites that attract visitors with common interests is a good way to build your organization's brand online.

Here are some examples of typical site-to-site connections you may want to explore:

✔ If your group supports animal rights, go to the Web sites for the American Society for Prevention of Cruelty to Animals (ASPCA) (www.aspca.org) and People for Ethical Treatment of Animals (PETA) (www.peta.org) to ask them to put a link to your site on theirs. Don't forget to also contact PetSmart, which has a charity to help homeless animals, as well as other pet food and supply companies.

- ✔ If you represent a health-related group, such as one that works for breast cancer research, consider any sites related to health concerns, sites directed toward women as a group, and sites related to medical associations.

- ✔ If your organization is raising funds for the arts, try the sites for your local arts council, record stores and bookstores, art supply stores, and libraries.

The point here is that the groups and sites you can partner with to build your organization's brand are limited only by your imagination. On the Internet, the rule is constant change, so go ahead and ask whether a site will add a link to your site; what can it hurt?

Part IV

Engaging Your Givers with the Right Campaigns

The 5th Wave   By Rich Tennant

"The university is certainly grateful for this check you're writing, and we all look forward to seeing your nephew, Grant, no pun intended, at our school in a few years."

In this part . . .

Being able to tell your story, connect with your donors, relate to your board, and create a good plan for fundraising are important parts of successful fundraising in any economic climate. All that work leads to the ultimate goal: raising the funds to operate your organization.

Knowing how to use the various campaigns at your disposal — annual fund drives, special events, capital campaigns, major gift programs, corporate-giving programs, and endowments — helps you make a great connection between your donors' ability to give and your organization's needs. This part of the book introduces you to each of these fundraising campaigns and shows you how to start, run, assess, and reuse these various campaigns so you get the biggest possible benefit from your fundraising efforts.

Chapter 18

Organizing, Implementing, and Celebrating Your Annual Fund

In This Chapter

▶ Checking out what annual funds are

▶ Setting up your annual campaign and putting it in motion

▶ Evaluating your campaign and preparing for the next one

*Y*our annual fund is the heart of your fundraising program. In both good and bad economic times, your annual fund is what keeps your organization going — which means it also needs to be at the center of your fundraising efforts.

Most people are familiar with the annual fund drives held in their communities. You receive requests from the local zoo, churches, and schools, just to name a few. Even with this familiarity, however, most people who are approached to give have no idea of the work involved in running an annual fund campaign. Although each annual fund drive is different, careful planning, collaboration, and good management — along with effective result tracking — are key ingredients to the successful annual fund that has the potential to grow over time, no matter what the economy is doing at the moment.

This chapter introduces you to the basics of annual funds. Here, we offer you ideas for setting up and running a successful annual fund, as well as warn you about the "plan busters" that can hang you up along the way.

Understanding the Basics of Annual Funds

The *annual fund* is the fundraising drive that supports the operating costs and day-to-day program costs of your organization. Unlike large gifts that come from major donations, program initiatives, special events, or grant funding, the annual fund is comprised largely of smaller gifts from a wider variety of givers. The annual fund may pay your staff's salaries, keep your lights on, put the roof over your heads, and pay for the vehicles that allow you to deliver your services. For this reason, annual funds can sometimes be difficult to maintain and grow thanks to their appeal factor — or lack thereof. After all, would you rather contribute to a fund that will pave the organization's parking lot or to a program that directly impacts people in need?

The important connection to make here — both for yourself and for your donor — is that both the annual fund and programmatic support work together to make realizing the mission of your organization possible. The annual fund provides the foundation on which you build all other programs and services. When you have a healthy annual fund, you not only have the start on some security for your organization, but you also have an engaged group of donors. And if you can provide those engaged donors — even if they currently give only $25 a year — with a good experience of your organization (which means being respectful and responsive as part of your annual fund drive), you have the potential to increase that donor's involvement with your organization. Perhaps the donor will become a volunteer. Maybe she'll increase the size of her gift. Maybe she'll have such a good experience that she tells others about your organization, leading them to get involved, too. Simply put, the success and growth of your organization's work starts with a well-planned annual fund.

Your annual fund may be large or small; you may spend weeks or only days planning it. Regardless, the system you develop and the planning you put into it are closely related — the more well thought out your plan is, the greater the return on your annual fund investment is likely to be.

Some big organizations hire fundraising consulting firms to help them determine whether expanded fundraising expectations are realistic. If you don't want to hire an outside firm, go out and interview some prospective donors. Ask them to look at your mission statement and then ask, "Is this doable? Are our expectations out of line? Would this be a realistic donation option for you?" Using a focus group in this way takes a lot of legwork, but the result can be a tested fundraising goal with a number of people getting on board before the fundraising train leaves the station.

Annual Fund Buster #1: Not having a plan. If you think you can simply work toward your annual fund all year long without a specific strategy in place, think again. If you don't have a specific plan in mind for your annual fund campaign, the funds that come in for that campaign will be spotty and short lived. With a carefully prepared annual fund plan, on the other hand, you know what you're spending, how much you anticipate raising, who your key players are, and how you need to evaluate the effectiveness of the various parts of your plan after you reach your goals. Most importantly, you can demonstrate clearly how your annual fund relates to your cash flow needs. If your plan enables you to share that story with your donors, they'll be more likely to make the connection about why contributing to your annual fund is vital to the health of your organization.

Helping your donors help you

One of the most compelling reasons for putting your best thought and effort into your annual fund is that your annual fund has the potential to reach donors you rarely get to reach through other campaigns. Unlike major givers, who most likely have some kind of continuing contact with your organization, annual givers are those small donors who may give a small, single donation once or twice a year. They may decide to give a small donation after visiting your Web site or after receiving an e-mail message or a newsletter about new programs or announcements. Or they may become fans on your Facebook page. For the most part, though, this large group of donors and potential donors isn't very involved with the day-to-day operation of your organization, which means huge potential for you.

When you approach your annual fund givers in tough financial times, consider sharing information on how to help them find a sense of financial security while still continuing to give. In doing so, you share your need with your potential donors while simultaneously showing them how making even a small gift helps your organization and enables them to make a difference in a cause they care about. As you prepare your annual fund approach, check out the book *Financial Peace Planner* by Dave Ramsey (Penguin), which includes practical ideas on giving as one part of building a healthy financial future. You can find many other books on the subject, as well.

Designing Your Annual Campaign

As you can see, the annual fund is the center of all the fundraising efforts for your organization. The time you spend planning and implementing your annual fund campaign relates directly to the success of the drive (and indirectly to the success of your other campaigns) — spend the time now, put the systems in place, and go about your other fundraising efforts in an organized way. Taking the time to plan your annual fund drive beats the socks off launching blindly into the unknown and hoping a certain percentage of donors will want to support your continuing efforts.

To have a successful annual fund drive, you need to do the following:

- ✔ Know your goals.
- ✔ Plan your timing.
- ✔ Have a well-prepared team.
- ✔ Know which tools to use.
- ✔ Evaluate your efforts.

The following sections explore each of these important areas in more depth. In essence, these five areas provide the blueprint for putting together a well-thought-out annual fund drive.

Communication *is* education

Especially in a tough economic climate when people are tempted to clutch their purse strings more tightly, you need to make sure you tell your story well. You need to be able to articulate why contributing to your annual fund is a good idea for donors — and why their contributions are vital to the accomplishment of your mission. If you can tell your story well, with heart and creativity, you can show your donors what your annual fund is all about and inspire them to help keep the organization rolling.

When you create your appeal for the annual fund, think of it as a way to educate your donors about the importance of ongoing support.

Connect the appeal to real stories and real people. Invite your donors in to see the day-to-day details; show them where their hard-earned dollars go.

To build awareness for your annual fund, you can even host a series of workdays in which donors can come to your facility and assist with daily operations. This kind of up-close-and-personal experience may remove some of the distance that unfamiliar donors feel with your organization and draw them closer to the heart of what you do, which, as we're sure you know, is a win for everyone.

Setting your goals

Most organizations rely on their annual funds to bring in the money they need to cover their standard operating expenses or to fund vital programs not supported by grant funding or government programs, plus whatever other expenses they need to cover growth in the areas where they've planted seeds. For example, an organization may use annual fund donations to pay for a donor recognition holiday luncheon or to purchase back-to-school kits for an afterschool program.

So what do you hope to cover with your annual fund campaign? You and your board need to put together a list of the goals you want to reach with your annual fund. For best results, appoint a development committee that's willing to devote itself to setting up, carrying out, and evaluating your annual fund drive. And don't forget — your board members and all those serving on committees should be givers themselves.

Be sure to include the following goals for your annual fund, as well as other goals related specifically to your organization's mission:

✔ **Bring in the specific amount of funds you need to reach your annual fund's fundraising target goal.**

Use a giving pyramid, which we describe in Chapter 6, to determine your giving levels and the number of gifts you need in each area to meet your goal. Be sure to spend some time exploring what's realistic for your organization right now.

✔ **Based on the current economic conditions, determine a realistic goal for your organization.**

In good financial times, you may plan to surpass the previous year's budget, but in times of hardship you may decide to lower your budget instead. Whether or not you publish the budget reduction in your budget is up to you, but showing the reduction in tough economic times may say something good about your organization — it sends a message about your willingness to be frugal when you need to be.

✔ **Find new donors and upgrade existing donors.**

A great way to gauge your opportunity for engaging donors is to take a look at the recent history showing how many regular donors have lapsed in the past year. Simply look at your donor records to find out who gave two years ago but didn't give in the previous year. Then do what you can to bring those lost donors back to your cause. Especially in a turbulent economy, you're likely to get the greatest return on your fundraising investment by working to upgrade your current donors and invite back individuals who have given to your organization in the past.

✔ **Enlist and train a dedicated volunteer corps.**

✔ **Identify potential higher-level donors.**

Every organization is different, and all donor groups have their own unique personalities. For this reason, the best advice we can offer you in terms of setting goals for your annual fund is to *talk to your donors.* Know what situations and issues your donors are facing. What's on their minds right now? What are they feeling good about? What are they worried about? How does your organization fit in? One large nonprofit organization recently decided to cut its annual fund budget during a tough financial situation. After making the decision, some members of the organization went out and did a focus group to find out whether there's a difference between big donors and small donors in troubled times — and they found that everyone was hurting. As a result of their research, the organization was able to change its messaging to connect with its donors in new and unique ways. For the best results for your own organization, let your donors tell you about the factors that are influencing their giving decisions today.

Setting an annual fund goal can be a struggle in organizations large and small. Why? Because you don't establish your campaign goal in a vacuum. You need to budget all the activities you support with your annual fund, adding the necessary percentage of increase for inflation over last year's budget, and consider how you want to enhance your programs.

Struggles may result between your planning committee ("We want to add services for the kids with no hair this year!") and your budget committee ("That's too much of a stretch for this year — let's try that next year!"). Ultimately, you face a moment of truth when everybody involved in your organization has to come together and ask, "Can we do it?" For many organizations, that moment's a tough one.

Reaching a consensus on your specific fundraising goal for your annual fund is a major part of setting up your annual fund — and doing so may take considerable talking, planning, and reevaluating. Fortunately, all this talking gives your organization the chance to return to its mission statement, take a look at its priorities, and ultimately get everybody working together for the good of the cause.

Timing your annual fund

When the economy is pitching and swaying, remembering the needs of your donors and being creative with your annual fund approach may help you keep the funds coming and draw your donors closer at the same time. By thinking through the timing of your annual fund and giving donors the option of sending gifts in installments (even $10 a month), you show flexibility as well as compassion for your donors. You can also offer the option of automatically debiting donors' bank accounts, depending on who your audience is and how comfortable they are with automatic withdrawal. If your donors see this option as a convenient customer service, it can mean great things for your campaign, but if donors perceive this automatic service as a narrowing of their options, you may not have many takers. This is one reason why knowing your donors is so important as you work through any campaign; see Chapter 7 for details on how you can get to know your donors.

Assembling your team

In larger organizations, the executive director or director of individual giving is in charge of leading the annual fund effort, with the help of an active board and development committee. In smaller organizations, the annual fund drive may be run entirely by volunteers. In churches, for example, one lucky volunteer often gets the lead role in the management of the annual fund; that volunteer's job is to assemble the rest of the team and get the ball rolling. The following sections offer a few tips to get you started as you pull your team together.

Choosing the team leader

Although annual fund leaders come in all shapes and sizes, you want to make sure your leader is a person who's fully aware of your mission. In addition, as with the leaders of other types of fundraising campaigns, the person in charge of your annual fund effort needs to be

- Passionate about your cause
- Able to both see the big picture and focus on the details
- Capable of creating a plan, getting it approved, and inspiring others to work on it

- Recognized as a person with whom people like to work
- Trained in leadership — either in a volunteer or professional capacity
- Respected by your constituency
- Able to put in the hours involved in leading a fundraising campaign

Putting your team in place

After you choose a team leader, you need to focus on assembling the rest of your team. The fundraising team you assemble has a direct impact on how well your annual fund meets its goals, so put some thought into choosing your team members.

Some members of your development committee may double as members of your annual fund team — in fact, you should have at least a member or two represent both groups. Your other team members can be anyone you think would do a good job. Just make sure they understand and feel passionate about the work you do. Important attributes of a team member include the following:

- Ability to communicate effectively
- Track record of following through on what he says he'll do
- Training in basic fundraising skills
- Some experience in fundraising
- A reputation that promotes trust

Ask your board to help identify key volunteers who would be good annual fund team members.

Creating a successful team

You can help make sure the time and effort your annual fund team puts into the project pays off by making sure all the team members have what they need. For instance, your annual fund has a better chance of being successful if you make sure the team members have the following:

- Regular meetings to discuss the goals, strategies, and plans for the annual fund
- Materials used to compile annual fund publications
- Resources for compiling materials
- Access to existing and former donor lists and donor histories
- Prospective donor lists that show how the prospects are related to your organization and give some rationale for their ability to pay or their payment levels
- A system for easily tracking prospective donor responses

Annual Fund Buster #2: An uncommitted board. A lukewarm board won't bring in large checks — and it won't be able to do the day-in, day-out follow-up required to run an effective annual campaign. Be sure that your board understands its role in the fundraising function of your organization before you launch an annual fund drive.

Choosing your fundraising tools

Because you want your annual fund plan to make the most of your resources and to be as effective as possible, take some time to think about which fundraising approaches you want to spend the most time on. We rank the main fundraising approaches here, from most to least effective.

Meeting face to face

A national survey by United Way indicates that seven out of ten people will say yes to a request from one of their peers when asked face to face for a donation. The biggest problem fundraisers have is not asking enough people in person or not involving volunteer leadership in "the Ask" often enough (see Chapter 10 for more on "the Ask").

In a smaller organization, face-to-face contact may not get the same return, but it may very well get a bigger response than any other approach. After all, as the old fundraising saying goes, "People don't give money to causes. People give money to people with causes." The human element is extremely important in any campaign, including the annual fund drive — and a face-to-face meeting gives your donors the easiest way to connect with you.

The best people for face-to-face meetings are those who are peers of the potential donors in the general organizational structure. For example, if you send a CEO in to talk to a top-level manager and the CEO makes a case for the organization, the manager may be left feeling that his donation or refusal could affect his job down the road. Better to avoid the situation altogether and select people for meetings based on their peer status. So instead of sending in the CEO, send in a fellow manager or someone in a comparable role.

When you're fundraising in the workplace, people are likely to take note when you get one of their colleagues to solicit for your cause. After all, the person doing the asking is someone with whom others have an established relationship — in other words, trust already exists between the person with the cause and the person being asked. The thinking is, "Oh, well, if Sarah thinks this is a good organization, it probably is!"

Making personal calls

When you can't be physically present with another person, a phone call really is the next best thing. A telephone call carries your voice — offering a connection that's more intimate than a letter or e-mail message. Don't underestimate the power of this personal connection — even when you're just trying to decide whether or not to call a donor back after business hours so you can leave a message on his machine. (Don't feel bad about making that call — we've certainly done it.)

Your responsiveness in a phone conversation helps build the relationship with the donor, which helps bring the donor closer to your organization (and may lead him to donate to your annual fund). Experience shows that people have more trouble saying no to a "live" person on the phone than they do ignoring a fundraising letter or a more impersonal solicitation.

Writing personal correspondence

Personal correspondence says to the donor, "You're important enough to me that I took the time to write to you personally." Like the personal phone call, this personal communication carries a bit of weight in the psychology of answering yes or no to a donation. However, a letter is more impersonal than the call or the visit because the real human contact is missing.

Nowadays an e-mail message sent directly to the donor — if the donor recognizes your name — may feel slightly more personal than a letter. With a letter, donors have the option of never opening it, pitching it unseen into the trash, or misplacing it in a pile of other papers. With an e-mail message, donors may press Delete before they even open it to see what it's about, so you risk not being heard either way. Both approaches have their pros and cons, but the best approach for your particular donors depends on their comfort levels with technology and their preferred methods of communication.

A personal letter *with* a phone call follow-up makes the contact more direct and alerts you if the recipient never received your letter. Take the time to write the note by hand, and you'll improve your response rate.

Sending e-mail

Personalized e-mail contacts that are sent directly to the donor may elicit a quicker response than traditional mail because of their fast nature. For that reason, some nonprofit organizations conduct huge e-mail campaigns to take full advantage of online fundraising. E-mail also enables you to use the information from your donor list to determine the groups you want to approach in your annual fund drive.

One flaw with some e-mail annual fund campaigns is that they often don't offer an obvious way for the recipient to take action. You can ask the recipient to mail in a check, but you provide no envelope or pledge form. And clicking Reply to respond to a mass-produced e-mail message often ends up at a dead-end address. You can improve results with e-mail campaigns by including a button or link in the e-mail that takes interested donors back to your site so they can make an online donation using a credit card. See Chapter 16 for more information on setting up donations online.

Sponsoring special events

If you can get somebody to come to your special event, you already have one foot in the donation door. After all, someone who cares enough to come to your event is already interested and able to provide something to your organization. You just have to get that person involved specifically in your annual fund. Be sure to gather important data about your attendees at special events, and save the comments they make about the evening. When the annual fund campaign rolls around the next time, you can mention that you appreciated their support at the special event last year and hope they'll consider contributing to the annual fund this year, as well. See Chapter 19 for information on planning special events.

Going door-to-door

As any Avon representative will tell you, cold door-to-door calling is an expensive and time-consuming venture. Of all the "personal contact" options, this one is the lowest on the ladder in terms of effectiveness. If your prospective donors open their doors (and they may not if you're holding something that looks like a sales kit), you need to cover a lot of ground in less than 30 seconds. Can you make someone see the heart of your organization — and want to donate to it — in that amount of time? Doing so isn't impossible, but it's certainly challenging and potentially dangerous if there's an unfriendly dog around.

Using direct mail

As we mention in Chapter 12, direct mail is a very sophisticated operation today because of the ability to buy and sort mailing lists. Targeting people who already know about you — such as existing donors, last year's members, attendees from events, or even people who have gone to or who are givers to similar organizations — allows for much more powerful niche mailing. A mail campaign may include an annual fund mailer (maybe in the form of a membership renewal), a brochure, postcards, newsletters, or catalogs.

Getting on TV and radio

As you may have seen, TV can be an effective means of generating support. For example, the televised videos and cries for help that followed the tsunami in Indonesia brought an outpouring of support that was funneled through the American Red Cross. TV and radio also give a sense of authenticity (whether it's warranted or not is another matter); viewers and listeners often think that if they see something or hear something in the media, it must be true. TV and radio can be a great friend to your mission. Particularly if you have a noteworthy cause that has ties to current issues and events, you can use that event-related exposure to help gain recognition for your organization, which translates directly into more dollars raised for your cause.

Media coverage on the radio and TV is expensive and often prohibitive for nonprofit budgets. Try instead to get human-interest coverage on local cable channels or place stories in news programs. Or add a podcast to your Web site that others can listen to at their own convenience.

Using social media to spread the word

As we illustrate in Chapter 14, social media is spreading like wildfire throughout the Internet. You can use Facebook, LinkedIn, Twitter, and your blog to spread the word about your annual fund drive. Tell your stories, and invite friends, donors, fans, and followers to help you get the word out. If you have a special event planned as an annual fund kick-off, be sure to publicize it on all your social media sites. And use social media to keep your donors and public engaged, as well — ask and answer questions, post fun trivia facts related to your mission, and try to keep a buzz going that will draw others back to your organization's Web site, where they can find out more about your annual fund.

Rating your organization

Does your organization have all its fundraising approaches in place? In Table 18-1, we present a way to rate your organization that encourages you to think about each of the approaches we discuss in the preceding sections. This rating is based on a scale of 1 to 10 (1 being "We haven't even thought about it yet!" and 10 being "Been there, done that, and it's working great!").

Table 18-1	Rate Your Organization: Fundraising Tool Effectiveness		
Approach	*Included in Your Annual Fund Plan?*	*Rating Value (1 to 10)*	*Next Step to Take*
Face to Face			
Personal Calls			
Personal Correspondence			
E-Mail and E-Newsletter			
Special Events			
Door-to-Door			
Direct Mail			
TV and Radio			
Social Media			

Annual Fund Buster #3: Bad timing. Evaluating where you are in your fundraising planning is important before you embark on an annual campaign. Is your board ready? Do you have leadership for the campaign? How experienced are your volunteers? Do you have the budget? These and other issues can have a lot to do with the success of your campaign — or lack thereof — so make sure you take your time in setting up your annual campaign. Be sure you're comfortable with the overall rating you give your organization in Table 18-1 before you start putting your annual fund plan in place.

Putting the Plan in Place

After you've identified your goals, chosen your team, and evaluated the fundraising tools at your disposal, you're ready to get to work on your annual fund campaign. The first step is to identify prospects. Then you need to make sure you have the materials you need for support. Finally, you need to ensure that your volunteers are trained and ready. After completing these tasks, you're ready to launch out into your community and begin your annual fund drive.

Understanding your approach: Donor research and planning

The annual fund campaign targets the following three types of donors:

- ✔ Prospects who have never given to your organization but who have interests or involvements that make them qualified candidates
- ✔ One-time donors whom you can approach for a repeat gift
- ✔ Repeat donors who can be upgraded to a higher giving level

Use the donor research strategies in Chapter 6 to find out more about the specifics of researching your donor audience.

 Schedule at least one prospective-donor brainstorming session with your annual fund team and selected board members. Everybody needs to be ready, willing, and able to come up with names of potential donors that the annual fund team can use as they begin implementing their plan.

 One of the items you need to research during this planning phase is the percentage of people helped by the work you do. Specifics ring true in the mind of the donor. For example, saying, "Your donation of $150 last year helped us warn a classroom of 30 preteens about the dangers of smoking" is much more effective than offering a generic thank-you.

Choosing your materials

After you identify the donor audience you want to target with your annual fund campaign, you need to take inventory of what you need to reach that audience. Your annual team members likely need one or more of the following items to support them in their donor contacts:

- ✔ **Online communications:** Online fundraising approaches are becoming more and more popular because they offer fundraising professionals a low-cost, fast way to connect with donors. As you develop your approach for your annual fund, be sure to think through all online opportunities, but also be aware of how your own donor base will expect to receive the information you provide. Provide these details — drawn from your own donor list — to all members of the annual fund team.

- ✔ **Brochures (if your budget allows them):** Printed brochures, flyers, or other publications explaining your annual fund are a nice touch to your campaign, but they can be pricey. Regardless of whether you include print pieces in your annual fund campaign, make sure you give any marketing pieces your organization uses to promote itself to your annual fund team members so they can at least consider them in their campaign plans. If your organization publishes an annual report, give it to your team members, as well, to help them understand what the funds are used for during the year.

  A lower-cost alternative to printing and mailing (or delivering) four-color print materials is to save the brochure, flyer, or report as a PDF file and make the file available to your donor on request or downloadable from your Web site.

- ✔ **Your case statement:** The all-important case statement gives a clear picture of your mission and explains why you — and only you — can offer the services you provide in the way that you provide them (see Chapter 4 for more on the case statement).

  Come up with a revised case statement for each annual fund you do. Nobody wants to see the same information served up year after year. The donations from the previous years should be making some difference, after all. Your team members need to tell donors how their donations have helped and how you plan to use this year's donations. Be sure your team members also communicate the continuing need — and your unique response to it — with enthusiasm and interest.

- ✔ **Donor information sheets:** Your annual fund team members also need information sheets on donors giving them donation history and pertinent background information. The information on these sheets can help your team members effectively relate and reach out to all your donors. These sheets are in addition to the donor list.

- ✔ **Pledge cards:** Givers to an annual fund often like to break their gifts into installments, which makes it easier for them to give larger amounts and easy for you to allocate income through the balance of your fiscal year. So make sure you arm your annual fund team members with plenty of pledge cards.

Five signs your plan is falling flat (and what to do about it)

Suppose that your annual fund team put together a great plan and you're now midway through the first leg of the campaign. You thought your online donations would be picking up by now. Even in a challenging economy, you expected more interest. Is this lukewarm response the result of the times, or is something going wrong with your plan?

Although you certainly don't like to think about all the hard work and effort you put into your annual fund campaign coming up empty, you need to be ready to identify any problems that creep up as you make your way through your plan. After you find out what's going wrong, you can focus your efforts on fixing it. Here are a few symptoms of an annual fund plan in trouble (and what to do to eliminate them):

✔ **Nobody wants to help.** If you're having trouble recruiting volunteers to help with the annual fund, people aren't making the connection between your mission and their passion. The first gift people give in any campaign is the gift of their belief — if volunteers don't believe in what you're trying to do, ask yourself why. How can you communicate your vision more effectively? How well is your leadership telling your story?

✔ **Your leadership is ho-hum.** If the leaders of the annual fund effort aren't passionate about what they're doing — or worse, if they're negative or disheartened — keeping the energy up for everyone else is going to be next to impossible. Your volunteer leaders need to see the goal and believe they can reach it. Their passion then ignites possibilities for the rest of the group (and, as a result, you probably find more and more people wanting to help — which can help you solve the first problem in this list).

✔ **People don't show up for meetings.** If you hold a meeting and nobody comes, you can be sure of two things:

   • People don't think it's an important use of their time.

   • You won't raise money that way.

Be clear about your expectations for meetings, and ensure that your volunteer leadership is onboard to do whatever is necessary to get people in the seats, even if doing so means making night-before phone calls or e-mailing the 20 volunteers who are supposed to be at the meeting the next day.

✔ **Your volunteers aren't giving.** Getting the buy-in of everyone involved in the fundraising campaign is an important part of building the energy you hope will inspire your larger donor base. If your volunteers aren't giving to the program they're helping to support with their time, how do you expect them to be effective in bringing funds into the organization? Even a $5 or $10 gift is a gift, so encourage all your annual fund volunteers to be givers to the campaign — 100 percent volunteer giving sets a great example.

> ✔ **Giving is down, down, down.** When you compare the numbers — what you achieved by this time last year as compared to what you've brought in this year — the results are dismal. What do they mean? To some degree, the economy may be impacting what you're bringing in, but if you're still raising less than you expected even after you adjusted for the economy, check your plan and the engagement levels of your volunteers and leadership to see whether any red flags show up.

Evaluating (And Celebrating) Your Annual Fund Drive

Going through a debriefing process can be helpful not only to give your annual fund team some closure, but also to provide next year's team with information on what worked, what didn't, and where improvements can be made.

Before you finish a campaign, make a point to identify the people who seem to be stepping forward as leaders for the next one. Some large organizations help new leaders learn the ropes by identifying future leaders two years in advance. For example, an incoming leader may serve in a support role to the current leader to figure out how the campaign is run; then next year, the new leader knows what's expected and can run a great campaign.

Your evaluation of your campaign can include the following questions:

- ✔ Did we meet our financial goals?
- ✔ Did we meet the goals we had for the number of prospects and donors contacted?
- ✔ What was our response rate in direct mail and telephone solicitation?
- ✔ Which fundraising tools were most effective?
- ✔ Was our team prepared and provided with the tools they needed?
- ✔ How effective was our annual fund leadership?
- ✔ What were the three biggest factors in the success of the drive?
- ✔ What were the three biggest challenges we faced?
- ✔ If we were starting this campaign again today, what would we change?

After you finish your evaluation, don't forget to take time to celebrate! Celebrating is an important part of the annual fund process. You need to thank all your volunteers, recognize extraordinary efforts, and praise people all around. After all, the seeds you plant today may germinate and grow into the annual fund team you have tomorrow.

One big celebration you can't afford to miss is the big thank-you event. Find a way to get everyone who helped put on your annual campaign together one last time — even if the "event" is a clean-up day at your facility or a free trip to a ball game. Telling people thanks in person is an important part of letting your volunteers know you truly value the time and effort they contributed. And, feeling appreciated, they'll be that much more likely to want to help you next year.

Planning for Next Time

One of the challenges of the annual fund is that it really is an ongoing process. It may feel like as soon as you finish one campaign, it's time to start another! But don't be overwhelmed. By taking a deep breath and bringing your board and committee together to plan early for next year, you can make your next annual fund campaign even more effective than the one you just finished.

Here are a few ideas to help you get started on planning for your next annual fund campaign:

- ✔ Spend some time discussing what worked in the current campaign. Look at the numbers, and review the experiences of volunteers and the board. Was your leadership effective? Did leadership have everything it needed to run a good campaign? Make a list of the items that worked well and put them in your plan for next year.

- ✔ Talk about the things that didn't go so well. Where did your plan fall flat? Did you reach your financial goal? How many new prospects did you bring in? Explore the pitfalls your fund experienced, and discuss ideas that could — in hindsight — have helped avoid them. Write down the challenges your campaign faced and your responses to them, and put them in the file for next year so your next leadership team has the benefit of your experienced view.

- ✔ Prepare a detailed budget-to-actual analysis to determine how accurately you budgeted for the expenses of the annual fund campaign and what kind of result your efforts produced.

- ✔ Think carefully about the leadership for your campaign, and plan out the types of resources your leaders need to be successful next year. Make a list of resources to provide, and schedule a planning meeting for the next annual fund well in advance of the kick-off date.

- ✔ Most importantly — know that the planning energy you invest now will help your next annual fund go more smoothly and be more effective. Remember that you're already on your way to your next annual campaign!

Chapter 19

Planning a Special Event

. . . .

. . . .

*W*hen you say *special event,* people often think of black-tie, high-society events with fancy catered food and a fine orchestra. Although major organizations hold these black-tie events regularly (and with finesse), there are many different types of special events — with different costs and constituencies — you can plan to raise funds for your organization without overwhelming your budget.

When considering what type of special event you want to throw, one of the first questions you have to ask yourself in tough times is: "Is this appropriate for the economy we're operating in?" Maybe a lower-cost event would be more suitable, considering the economic climate in which you're operating. Your donors are more likely to support a mission-focused event when times are tough. Or maybe you've scaled back the event over the last few years, and now the local economy has recovered enough that you can kick your plans up a notch.

In this chapter, you discover how a special event, done well, can raise visibility for your organization and how it can mean substantial fundraising bucks down the road. The key to planning a successful special event is to have a person who wants to champion the event, a committee to plan and execute it, and enough time to find the right event and pull it together.

Seeing How a Special Event Benefits Your Organization

Put simply, a fundraising *special event* is an experience that brings people together, raises awareness for your cause, and gives you an opportunity to ask for donations. The event can be anything from a celebrity car wash to a walk-a-thon to a kissing contest to an evening of ballroom dancing.

The advantages of hosting a special event go beyond money raised. The single biggest benefit of a special event is raising awareness. Through your publicity efforts — and hopefully by word of mouth — people in your community become aware of your organization. Raised awareness benefits you in a number of ways, including the following:

✔ Increases your prospective donor list

✔ Involves donors as volunteers, giving them the chance to form a closer relationship with your organization

✔ Expands media coverage

✔ Raises funds, the amount depending on the type of event — expensive events may yield less financial gain

How big does your special event need to be? Only as big as your budget and community support. Because the focus of a special event is more about building awareness than raising money, the selection of the event itself is more important than the money spent on that event. Know where your break-even point is and keep focused on how the special event benefits your organization. If you steer by those two items, you will find it easier to make choices that help keep your costs within reasonable limits.

Planning, Planning, Planning!

As with most things, the secret to a good special event is in the planning. If you want your event to be truly *special,* detailed and thorough planning is a must because a single misstep could sink your results. If you're ready for the event and do it well, you maximize awareness in your community, build goodwill with your volunteers, have fun, and raise money. If you're not ready, an event that unravels can give the community the impression that your organization doesn't manage itself well, which can be a devastating perception for agencies trying to build credibility and trust.

Planning your special event involves making the following decisions right at the start:

✔ Who takes the lead? Which volunteers serve on the committee?

✔ What kind of event do you have? Whom does it reach? How do you reach those people?

✔ What do you want to accomplish? Are you raising awareness, money, goodwill, or all three?

✔ Can you afford to do a special event at this time? Do you have enough lead time for successful planning?

✔ What is the break-even point for your organization, and can you get a sponsor to offset the expense?

The following sections contain specifics to help you answer these questions.

Putting together the best team

The right leader (one who is enthusiastic, engaging, persuasive, and passionate) can energize your volunteer group. With the right leader, people want to help, and the event becomes a major team-building activity.

With the wrong leader — someone who looks at the event as a chore or someone who is already overcommitted, lacking the time or energy to take on another duty — the event looms as a continual albatross around the neck of your organization. Because leadership is so vital to a successful event, postpone your plans for a special event until you have just the right leader to forge ahead with heart and soul. A lukewarm event drains your organization's financial and volunteer resources and becomes a negative experience that nobody wants to attend.

As you begin to put together your special-event team, select a committee chair who

✔ Has the time to commit to the effort

✔ Has people skills to motivate others

✔ Understands and is able to communicate the vision

✔ Has some fundraising and event experience

✔ Has passion for the mission of your organization

After you choose a team leader, it's time to put together the rest of your team. Your special-event committee should consist of volunteers who

✔ Love to get out there and promote your cause with enthusiasm

✔ Get things done

✔ Can work as a team to pull the event together

The growing special event

Some events become annual events and grow precisely because they're annual events. For example, some organizations have an annual silent auction or dance. The anticipation and repeat promotion of the event from year to year helps the community recognize the organization and the cause.

One special event started by the Indianapolis Zoo as a way to bring more people to the zoo has grown into a major special event for the city. Zoobilation, which raises close to half a million dollars each year, has become the social event of the year for young couples. Attendees dress in formal wear — they come in ball gowns, tuxedos, and, occasionally, safari gear. The event now features five different bands and food from 20 local restaurants. Demand has grown to a point that tickets sell out every year well in advance of the event — even in a down economy.

Be sure to provide enough lead time before the event (see the section "Setting a timeline" later in this chapter for details). The committee needs to meet monthly at first to solidify the plan and keep it in motion. As the event draws near, the committee may meet weekly to ensure that all aspects of the event are under control.

Selecting an event

The type of special event you choose to put on is just as important as the people you choose to lead it. Is the event linked logically to your organization's mission? Will the people who care about your cause sit up and take notice of the event?

Here are some guidelines for choosing the right event:

- ✔ Look for an event that's a logical fit with your organization's mission.
- ✔ Think about who you want to attend your event — and why.
- ✔ Know the net return you want to get from the evening.
- ✔ Consider how you can get exposure from the local press for the event.
- ✔ Be aware of the budget for special events and stay within your means.

Involve the people your organization serves in your special event. One mental health association nearly always includes in the audience people who have received their services. At first, other audience members did a double take to see clients in the audience, but including clients in the celebration shows that the organization means what it says about encouraging the rights and dignity of the people it serves.

Deciding the when and where

After you select the event leadership and the event itself, you need to decide when and where you want to host it. As far as the when is concerned, select the date and time of the event after carefully considering the wants and needs — and schedules — of your target audience. Here are some questions that can help you determine the when for your special event:

- **What time of year fits logically with your organization's mission?** For example, a program that raises donations for holiday gifts for kids may have its special event the weekend after Thanksgiving, when the holiday buying season officially begins.

- **What else is going on in town at that time? What other obligations may your audience have?** For example, if you schedule your fundraiser when the big city orchestra hosts its black-tie ball, you may lose some of your higher-level donors.

- **Do you know of a time of year when you're likely to get more help than others?** If many of your volunteers go to Florida for the winter, for example, you may wind up having that Valentine's Day dance all by yourself. Remember that your volunteers are an important part of the overall success of the event — both for the word-of-mouth publicity they offer and for the team-building experiences they have.

Equally important may be the where. Be sure the where is logically connected to your organization. For example, why have a school-related special event at a location other than the school? As you consider the where for your event, ask yourself these key questions:

- **Where in your town can people get to easily and park near?** Logistics can kill your event. If people can't get to the event easily, they won't come.

- **What locale fits the event?** For example, if you're throwing a black-tie event, don't hold it at a soup kitchen in the inner city. If your event involves art, a museum or theater makes sense. Just make sure the venue matches the mood and is a destination that's attractive to your potential donors.

- **Is the location in your budget?** Renting a swank country club for a black-tie event may be swell, but can you afford it? Your potential donors don't want to see you bleeding money for the sake of a fundraiser. Look for someone to donate a locale or swap it for free, positive publicity.

One of the best kinds of events revolves around people's homes. For example, an art museum has a progressive dinner for major donors at six different homes. Being invited to participate in the dinner is seen as an extra-special thing. The people who open their homes for the dinners contribute everything from the food to the dinnerware. Involve your board and volunteer leadership in your special-event initiatives to inspire others to increase their engagement with your organization.

Setting expectations

Clearly, making a mountain of money isn't a realistic expectation of your first fundraiser. After you put together your special-event committee, spend some time discussing and carefully thinking through the goals for your event. How will you measure your success? Keep in mind that realistic goals help you set a realistic budget.

As you consider what expectations you have for your special event, you may want to set goals for the number of people attending, cost per person, the coverage you get in the media, the number of volunteers involved, the amount of money you raise, and the overall happiness quotient.

What exactly do we mean by *happiness quotient?* How can you rate people's happiness with the event? It's quite simple. Set a scale from 1 to 5. People with a happiness quotient of 1 leave the event looking seriously bored or disgruntled. People with a happiness quotient of 5 leave the event looking euphorically happy, singing the praises of your organization all the way down the street. Include volunteer and staff reactions in the happiness quotient, too. The 1-to-5 scale isn't a scientific method of tracking event results, but the good feeling that results from a successful event may be the single biggest lasting effect your efforts make in the year to come.

Budgeting for the special event

As you plan your special event, don't forget the budget. Even if the goal of your event is mainly to generate awareness and goodwill, the event shouldn't break the bank. If your organization has a history of special events, you probably already have a hefty allotment for this year's event. If you're putting on a first-time event or are trying a new event that presents new costs, you need to be mindful of the upfront investment involved in setting up services and reaching your target audience.

As your special-event committee works with the budget, be sure to prepare for expenses in each of the following areas:

- Facility (rental fees, insurance, permits, lighting)
- Parking (parking-lot fees, valet fees)
- Equipment (tables and chairs, audio-visual equipment, tents)
- Services (catering, housekeeping, transportation, security)

- ✔ Entertainment (speakers' fees, performers' fees, band fees)

- ✔ Publications (invitations, flyers, posters, tickets, banners, thank-you cards)

- ✔ Decorations (table centerpieces, flowers, balloons)

- ✔ Recognition (gifts, cards, discount tickets, plaques, pins)

Remember, even if you do have a healthy budget for special events, you don't have to use all of it. Try to attain sponsorship for as many components of the event as you can — from the napkins to the catering to the limo service for your entertainers.

Setting a timeline

How far in advance do you need to plan your special event? Many organizations begin planning for next year's event the same day they evaluate the one they just had. If you do a repeat event every year, this process is fairly simple. If you're starting from scratch and putting together a brand-new event, you need all the time you can get. So if you can begin planning a year before the event takes place, do so.

Suppose that you're going to put on a gala with a catered dinner, a speaker, and dancing. You hope for the black-tie and evening-gown crowd. If you process the staging of the special event, you can break the pieces down into a timeline that helps you stay on track and get everything done in a comfortable time frame.

Here's an example of a timeline for a special event that will occur in July of next year:

- ✔ **August:** Begin planning; select the event committee; hold your first committee meeting; select the speaker and theme. Follow with monthly committee meetings (with more frequent meetings as you get closer to the event) to keep the momentum going.

- ✔ **September:** Divide tasks among the committee. Contact the speaker. Determine the location and equipment needed. Remember to consider permits, security, and insurance.

- ✔ **October:** Draft the agenda for the evening. Be specific, writing down what you want to happen from start to finish in 15- to 30-minute increments.

- ✔ **November:** Identify potential sponsorships and create a plan to pursue them.

- ✔ **December:** Identify potential participants from your donor list and the community at large. Begin to pursue sponsorships.

- ✔ **January:** Contact food-service, housekeeping, and entertainment vendors.

✔ **February:** Approve the menu; select the music.

✔ **March:** Print invitations, flyers, and tickets. Finalize your publicity plan.

✔ **April:** Do a reality check. How much will this event cost? What kind of return do you anticipate? Gauge the general interest for the event and determine whether, in light of your budget and your objectives, you need to adjust your plan or move forward.

✔ **May:** Start publicizing your event; organize your volunteers; send invitations (the last week of May).

✔ **June:** Coordinate all elements of the event; divide into work teams or groups; practice a run-through; do a last-minute function check of the facility — housekeeping, food services, sound system, audio-visual equipment (projectors), and entertainment.

✔ **July:** Put on the event! Don't forget follow-up activities, such as sending thank-you notes to volunteers, hosts, and donors, and beginning to lay the groundwork for next year's successful event.

With sufficient time and detailed planning, your event should go off without a hitch. Relax and enjoy it!

Black Tie Optional: Organizing an Online Event

These days it's possible to hold interactive events from your Web site. You can hold a seminar during which you present information about your cause that interests your donors. Or you can hold an online event (perhaps using a Webcast) with a special draw, such as a celebrity chat, during which attendees can submit questions and watch and hear the celebrity respond in real time.

Online events won't be as splashy as a black-tie dinner, but they are virtually free ways to keep your name in front of people on a much more regular basis.

Using Webinars to inform and persuade

Does your organization collect funds to save the rain forest? What about giving an online travelogue presentation about the rain forest and its various birds and beasts? Are you an arts group preparing for your annual Christmas show? You can use different programs to easily create behind-the-scenes photo albums, video clips, or Webinars that tell people more about your organization and its cause and programs.

Webinars are new, low-cost ways to bring potential donors together for an online meeting. During a Webinar, you can offer a presentation, run a video, chat about a program, show a slide show, and much more. Your donors log in to the specific site where the Webinar will be held and then call in to participate in the discussion. This type of online event enables you to gather people together around your cause without incurring the costs of hosting a larger, physical event.

If you want to make the Webinar a real online event, you can invite a book author or researcher in your industry area to host the Webinar and invite key donors to the online event. You can raise funds before the event by charging for tickets or invite participants to make a gift offering at the close of the event.

Many Webinar services, such as www.GoToMeeting.com, enable you to save the Webinar transcript so that others who can't attend the actual online event can view the file or receive the information later.

Chatting online with celebrities

If you know someone with a big name who supports your cause but who doesn't have the time to travel to an offline event, consider setting up an online chat. This format allows you to associate a famous name with your cause and to get that person to chat with your donors online. Designate someone from your organization as a moderator, and, if possible, allow visitors to request an audio recording or transcript of the chat after it's over. When you send them the saved chat, include a pitch for a donation.

It's beyond the scope of this book to go into the technical ins and outs of setting up online meetings and chats, but trust us — it's not that difficult to do. Go to the online expert in your organization or ask a local Web design group to donate its time to set up one for you. With a simple-to-use online meeting product, such as Windows Live Meeting from Microsoft, you'll be amazed at what you can do.

Following Up after the Big Event

The auditorium is empty. Confetti covers the floor; dishes, flatware, and crumpled napkins cover the tabletops. Soon the crew will arrive to disassemble the furnishings and the tent. Your special event is over — or is it?

You may think there's nothing left to do but go home and collapse from all the work of the past several months, but not so fast. Soon after the event, you need to figure out whether the event was successful, thank the volunteers and sponsors who helped out, and start thinking about next year's event. The following sections outline how to wrap up the event and look ahead to the next one.

Measuring goodwill

The result of special events — both in the "real world" and online — can be all over the board, and the amount of money you raise in your special event may turn out to be secondary to the goodwill you generate. Because goodwill is hard to rate, you may walk away from the event wondering whether you hit your mark.

You can use the goals you set during the event-planning stages to help you determine whether you reached the desired objectives. You can also watch for longer-term positive results by being alert for the following:

- People smile as they leave.
- Your event is mentioned — in a positive way — in the paper or on social media sites.
- People mention to you that they heard about your event.
- You get an increase in calls and/or visits.
- People sign the guest book to get on your mailing list or fill out a pledge card at the event.
- You feel that the community has a better understanding of who you are.
- Participants send you thank-you notes.
- People ask you whether you plan to have the event again next year.
- Participants complete online surveys about the event they attended, and the feedback is largely positive.

Evaluating the event's outcomes

When the dust begins to settle and you've recovered from the stress of putting on your special event, take some time to evaluate your event. After all, learning from this one can help you run the next one more smoothly. Here are some of the questions that you — and your special-event committee — can ask as you evaluate:

- Did we meet the goals we set in the beginning?
- What kind of publicity did we get?

> ✔ How many new people did we reach?
>
> ✔ What was our per-plate (or per-participant) cost?
>
> ✔ Did we use all possible means to publicize the event?
>
> ✔ Did we raise any money?

Is it possible to have a good event without raising any money? Yes! Although you may put on your special event with the objective of raising substantial funds, the more direct benefit is the exposure you get and the awareness you raise for your organization and its cause. The money comes, over time, as a result of these other benefits.

Same time next year? Depending on whom you ask, some event planners feel that having the same event several years in row is important to help brand the event in the mind of the community. Although this approach works well for some organizations (especially those that know they've selected an event that fits well with their mission), an argument can be made for not repeating an event that clearly didn't work. If your event was a royal flop, don't buy into the argument that you really need to give it three years before you see any kind of return on your investment. A good rule of thumb, especially for organizations on a shoestring, is to do more of what works and do less of what doesn't.

Saying "Thank you!"

Whether you plan to repeat your event next year or not, don't forget the last step! Say "Thank you!" to everyone involved. As anyone who has ever been through a special event can tell you, the thanking is no small feat. It requires your heartfelt recognition of the various parts of the whole, from the person who stuffed the invitation envelopes to the catering manager who oversaw the meal and dessert to the volunteer who desktop-published the flyers in her spare time.

How do you thank all your participants? Here are just a few ideas:

> ✔ A personal visit to the volunteer to say, "Thanks!"
>
> ✔ A phone call and a follow-up letter
>
> ✔ A personal letter to the helper
>
> ✔ A thank-you luncheon for everyone involved
>
> ✔ A group thank-you in the next agency newsletter (which is a good idea to do in conjunction with another form of recognition)

Remember that the ladder of effectiveness ranges from personal contact to impersonal contact, but the biggest thank-you comes from you, personally.

It's easy to leave out a name or two in your thank-you list, but doing so isn't acceptable. As you move through the planning stages and the event itself, make sure that everyone involved in the planning keeps a list of the people who helped throughout the planning for the event. Then, when the event's over, just pull out your list and go through the thank-yous one by one.

Gathering event lessons for next time

Evaluating what worked and what didn't for your special event is an important part of the planning for next year. Within a few weeks after finishing and celebrating your event, get the board together for a debriefing. You may want to take half a day to discuss your thoughts on the following questions:

- ✔ What did we learn from this event?
- ✔ Whom did we identify as our leader for next year's event?
- ✔ What worked and what can we improve next year?
- ✔ Did this event really connect with our donors?
- ✔ Did we use all available methods to publicize the event?
- ✔ Did the event accomplish what we intended it to accomplish? Should we do it again, as we did this year, or should we try something different?
- ✔ When should we have our first planning meeting for next year's special event?

Whether or not this year's event was the fulfillment of all your event hopes, you can learn valuable lessons from the experience. Your increased knowledge of your donors, your economic climate, your volunteer base, and your organization's ability to host special events will all contribute to making future events even more successful than this one.

Chapter 20

Building Buildings, Nonbuildings, and Futures: The Capital Campaign

. . . .

In This Chapter

▶ Getting ready to run a capital campaign

▶ Designating a leader for your capital campaign

▶ Following through each step of the campaign

. . . .

*W*hen you think growth, think capital. *Capital* means big money — enough to build a building or provide income for your programs for many years to come. A capital campaign is the biggest campaign your organization can ever undertake. This type of campaign requires a massive, all-out planning effort to secure large amounts of money for a specific purpose.

Understandably, launching into this type of campaign takes considerable thought and planning any time, but planning is especially important in times of economic challenge. Even if you have a long-term physical development plan in place, pay attention to the economic landscape and weigh out your chances of running a successful campaign. Take the time to discuss options thoughtfully with your board before you move full-speed into your capital campaign.

This chapter helps you think through all the basics, including timing, involved with planning and implementing a capital campaign. Of all the advice we can give you on this topic, here's the most important: Be sure that your organization is ready to take this step. A premature capital campaign can do more harm than good, so make sure you organize a capital campaign that has the support and enthusiasm of both the fundraisers and the planners.

Gearing Up for the Big Campaign

Generally, you use the *capital campaign* to bring in special funds over and above your *operating budget* (which is the money-eating animal you feed with your annual fund). A capital campaign raises the funds for the new wing of your hospital, the new program for teen mothers, or the funding of an endowment that supports the chair of your philosophy department (more on endowments in the "Checking out endowment campaigns" section later in this chapter).

Most capital campaigns share the following characteristics:

- The campaign encompasses a massive, organized fundraising effort.
- The campaign is designed to raise a specific amount for a specific need.
- The campaign cycle stretches over a long but specific time frame.
- Lead gifts make up half the campaign's fundraising goal. Lead gifts are dependent on face-to-face solicitation. (We talk more about lead gifts in the "Identifying lead gifts and challenge gifts" section.)
- Donors pledge large gifts to be paid over a multiyear period.

If you've determined that your organization is ready to implement a capital campaign to meet its current and future needs, how can you be sure that now is the right time to start such a campaign? Part of the answer to this question depends on the enthusiasm of your supporters. If your supporters are excited about the new library you plan to add, you have a ready corps of volunteers who will tell your campaign story with passion. (Let prudence be your guide here — as John says, "You don't have to have a building to do good things.")

The other part of the answer to the timing question involves circling the wagons before you proceed with your capital campaign to find out whether your major givers are still on board. Find out how your big givers feel about the timing of the campaign. Be clear that you're not talking about ending the campaign altogether but rather exploring the right timing for it.

Your major givers will be the ones giving you the lead gifts for your campaign, so it's important to know how they feel about the campaign's feasibility in light of the current economic landscape. Although the donors who give to a capital campaign are, in general, not as severely impacted by economic changes as your other donors, you may want to consider offering an extension on pledge payments — extending a three-year pledge to five years, for example — to accommodate the needs of your major donors.

Running a capital campaign every year is the fundraising equivalent of forcing your giving well to run dry. Capital campaigns should be, by their nature, rare, which is why you need to think carefully through your decision to run one.

Exploring Capital Campaign Types

The needs of your organization determine the type of capital campaign you develop. In general, your intention is the same — you need to raise a large amount of money for a substantial need. Like ice cream, capital campaigns come in several common flavors (which we discuss in the following sections):

- Bricks-and-mortar campaigns
- Endowment campaigns
- Project campaigns
- Combined campaigns

In some special circumstances, organizations have been known to create capital campaigns to help fund special equipment. For example, one organization John works with launched a major capital campaign to fund exhibits for a newly renovated state museum. But this type of campaign is rare enough that we don't spend a lot of time on it here.

Building bricks-and-mortar campaigns

The *bricks-and-mortar capital campaign* is probably what most people think of when they hear the term *capital campaign.* A bricks-and-mortar campaign raises money for tangible things, such as a new wing for your hospital, a new school, a new library, or improvements to a community center. Whether you're renovating an old structure or building an entirely new one, a capital campaign brings in the high-level funds you need to meet your goal.

Many foundations and other funding entities these days exclude bricks-and-mortar capital campaigns from their giving agendas. Be sure to check to see whether a foundation or other source of money is receptive to capital campaign proposals before you bother to write one up.

Raising funds *before* a building is built is much easier to do than raising funds to pay for it *after* it's been built. Why? People love to be part of dreaming a dream and watching it come to fruition.

Checking out endowment campaigns

Another kind of capital campaign is the *endowment campaign,* a campaign in which the money raised is used to invest in your organization's future instead of in a new building. With an endowment, a donor pledges a substantial gift that's given over a period of several years; sometimes the interest or appreciation of the assets can sustain a program over several years. Many grantor foundations were built through endowments of their own. A gift to an endowment campaign typically goes into a fund for ongoing support of specific programs.

Endowments are often the result of planned-giving instruments or bequests. See Chapter 21 for more about planned giving.

The one thing all endowments have in common is that they're large enough to be able to generate significant income from the principal. You can generate income from an endowment in several different ways. One form of endowment allows organizations to make use of the interest earned each year on the endowment balance. Another endowment form may allow organizations to draw down a fixed percent of the value of the endowment each year. This idea is based on the fact that endowments normally earn interest and gain additional value through appreciation. In difficult economic times, endowments don't always do so; as a result, the management of the endowment has to decide what the appropriate amount is to draw down. (Turn to Chapter 23 for more details about endowments.)

Regardless of the type of capital campaign you choose to run, remember that big gifts create big names and, not coincidentally, that big names create big gifts. Use naming opportunities to attract and recognize your high-level givers, giving them a publicized stake in your organization's mission for today and tomorrow. Just think — each time your high-level donors come to visit their namesake buildings, they're reminded of the importance of their generous gifts.

Putting together project campaigns

A *project campaign* is another type of capital campaign, but it has a narrower focus than either the bricks-and-mortar campaign or the endowment campaign. This type of capital campaign raises funds for a program that requires a specific amount of money for a specific time. For example, suppose that you're currently serving 15 teenagers in your teen parenting program, and you need to increase that number to 25. To do so, you need more physical space, more funds allotted to the annual fund, more program materials, and more personnel. You can use the same planning you do for a larger capital campaign to accomplish your goals in a more focused project campaign.

Running combined campaigns

A *combined campaign* orchestrates all your needs in a single plan — bricks and mortar, program goals, equipment, and even the annual fund may all be interwoven with the overall combined campaign goals. If you want to see a combined campaign at its finest, look at any major university. Universities are quickly mastering the techniques for weaving together the goals of combined campaigns.

 Unless you're part of an institution that has substantial giving bases and naming possibilities, think long and hard before you try your hand at a combined campaign; running a successful one is very hard to do without the donor foundation that many large institutions already have in place. Many donors — especially in times of economic hardship — think, "I gave to the building campaign, so I'm not going to give to the annual fund." You don't want to jeopardize your operating fund because you launch a capital campaign at a time when your donors can't support it.

Selecting a Champion

In any capital campaign, leadership is everything. The person you select to head the campaign — called the *campaign chairperson* or *leader* — often makes the difference between achieving your goal and falling short. The successful capital campaign is a thoroughly planned event that requires a leader with vision, experience, and the connections and means to secure the highest-level lead gifts possible. (*Lead gifts* are major pledges that come in early and really start your campaign rolling. We talk more about them later in the "Identifying lead gifts and challenge gifts" section.)

The best approach for choosing a campaign leader is selecting someone from your board because your board members are dedicated to your mission, are familiar with the workings of the board, and are committed to the long-term success of the organization. After choosing a leader, don't forget that you need to select dedicated volunteers to serve on the committee, as well. As you begin to select committee members, consider these characteristics:

✔ Commitment to the mission of the organization

✔ Position in the community

✔ Experience with the organization

✔ Ability and willingness to give

Each of these characteristics is vitally important. The dedication and commitment your committee members show toward your organization serve as a model for all your volunteers and supporters. The visibility of the people you choose helps to inspire others in the community who admire those people and may attract new donors and supporters to your cause. When your committee members have experience with your organization, you already have that relational link you try so hard to build — they're already engaged with the work you do and feel good about being part of your mission.

In a capital campaign, each of your committee members must be a giving member. After all, the members of the capital campaign committee have much more credibility as they go face to face with potentially high-level donors when they can back up their donation requests with their own giving experience and the giving experiences of the organization's board members. As we explain in Chapter 10, "the Ask" is more powerful if, for example, when your committee member invites Bob to make a donation, she can say, "Bob, our board consists of 14 members, and we have each contributed between $3,000 and $50,000."

Staging the Campaign

Planning is a particularly high priority in a capital campaign because of the campaign's sheer scope. Don't start before you're ready, or your results will reflect your hasty actions.

Before you launch the capital campaign, you may want to create a capital planning committee to evaluate the institution's readiness for a capital campaign. This committee may hire an outside firm to do a feasibility study; it may also identify and cultivate prospective high-level givers. The planning committee shares the study's report with your campaign's leadership, and your campaign committee makes any decisions necessary to implement the planning committee's plan.

You may need to organize more than one committee to take care of each step of the campaign process because the planning and implementation of a capital campaign involves so much time and effort.

Planning and implementing a capital campaign usually involves the following stages:

1. **Readiness:** Determine whether your organization is really ready to launch a capital campaign. You can do so yourself or use an outside agency to make sure your basic fundraising structure is in place and functioning before you take on the massive and very public capital campaign. Making sure your organization is ready to withstand the hurdles of the capital campaign before you start is extremely important because the outcome of your capital campaign — whether you pass the goal with flying colors or you fall flat on your face — can have an impact on the public perception of your organization for years to come.

2. **Testing:** Identify key potential donors of influence in your area, and get their opinions on the readiness, practicality, and appeal of your campaign.

3. **Setup:** Put in place the basic organizing systems, such as research, record keeping, staffing, and so on, in preparation for the campaign.

Don't forget about the additional maintenance and ongoing expenses you incur because of this new campaign. Those expenses end up becoming part of your annual fund's requirement. If your campaign involves creating an endowment, you won't have a lot of additional expense beyond staff time. But if you're working on a capital campaign for a building, you have to account for considerable additional expenses. Think through every part of your capital campaign and plan accordingly.

4. **In-house preparations:** Finalize your case statement, develop materials, train committees, solicit challenge gifts, and recruit volunteers. The case statement for this kind of campaign includes elements from your regular case statement, but it probably includes elements specific to this new purpose, as well.

5. **Lead gifts:** Have your committee members acquire lead gifts from board members, individuals, corporations, and foundations.

6. **Public fundraising:** Publicly announce your capital campaign (when you have acquired pledges for more than 50 percent of your goal), and build the public-solicitation portion of your campaign.

7. **Completion and evaluation:** Focus on smaller gifts and bring the campaign to a close, evaluating the entire process, managing recognitions, and making suggestions for improvement in the next campaign.

Note that much of the work of the capital campaign is actually done behind the scenes during the first five stages of planning. The campaign only goes public in Stage 6, when you've reached more than 50 percent of your campaign goal. We talk about these stages in more detail in the following sections.

Testing the waters: Campaign feasibility

Testing for readiness is a major part of the success of the capital campaign. Is your organization ready? Is your board ready? Is the public ready? Many factors, both internal and external, affect the overall success or failure of your campaign.

Delaying a campaign doesn't have to send a negative message to your constituents. Making a prudent decision in tough times can demonstrate to your donors that you're discerning the best time to move forward with your plans — which, we might add, is good stewardship.

Many organizations rely on consulting firms to do *feasibility studies* as they prepare major campaigns. Having people outside your organization evaluate your organization's readiness to start a capital campaign enables those people interviewed to be open and honest in their responses. If a person from your organization asks another person from your organization questions like "Do you think our organization is ready for this campaign? Do you think the goal is realistic?" the person from your organization may not feel free to answer candidly.

You can also rely on the objectivity of the outside consultant to recommend whether now is truly the time for a major campaign. Someone inside the organization who's excited about the prospect of a capital campaign, on the other hand, may push for a major campaign before the time is right.

In general, a feasibility study helps you do the following:

✔ Determine whether your case statement is solid.

✔ Evaluate your board's readiness.

✔ Test the overall campaign goal.

✔ Test whether donor record-keeping systems are ready for a capital campaign.

✔ Test your markets for giving and develop a giving pyramid for the campaign (see Chapter 6 for more on the giving pyramid).

Your feasibility study may also let you know how your organization's messaging is being received by potential givers. Your committee may feel the appeal is right, but your testing may show that your organization's message needs to be altered or augmented to some extent. In the process of testing your message, you may find another market, as well. For example, the feasibility study for a zoo showed that a growing portion of the donor base cared deeply about preservation issues, so the zoo launched a new initiative targeted to this specific interest. In this way, asking the right questions at the right time can help you discover something new that may have enormous appeal to your donors.

Even if you're a three-person shop, do a feasibility study before you launch a major campaign. Although your study may not be something coordinated by a national consulting firm, you need to test your case statement, your goals, and your giving pyramid with a number of high-level donors.

It's okay to go out to your stakeholders and say, "Here's what our board is talking about. Does this sound feasible to you?" Take along a questionnaire and do the interview in person. Doing so builds the donor-organization relationship and makes the donor feel as though she has really helped.

This type of interview accomplishes another goal, as well: The interview and the questions you ask often give you a sense of which pitches are most and least desirable in the minds of your donors. The interview helps you decide which appeals to leave out of the overall plan.

Sometimes a feasibility test lets you know that you're trying to do too many things at once. If the recommendation that you need to divide your campaign into smaller segments comes back from the feasibility test, don't despair. Instead, look at it as an opportunity to celebrate a greater number of successes.

If you've never hired a consultant before and need some help exploring your options, you can contact your local community foundation for ideas or ask other nonprofits for names of consultants they've used. If you work for a small nonprofit, you don't need to hire a national consulting firm; you may be able to find a local consultant who can bring just what you need.

Setting your goal

Setting the goal for your capital campaign may be the subject of long and hard debate. You hear the clashes between risk takers and stability; you see the different priorities and definitions of a number of people who care about the organization and want to see it grow in the right direction. The financial goal for the capital campaign is wrapped up in the vision and agenda of many individuals, so be prepared to deal with a lot of discussion before you finalize your capital campaign goal.

When you arrive at a consensus about the amount of money you need to raise and the realistic possibility of attaining it, test the number. In interviews with donors during your feasibility tests, ask people questions like "Do you think this is a realistic amount?" Listen carefully to the responses and evaluate them. If you get too many noes, go back to the discussion table with the responses, and reevaluate your position.

If your organization regularly undertakes major campaigns, cultivate the wisdom and experience of those involved in the experience by inviting all your previous campaign chairs to test the theme of your campaign and your overall goal.

Here are a few examples of capital campaign goals:

- ✔ Solicit large amounts.
- ✔ Stretch out pledges over multiple years.
- ✔ Use challenge and matching grants.
- ✔ Include corporations and foundations.
- ✔ Stress lead gifts.

The best-laid plans — especially when physical construction is involved — often overrun their boundaries. Be sure you create a contingency fund to take care of overages on projects and unexpected expenses. As a ballpark figure, plan on putting aside a minimum of 10 percent to handle those unexpected construction overruns.

Identifying lead gifts and challenge gifts

A *lead gift* is one of the first — and biggest — gifts you can expect during your campaign. Lead gifts take a lot of time and cultivation; you develop and solicit them strategically, over months (or perhaps years). A relatively low number of lead gifts comprise a high percentage of your overall fundraising goal. According to the Center for Philanthropy at Indiana University-Purdue University Indianapolis, the numbers break down like this:

- ✔ The top 10 to 15 gifts comprise the top 34 percent of your total goal.
- ✔ The next 75 to 100 gifts make up the next 33 percent of the goal.
- ✔ All other gifts make up only 33 percent of the total goal.

As Chapter 6 explains, a giving pyramid helps you plot out the number of major gifts you need to make your overall fundraising goal. This pyramid is extremely important in capital campaigns, as well, and can help you determine not only how many of each type of gift you need, but also the number of people you have to approach to reach your goal.

The first few gifts of a capital campaign are important pieces of your overall capital campaign strategy, but just who will be your first lead givers? Here are a few of the likeliest candidates:

- ✔ **Board members:** You must have a giving board to run a successful capital campaign.

- ✔ **High-level donors:** Your major givers in other areas of your fundraising program are also likely to step up to the plate with substantial gifts in your capital campaign. You need to think of gift incentives, such as naming opportunities and other forms of recognition, as well as a revitalized case statement that helps donors see why now is the right time to give that large gift.

- ✔ **Stakeholders in business and philanthropy:** Lead gifts may also come from the corporate or philanthropic community. Companies may be interested in sponsoring a portion of your campaign by providing a challenge gift that inspires others to give at a higher level. (See Chapter 22 for more on soliciting corporate gifts.)

One of the most effective vehicles in a capital campaign is the challenge gift. A *challenge gift* is one in which a lead giver (an individual, a corporation, or a foundation) says something like, "I'll give you $100,000 if you can get it matched by July 1, 2011." This kind of gift enables you to go to other prospective high-level donors and say, "If you give now, your money will go twice as far." Because of the matching funds, a donor who gives $25,000 gets the good feeling of knowing that his gift actually takes you $50,000 closer to your campaign goal. See Chapter 21 for more about challenge gifts.

Before the economic roller coaster of 2007 through 2009, experts were estimating that the largest transfer of wealth in history would soon be transferring from one generation to the next. Even though the economy has no doubt had a big impact on inheritances, you still have huge opportunities to solicit major gifts. (Check out Chapters 9, 10, and 21 for more about your major gift opportunities.)

After you've identified your prospects and put your goals and approaches in place, your fundraising for these larger lead gifts can involve all the fundraising techniques we discuss in Chapters 10 through 17. However, your donor prospect list is typically more targeted, the win for your efforts may be bigger, and the time you spend cultivating these big-hitter relationships can involve months or even years. Especially at this high level, the giving relationship between you and your donors is very important. Don't be afraid to spend a considerable amount of time and effort developing a connection with a major giver before asking for a gift.

Going public

Suppose that you've completed the campaign plan and the consultants have told you the time is ripe for your capital campaign. So you pull your committees together, begin prospect research, gather your materials, and secure all the necessary lead gifts. You're already two-thirds to your goal, and you're certain you're going to reach it. Now what do you do? Sit back and coast to the finish line? Nope. Now's the time to go public with your campaign.

A successful capital campaign is a big boost for the morale of your supporters and the public perception of your nonprofit organization. It says a number of things to the public at large:

- ✔ This organization knows what it's doing.
- ✔ This organization is responsible with its money.
- ✔ Other people believe in this organization — look who's giving!
- ✔ This organization is worth a lot — look at the size of its goal!
- ✔ This organization is doing good work.

Each of these messages is important in a dollars-and-sense kind of way. Because fundraising is more about relationships than it is about money, and because relationships are built on trust, which is built on credibility, you have a great opportunity to further the trustworthiness of your organization by taking a successful capital campaign public. The more trustworthy your organization is, the more people will want to identify with you. To go public with your campaign, you need the following in place:

- A spokesperson (perhaps your campaign chairperson)
- Visual aids (such as a beautiful rendering of the finished building, with the parts not yet funded only penciled in)
- Printed materials (brochures, pledge cards, flyers, and so on)
- E-mail lists and a Web site, as well as social media accounts with Facebook, LinkedIn, and Twitter
- Media contacts, such as radio, television, and the Internet
- Donors willing to say why they believe in your organization

Make sure you prepare for going public in your campaign plan. Most importantly, be sure you've budgeted the necessary funds, prepared and printed the necessary materials, and established the ground rules for your publicity effort. See Chapter 13 for more about working with the media.

Following up with your capital campaign

Your campaign has been a success. So, how do you wind down the campaign? The key is follow-up.

As you bring the public campaign to a close, you need to organize the following to make sure the gifts promised are delivered and the goodwill created continues:

- Effective and quick responses to gifts from all donors
- Timely follow-up with thank-you notes and receipts
- Accurate accounting and data tracking
- Evaluations and reports on various stages of the campaign
- An open letter of thanks to the community, published in the local papers, for support in reaching your now-successful campaign goals

Follow-up to your campaign also includes major celebrations, which should be part of your campaign's overall publicity component. Have dinners to thank the volunteers — and invite the media. Hold a ribbon-cutting ceremony for the new wing — and invite the media. Make a fuss over the first new teen mom to graduate from your job-training facility — and invite the media. After doing so much work quietly, the time has come for you to pat yourself on the back in a very public way.

Debriefing everybody

Especially with something as big and far-reaching as a capital campaign, learning from your successes as well as your mistakes is important. What went right in your capital campaign? What would you like to avoid like the plague in the future?

Before you disperse your committees, ask them to meet one last time for a debriefing. Prepare a questionnaire related to the individual tasks you assigned. Ask people to rate their own effectiveness as a team and to list any suggestions they would make for the next team who steps into their shoes. Ask them about their likes and dislikes about the process, and glean any important insights for the next capital campaign team that comes along.

Finally, summarize all the information you gather (and archive it for the future) before closing the book on the capital campaign altogether. Remember that the effects of your work, resulting in long-term pledges that will pay over a number of years, will be felt for many months to come. The knowledge that you gained from your campaign experience can help others begin where you left off and can take your organization into the future.

Chapter 21

Securing Major Gifts, Planned Gifts, and the Challenge Grant

. . . .

In This Chapter

▶ Matching the donor's cause to your mission as you develop your major gift strategy

▶ Taking advantage of planned gifts and knowing how to get them

▶ Understanding the ins and outs of challenge grants

. . . .

*P*icture this: You're sitting on Mrs. Lewis's divan. Your mouth is dry. You've been preparing for this moment for months. You've had several lunches and follow-up conversations with Mrs. Lewis, and you've exchanged personal correspondence repeatedly. You know her dog on a first-name basis. From your relationship to date, you expect Mrs. Lewis to be a major giver in one way or another. Now's the time to see how substantial her support will be.

In this chapter, we explain the important role of the big-time giver in your organization, whether that person (or in some cases, that corporation or foundation) presents you with a huge check as a *major gift* or offers to match other donors' contributions with a *challenge grant.* We also explain how to deal with *planned giving,* a scenario in which an individual provides for your organization in his or her will or through other kinds of planned gifts. Not everyone has the means to give that $5,000, $20,000, or $100,000 gift, but those people who do — and who have an interest and a heart for your mission — can help you greatly through one of these three giving opportunities.

Note: In this chapter, we provide a basic introduction to the major gift and planned gift concepts. We encourage you to talk to planned gift specialists for particulars on how to develop a planned-giving program that's right for your organization.

Making a Perfect Match

Making sure your organization's mission and the interests of the donor are compatible is the most important part of securing a major gift. Yes, the giver's ability to give is important, but even more important is the giver's interest in giving specifically to your organization because of the work you do. Chances are a major donor gives to many different organizations, but she likely makes a major gift to only a select few. For this reason, making sure you have the right match for your donor's interest is very important. Don't panic; we explain how to do so in the following sections.

Deciding on the major gift amounts for your organization

What exactly is a major gift? Well, the word *major* here is relative. To a small organization, it may be $5,000. To a university, it may be $5,000,000. To a tiny, shoestring agency, a major gift may simply be a gift that's bigger than the norm.

Consider what your organization considers a major gift. Take a look at your overall operating budget and ask yourself: What type of gift would be a major help to us? Five percent of the operating budget? Ten? Two?

As you decide on the level of major gifts for your organization, ask yourself the following questions (for guidance in answering these questions, head to Part II):

✔ Who are our major givers likely to be?

✔ What people on our board and on staff will work on building relationships with our major givers?

✔ Do we have any current givers whom we can cultivate into major givers? If so, who are they?

✔ Does our board have expertise in the area of major gifts? Do we need to have board training on how to ask for major gifts?

✔ Is our board currently giving at a major gift level? If not, why not? If so, who are our highest givers?

✔ How do we recognize our major givers?

Deciding the amount that represents a major gift for your organization can not only help you plan to solicit for that amount but also keep you from settling for a $2,000 gift when you really need to move your givers toward $5,000. So make sure you take some time to carefully consider the questions posed in this section.

What is a gift?

In daily life, you most likely give and receive gifts all the time. You give someone else your attention. You receive ideas from other members on your fundraising team. You accept your Aunt Mildred's parakeet gracefully because it's her gift to you. But what makes a gift a *gift?*

In its most basic form, a *gift* is something you offer to somebody else with no thought of compensation. In fundraising, a gift may mean any number of things that all build on this basic definition. For example:

✔ A *general gift* is one a donor gives to your annual fund or contributes to your organization's operating expenses. Find out more about this type of gift in Chapter 18.

✔ A *lead gift* is the first, usually sizeable, gift to a capital campaign. Check out Chapter 20 for more details about capital campaigns.

✔ A *major gift* is another type of large gift that a donor may give to support a particular program, launch a campaign, further a cause, or be applied in another specific area of service. Major gifts are the subject of this chapter.

Despite the many types of gifts, a gift is still just a gift, freely given, with no arm-twisting and no product or service given in return.

A major gift for your capital campaign is different from a major gift for your annual operating campaign. In a capital campaign, you strategize with big gifts at the top — in that kind of campaign, $1,000,000 is definitely a major gift, but $10,000 might not be. In your annual operating campaign, $10,000 could be considered a significant major gift. See Chapter 20 for more information about capital campaigns and Chapter 18 for more about annual campaigns.

Getting to the heart of the major giver

The most important concept to remember about potential major givers is that you build your relationships with them by working with them over time — sometimes over many years. More specifically, you and your organization establish a relationship with a particular major giver by following these steps:

1. **Identify the person as a prospective major donor.**

2. **Qualify the donor by determining her interest in your organization and her ability to give.**

3. **Cultivate the donor and bring her ever closer to the heart of your mission. Introduce her to volunteer leadership to help build her relationship with your organization.**

4. **Ask, listen, and respond to her needs.**

5. **Request the major gift.**

6. **Acknowledge the gift, and continue the relationship by letting her know how her gift is making a difference to the people you serve.**

7. **Find a way to involve her further in specific activities.**

Although you don't want to insult somebody by asking for an outrageous amount of money, donors are often flattered that fundraisers think they're capable of giving at such high amounts. Asking for more than you expect gives you another benefit, too — the opportunity to accept less. Being able and willing to accept less than you ask for initially lets the donor know it's okay to "bargain down" to an amount she's more comfortable with.

The following sections take a closer look at two specific major givers: major donors who give to capital campaigns and major donors who give through corporations. To find out more about the major giver, in general — who she is, what she wants, and how you can make sure the donor-agency relationship with her is a positive one — turn to Chapter 9.

The give-and-take in a major campaign

A major giver in a capital campaign gives a lead gift that can make a huge difference in the success of your fundraising effort. A major gift in your capital campaign — also called a lead gift — may be as substantial as $25,000, $50,000, $100,000, or more. When you ask for lead gifts in a major campaign, remember that you're looking for a few gifts that comprise 40 to 60 percent of your total goal. (Check out Chapter 20 for many more details about capital campaigns.)

The people who are regular and large donors to your annual fund are the best candidates for major, lead, and challenge gifts because they have a relationship with your organization and have demonstrated their commitment to your cause.

Be prepared for your major giver to want to contact a tax advisor or lawyer before agreeing to a pledge amount. In fact, if the giver doesn't suggest doing so, you should, as a donor service. Some major givers may want to draft contracts to stipulate certain aspects of their agreements with you. Work with your organization's legal team and your donor's tax advisors to come to an agreement that's in everybody's best interest.

Corporate giving and cause-related major gifts

Although corporations are still a source of some major gifts, they're increasingly leaning toward giving gifts whose purposes and any publicity associated with them align with the missions of the corporations themselves. This relationship between the corporation and the gift is called *cause-related marketing.* For example, a waterworks company may want to sponsor the water tanks at the aquarium at the zoo; in return for the company's gift, it may want to attach the company name to the tanks in some way. This public recognition not only builds the company's community-spirited image, but also provides lots of exposure as the zoo's crowds stroll by.

Another example of cause-related marketing is when companies that depend on research endow chairs in the subject matters they care about in well-known universities. Cause-related giving is happening more and more between for-profit and nonprofit organizations. Alliances, partnerships, and sponsorships between the two types of organizations are here to stay. Chapter 22 has more information on corporate giving and cause-related marketing.

Valuing the relationship: Stewardship in action

What kind of reporting method do you plan to use to let your major givers know that their donations are going where you said they'd go? Each individual major gift is a campaign in itself — which means that each individual giver deserves to be met with, listened to, and valued. After you receive a major gift, nothing about the effort you put into building a relationship with the donor changes. In fact, it's more important than ever to include every major donor in the loop.

When your major giver made her donation to you, she became a part of your organization. Thus, you need to include her in your organization's communication flow when you have both good and bad news to report. Keeping your major donors updated on the changes — positive or negative — that are taking place in your organization helps the donors know that your organization is about more than money; not to mention it makes them glad they gave to your organization as generously as they did.

You can report the use of donated funds through your *annual report,* which includes financial information about your organization as well as updates on programs, services, and staff. But for high-level, major givers, personalized letters with specific information about how your organization has applied their gifts are a great idea. For example, in your letter, you can write, "Your generous donation helped us provide training for 15 more teen moms than we helped last year." Or you can write, "Because of you, Sarah was able to finish high school, take a computer course, and get an entry-level job at a small publishing company. Her daughter, Haley, is healthy, caught up on her shots, and happy in our day-care center while her mom works."

Personalized attention makes your major givers glad they're in a relationship with you. Plus, as you honor the continuing relationship between you and your major donors, you keep the door open for potential planned gifts in the future.

Creating a major gift strategy

Before you begin your search for major givers, take time to develop a major gift strategy that can help you find, cultivate, and build relationships with your major donors. As you craft your strategy, think about what your major givers are looking for in any organization to which they decide to give. For starters, major donors want to know that your organization does the following:

- ✔ Cares about the issues they care about
- ✔ Is careful about spending contributions
- ✔ Values them as individuals
- ✔ Appreciates their gifts
- ✔ Practices good management
- ✔ Produces measurable results
- ✔ Plans intelligently
- ✔ Selects good people who represent it well
- ✔ Presents an image with which they want to align

Set the ground rules for major gifts before you need them. Come up with naming opportunities and other forms of donor recognition. Preparing ahead of time and knowing what you want makes you more able to attain it.

Get your board together and follow these tips to develop your major gift strategy:

- ✔ Brainstorm a list of major giving ideas.
- ✔ Get board approval before you proceed.
- ✔ Create ideas you can live with for quite some time — you can't remove a donor's name from a named gift at the drop of a hat.
- ✔ Don't be afraid to reach for some high-level gifts — but also be realistic, based on your current economic climate.
- ✔ Consider whether corporate sponsorships or in-kind contributions can be a part of your major gift strategy.

As you put together your major gift strategy, think about how to reward your donors when they enter into this high-level relationship with your organization. Some of the ideas you can include in your strategy are:

- ✔ **Keep in touch with your high-level donors often.** Send them newsletters. Contact them by e-mail every so often. Call when you feel direct, personal contact is appropriate. Ask your donors what their opinions are about new initiatives. Follow up in other ways, too.

✔ **Recognize your high-level donors' gifts.** Host a special dinner for your high-level donors. Take each major donor out to lunch. Invite your major donors to be part of an elite giving club.

✔ **Visit your high-level donors at home if they enjoy personal calls.** Personal visits build relationships in unique ways — being in someone's house creates a level of intimacy that you can't reach in a board room or via e-mail.

✔ **Consider unique naming opportunities.** Create a complete list of items that are available for naming, and keep careful track of which donors are offered and which ones accept these naming opportunities. Make sure two different staff or board members don't promise the same naming item to two different donors.

Naming opportunities work best when you plan them carefully and use them slowly. Doing so helps preserve the importance of the naming items and keeps you from making potentially embarrassing mistakes.

If you use naming opportunities, decide with your board in advance how much must be donated in return for the naming. Is it $40,000 for a garden, $20,000 for a fountain, and $10,000 for a bench? Make sure the naming items are planned, approved, and available before you begin publicizing your major gift plan.

Preparing for Planned Gifts

At the very top of the fundraising ladder, you find the planned gift. A *planned gift* is a long-term, high-dollar gift that may come to your organization in the form of a bequest, property, insurance, or one of several other planned-giving instruments (see the "Creating a plan for planned gifts and choosing gifts for the plan" section for more on these different instruments).

Some fundraisers build entire careers around the concept of planned giving, as well they should. This highly specialized area of giving requires continual education on current tax laws, financial instruments, best practices, and the application and development of gift strategies.

Changes in the economy have an impact on planned giving, but as the population ages, your donors know that estate planning gives them a way to plan for the legacy they want to leave. Because of the huge transfer of wealth that scholars expect to take place over the next two decades and the aging baby-boomer population, smart ways to preserve and hand down assets are in demand. Planned-giving instruments give donors ways to protect their holdings, provide for their families, and leave a legacy to an organization with a mission they believe in.

Getting the gift that keeps on giving

A planned gift can be a great thing both for your organization and for your donor's family — it's the gift that truly keeps on giving after your donor has passed away. Planned gifts range from a simple bequest to a complex trust. As you may expect, this kind of high-level gift comes from a much smaller percentage of your complete donor list than other types of gifts. However, don't eliminate people who don't seem to be potential big givers because you may be surprised to find out which of your donors has the resources to make a substantial planned gift. Even a modest annual fund donor can give you a gift in his will or leave you proceeds from a life insurance policy.

When you first heard the term *planned gift,* you may have thought "That's odd — aren't all gifts planned?" In actuality, the phrase *planned gift* refers to the high level of planning required — by fundraising officers, financial advisors, tax attorneys, and more — to develop just the right giving plan for a high-level donor who wants to leave a major gift to a charitable organization.

In addition to requiring a lot of planning, planned gifts can do the following:

- ✔ Provide estate planning for donors
- ✔ Give donors income and possible estate tax savings
- ✔ Be given during the donor's lifetime and be relatively small
- ✔ Provide an income to the donor or to someone designated by the donor
- ✔ Improve the relationship between the donor and your organization while the donor is still alive
- ✔ Involve the donor's tax and financial advisors

Now that you know *what* a planned gift is, you need to figure out *who* the planned giver is. A potential planned-giving donor will be

- ✔ Engaged with your organization at a high level
- ✔ Interested in making a long-term difference for the organization
- ✔ Able to make a large donation either now, by investing funds in a planned-giving instrument, or later, when the ability to get at the funds for the donor's own use (called accessibility and liquidity) isn't an issue

The most important rule to remember for any planned-giving program is that the needs of the donor come first. Your donors place high trust in you as you help them find, evaluate, and select the right planned-giving instrument for their needs and financial situations. Although you're working to secure a gift for your organization, remember that the gift must be the right fit for both you and the donor, which is why each donor should have his own advisors review and respond to the planned-giving plan before either party signs the contract.

Differentiating planned giving from other types of giving

If you have a good, healthy donor program in place, in which you cultivate donors, bring them ever closer to the mission of your organization, and upgrade them to higher gifts each year, a planned-giving program is only a matter of education. It's a logical next step.

The concept of planned giving is only about 40 years old. A change in the tax laws in the late 1960s concerning how charitable contributions are made led to the development of the planned-giving instruments you can use today.

As you compare planned gifts to other types of gifts, take note of the following three primary differences:

- ✔ **The type of the gift:** A planned gift may be any amount of money, stock, insurance, property, or material goods.

- ✔ **When the gift is paid:** Although a planned gift is ordinarily paid to the organization upon the death of the donor, some planned-giving instruments pay the donor and/or other selected recipients an income during the donor's lifetime, as well.

- ✔ **The complexity of the gift:** A planned gift is a transaction that requires the collaboration of tax advisors, lawyers, financial advisors, and fundraising professionals, all working together with both the donor's and the organization's best interests in mind.

Your potential planned giver needs to find out over how many years he can allocate the deduction for his planned gift. After all, many people can't take the deduction all in one year. Make sure that your donor talks to his tax professional and gets all the answers he needs before either of you sign a contract.

Timing is key: Knowing when to start

If you've just begun putting a fundraising system in place in your organization, or you're a one-person development office, you may be wondering how important a planned-giving program really is and when you need to start one.

One big mistake many organizations make with planned giving is not starting it soon enough. When you create planned-giving opportunities, you generate gifts that will come to you later. Prepared organizations always know who their top-level donors are and what kind of potential gifts are "in the pipeline," which means future planned gifts as well as projected donations for other campaigns.

In general, you know you're ready to start a planned-giving program when

✔ You have an established donor base.

✔ You've demonstrated good stewardship consistently.

✔ You have the resources (on your board or through a consultant) to offer the high-end support a planned-giving program requires.

Many nonprofit organizations rely on the pro bono services of tax or legal advisors to set up and maintain their planned-giving programs. Traditionally, only the larger organizations (museums, symphonies, universities, and so on) can afford a full-time staff member who specializes in this area. Either way, as a best practice, be sure to have a planned-giving professional either on your board or available to consult as needed.

Gearing up for planned giving

As with all other aspects of your fundraising plan, your organization's mission is an important element of your planned-giving program. Yet, although we can assume that you have a crystal-clear mission and the publications to support it, before you embark on a program that takes you into the deep waters of planned giving, you need to be certain you have a sound planned-giving plan — and the people to work it — in place.

To get a planned-giving program going, you need three things:

✔ A board that's ready for planned giving

✔ A plan to implement a planned-giving program

✔ The professional resources to help you investigate, set up, and maintain the program

Not all organizations are set up the same way, but some boards organize a planned-giving committee to make important decisions like what the responsibilities of the committee members will be, how planned funds will be invested, what the board's legal responsibilities are, and how the invested funds will be used. Whether or not you have a planned-giving committee, you need a process by which the board supervises your planned-giving program.

The following sections help you gear up for your planned-giving program.

Starting with your board

Making sure your board is ready to implement a planned-giving program is an important part of putting your program in place. If your organization has a good reputation in the community and is led by solid, respected leaders, you may be ready to start a planned-giving program. As you explore this complex fundraising option, do the following:

✔ Open the topic for discussion with your board, and ask a local financial expert (if you don't have one on your board) to explain the various planned-giving instruments and their individual features.

✔ Pull together a focus group to discuss the pros and cons of a planned-giving program in your organization.

You may also want to do an informal survey among some of your closest donors that says, "We're thinking about starting a planned-giving program for the people closest to our mission. Do you think people would be interested in a program that . . . ?"

Because planned giving is such a highly specialized area, nonprofit organizations considering a planned-giving program for the first time need to get educated about the process before they begin. Look for classes in your area that offer the basics of planned giving; for example, a financial services firm in your area may offer classes on planned-giving instruments.

Regularly advising your board of all planned gifts you're exploring is extremely important. Some gifts may involve obligations on the part of the organization, and, for this reason, the board needs to be involved.

Creating a plan for planned gifts and choosing gifts for the plan

The largest part of preparing for a planned-giving program is determining your goals and guidelines for the solicitation, acceptance, and administration of gifts. Don't forget to get legal and financial advice as you prepare these guidelines.

After you get some input from legal and financial professionals, your planned-giving committee (if you have one) or your board needs to draft policies that determine the following:

✔ The type of gifts you offer

✔ The amount the planned gift pays to donors (if applicable)

✔ The legal and ethical responsibilities of you, the fundraiser

✔ The process you follow to preserve the confidentiality of the donor

✔ The distribution of assets

✔ The investments you accept

In planned giving, you can use a number of different donation instruments — which is one of the reasons why having a well-trained, knowledgeable, and up-to-date consultant or staff member is vitally important. The person who works with donors on planned-giving possibilities needs to be able to answer questions about the various instruments, use his resources to find the solutions to complex situations, and make recommendations in the best interests of the donor.

Marketing tips for planned giving

Part of getting your planned-giving program going is letting financial and legal professionals who advise their clients about such programs know about it. How exactly does speaking to these professionals help your program? Education is the key. If tax advisors, lawyers, and financial experts in your area know about your planned-giving program, they can recommend it to their clients, saying, "You're in an estate tax rate category in which you can designate the money for a charity you care about; otherwise, that same money will be paid to the state and federal government for estate and inheritance taxes." Who wants to pay money to the state when they could leave behind a legacy with an organization they care about?

Here are a couple of ideas for effectively marketing your program to professionals:

✔ Get out in the community and make presentations. Go to lawyers' and accountants' offices — two groups who will be interested in what you're offering their clients — and explain your planned-giving program and the instruments you offer.

✔ If you live in a small- to medium-sized town, go to your local banker and ask, "Who are the local lawyers in town who deal with most of the big gifts?" Follow those leads to have discussions with the attorneys in town who deal most often with planned giving.

Some of the more popular planned-giving instruments your organization will work with as you explore planned giving as a fundraising option include wills, charitable gift annuities, charitable trusts, insurance and interest gifts, and qualified plans.

Here's a rundown on each of these different gift types:

✔ **Working with wills:** A will is the simplest and most common planned-giving instrument. Because most people are familiar with wills, this instrument is the easiest one to explain and market. When donors work with your organization to draft their wills, they can protect their dependents, reduce their estate taxes, and control how their assets are distributed — and to whom. Some donors like leaving contributions to charities in their wills because the gift is revocable — if the donor changes his mind later, he can revise his will and erase the gift. In other gift forms based on contractual agreements, donors can't change their minds.

✔ **Assessing annuities:** In a charitable gift annuity, the donor makes a gift of cash or assets to your organization and your organization agrees to pay an income to the donor and/or his beneficiaries until the donor's death. The older the donor is, the higher the annual income you pay.

Your organization invests the donated funds and pays out a fixed income to the donor. The benefits to the donor include receipt of partially tax-free income capital, as well as estate tax benefits. The American Council on Gift Annuities (ACGA), a national organization of charities founded as the Committee on Gift Annuities, educates charities about gift annuities and other planned gifts. You can find suggested charitable gift annuity rates by going to the organization's Web site at www.acga-web.org/giftrates.html. Most charities rely on the ACGA to help them determine the payout rate for charitable gift annuities.

✔ **Tackling charitable trusts:** The *charitable remainder trust* is a three-way relationship arranged between a charity and a donor through a trustee, who manages the account. Using this type of giving instrument, the donor sets up a trust for the donation, using annual payments, which pays out to the charity upon his death. This type of trust benefits the donor by reducing the donor's estate tax and providing income and capital gains' tax benefits. A *charitable lead trust* is slightly different from a charitable remainder trust in that the donor specifies a certain number of years during which an annual payment is made to the charity. At the end of that specified time, the principal is returned to the donor or paid to a designated beneficiary. Both charitable remainder and charitable lead trusts can be either the *unitrust type,* which provides fluctuating income based on the value of the trusts' assets, or the *annuity type,* which provides fixed income.

✔ **Investigating insurance and interest gifts:** Donors can also give an organization an individual insurance policy. The charity collects the insurance proceeds upon the death of the donor. If the premiums are continuing, the organization typically pays the premiums and the donor sends in an annual contribution to provide for these payments. Insurance policies are fairly common planned-giving instruments. In some cases, you can use a two-fold system: A charitable remainder trust purchases an insurance policy on the person who donated the money in the first place. The charity gets the money in the trust, and the insurance proceeds go to a designated heir selected by the donor.

✔ **Using qualified plans:** Qualified plans include IRAs, 401(k)s, 403(b)s, and a variety of other investment plans. Simply by changing the named beneficiary on the plan, an individual donor can designate all or part of the proceeds of a qualified plan to a charity. Upon the donor's death, the amount contributed to the charity isn't included in the individual's estate.

State regulations on annuities and trusts vary, so check the regulations in your area before beginning such programs. You can get a listing of state regulations by going to the Planned Giving Resources site at www.pgresources.com/regs.html.

Web resources for planned giving

The Partnership for Philanthropic Planning, a professional group for charitable gift-planning professionals, lists various position papers related to planned-giving instruments on its Web site at `www.pppnet.org/resource/resource.html`.

If you crave more details about planned giving, check out *Planned Giving Today*, a publication for Canadian and U.S. gift-planning professionals, at `www.pgtoday.com`. Also take a look at articles about planned giving in the research library at `www.charityvillage.com`.

Marketing the plan to the giving public

When you announce to your organization's donors, "We now have a planned-giving program," your next task is to educate your donors about what that program involves, how it benefits them, and how they can best take advantage of it. As you look for ways to educate your donors about your planned-giving program, try doing the following:

- ✔ Mention your program in your newsletter and on your Web site.
- ✔ Send a flyer to prequalified donors in a targeted mail campaign.
- ✔ Write personal letters to individual donors.
- ✔ Create a new planned-giving brochure.
- ✔ Send an e-mail message to online donors.
- ✔ Advertise in publications with your audience base.
- ✔ Announce your program at a donor recognition luncheon.

One key to launching a successful planned-giving program is making sure you publicize it to the right audience. If you approach a mid-20s audience with a planned-giving strategy, they're likely to say, "Great. Let me get back to you in another 20 years." If you introduce your program to a select group of high-level givers who are also retirees, sooner or later they're going to come to you and say, "I'm putting together my will. . . ."

Making Money Go the Extra Mile: Challenge Grants

A *challenge grant,* one of the most effective fundraising tools around today, is a type of funding offered to your organization — sometimes anonymously — contingent on your organization's raising a set number of matching funds.

Because challenge grants force your organization to raise a set number of funds, all the gifts involved in a challenge grant go farther — which can mean happy givers and more good being accomplished by your organization.

In times of economic hardship, giving your donors the opportunity to participate in a *matched-giving program* (the kind of program that elicits challenge grants) can help them feel like they're truly making a difference, even though their gifts may be smaller than they were in previous years. Additionally, a matched-giving program builds a community of giving that can have payoffs far into the future.

In Chapter 11, we explain the ins and outs of grant proposal writing. Challenge grants also involve grant proposals, but with a twist: In a challenge grant proposal, the donors of the grant spell out the terms and conditions of the funding. The donor states that she'll give a substantial gift, if the giving public matches it. This type of grant provides a huge incentive for potential donors to make their dollars go much, much farther.

When you apply for a challenge grant, you say to your potential funders, "The program we're trying to fund is a program that covers not only all the standard grant proposal ingredients but also a plan for securing matching funding, projected amounts, intended sources, and measurable outcomes." In any challenge grant proposal, you want to communicate this message to the potential grantor: You have the possibility to be the whole inspiration for this new initiative; your challenge grant will make it happen.

Here are a few real-life examples of situations in which challenge grants made a big difference in a particular program:

- A donor who supports a small educational foundation pledged a $10,000 challenge gift to other donors with the intention of matching all gifts up to the $10,000 amount. This inspired year-end giving to the foundation.

- United Way created the Forever Fund with the intention of providing an endowment for the continuance of the organization. The fundraising effort floundered until the Lilly Endowment came along and gave a huge challenge incentive.

- More than 65 community foundations in the state of Indiana have used challenge grants to get started. Michigan and Ohio have now started community foundations using the same approach.

In general, challenge grants do three positive things:

- **Challenge grants spotlight your organization and provide an endorsement from a major player.** The person or entity giving the challenge grant is most likely someone in the public eye — the publicity they receive for their philanthropy benefits you both. For your organization, this alliance means respectability — the "good fundraising" seal of approval.

✔ **Challenge grants help people feel that their money goes farther than it would in a sole donation.** If a foundation gives you $10,000 to start a new family life program and you match it with another $10,000, all the donors who gave to your campaign can feel that their donation went twice as far. Plus, challenge grants can have different kinds of ratios — for example, 1:1, 2:1, or 3:1. In other words, a challenge grant funder can choose to match two or three times the amount your other donors give, depending on the program you're funding and the relationship you develop with that funder.

✔ **Challenge grants enable you to honor and reward the giver of the challenge grant.** This person is a "mover and shaker" and probably one of the closest constituents you have in your organization. The recognition you give her helps her feel good about her gift and gives her the satisfaction of knowing her generosity enabled the whole program to work. The recognition you give your challenge grant funder inspires others to want to make challenge grants in the future, as well.

The following sections cover some basic info you need to know as you explore the idea of starting your own matched-giving program.

Before you open up to the possibility of challenge grants, discuss the idea with your board. Feel out any resistance. Most likely, your board will approve the idea and want to participate. Often the first challenge gifts you receive are from board members themselves.

Understanding how challenge grants work

Both corporations and foundations typically play major roles in giving challenge grants, because doing so leverages their money. Their initial investments may be doubled, tripled, quadrupled, or more. One recent challenge grant began with a $5 million grant and raised more than $40 million. The corporation got publicity and credit for initiating a $40 million contribution — now that's potent stuff.

But not all your challenge grants will be multimillion-dollar affairs. In many fundraising drives hosted by churches or service organizations associated with the arts, social services, and education, the main benefit of challenge grants isn't that they raise millions of dollars, but, instead, that they take the money farther than the original gift. In each of these service areas, the grants are usually related to something new or to the enlargement of an existing program.

Live events, such as public radio fundraisers, often accept challenge grants of as little as $1,000 that must be met in the next hour from listeners. If you have access to such media, look for mini-challenge, short-time-period grant opportunities.

As you look for ways to get a challenge grant going, keep the plans quiet. Top-level donors will be interested in getting in on the front end of a big deal — advertising your intent may diffuse the excitement. Work out all your plans before you approach the selected donor with the idea. Then, when you're ready, say to the donor, "We're designing this program and we think you'd be perfect to lead the campaign with a challenge grant of $5,000."

Managing a challenge grant

As you design the proposal for your challenge grant, keep the following key concept in mind: You're giving this person (or funder) the ability to empower lots of other people to give. This powerful thought is the major difference between a traditional grant proposal and a challenge grant proposal.

When you begin your challenge grant campaign, you want your potential matching donors to recognize the opportunity to increase the effectiveness of their gift. You also want them to think, "Gosh, we'd better be part of this campaign — we certainly don't want to be left out!"

If you're leveraging a challenge grant to secure funding from another source, be prepared to provide proof of the challenge. A letter from the funding individual or entity, signed by the appropriate responsible parties, should suffice.

Generally, challenge grant funders don't specify how the remaining money must come in — the idea is to get the amount matched.

Challenge grants nearly always have deadlines, which are both practical and helpful — deadlines give you specific time frames for your campaigns. Having a specified time frame in which to raise the matching money enables you to put some urgency into your fundraising letters. For example, you can write, "If we don't raise the matching amount by December 31, 2011, we lose half of the challenge grant." Your potential donors won't miss that kind of urgency.

After you receive a challenge grant, the best way to motivate other people to give is by securing great gifts from people and groups that donors admire — with the promise that donors can extend the reach of their gifts by contributing now.

Chapter 22

Engaging the Corporate Giver

In This Chapter

▶ Understanding why corporations give

▶ Locating the right corporate donor match for your organization

▶ Convincing corporate donors to give to your cause

*N*ot all major givers are individual philanthropists interested in further-ing your mission and earning tax benefits and other perks at the same time — corporations are a source of major giving on an international scale. Whether they give from their corporate foundations or through corporate sponsorships, corporations generally want more than a simple feel-good feel-ing for their donations. They want to see measurable benefits for their com-panies, which is why corporations carefully evaluate the causes they support and the missions they engage in, especially in times of economic challenge.

Philanthropy is good business, and supporting charitable efforts enables companies to differentiate themselves from their competition. Favorable public opinion is a sought-after goal in both the for-profit and nonprofit sec-tors. Aligning with a good cause helps build the community feel-good quo-tient and benefits the company by boosting goodwill, perhaps increasing sales, raising visibility, and creating a sense of benevolence and involvement that may help it attract and keep good employees.

This chapter shows you how to go about finding the right corporations to approach on behalf of your cause. Then it offers you some pointers about pitching your message to a company's decision makers.

Understanding the Attitudes behind Corporate Giving

You can't really know how to approach donors until you understand the reasons why they give. Individuals may have hundreds of reasons for giving. Corporations can be a little more straightforward: a blending of practical and altruistic reasoning.

Many corporations donate in the interests of *cause-related marketing,* a way to associate themselves with the good guys of charity to spiff up their own public images. They get free publicity and free goodwill. People may buy more of the corporation's products than their competitors' when they hear of their good deeds. Some corporations even find that giving is a way to influence politicians regarding legislation related to their industries.

But many corporations give above and beyond the basic promotional possibilities, and different companies give for different reasons. Some may indeed have altruistic motives as well as the desire to give back to the community. In addition to self-promotion, corporations give major gifts because they want

- ✔ To show the community that they are people friendly (or arts friendly, or health conscious, whatever the case may be)
- ✔ To show their employees that they care about improving their community
- ✔ To help organizations that do work related to their particular industry (for example, a medical supply company that makes a major gift to a medical school)
- ✔ To give a seal of approval to a particular cause

Some corporations go even further in their commitment to doing good. They may develop a philanthropic plan or use cause-related marketing. We explain these concepts in more detail in the following sections.

Making a difference in the community

A quick review of most corporate mission statements shows you that businesses today are more aware of the community impact their products and services need to have. Corporate mission statements don't say "our goal is to make money;" instead, they may say "our goal is to provide reasonably priced ways to improve life for families affected by. . . ." This focus is more in tune with benefits to both the individual and the community. By understanding a particular corporation's approach, you can see how your cause may align with that company's giving program.

Some corporations today are developing philanthropic giving strategies that become part of the overall strategic plan of the business. A *philanthropic giving plan* is filled out and approved by a committee of the board and includes the *corporation's giving mission statement,* which states the corporation's belief in philanthropy and the way in which that belief aligns with the company's mission. The plan may spell out different strategies for specific initiatives — for example, providing different amounts to education, social services, and the arts.

The best giving programs relate their missions not only to the community but to their workforces, as well, and they try to engage employees in the giving process. These corporations are likely to encourage their employees to donate volunteer time to a nonprofit organization, and the volunteers are recognized for the hours donated and time worked. Some companies even have celebrations to reward employees who dedicate considerable effort to nonprofit organizations — this is a great way to encourage a culture of giving and boost the morale of your workforce at the same time.

The best place to start in researching corporate philanthropy plans is on company Web sites. Organizations that have a philanthropic arm promote their philanthropy through traditional marketing channels and include information about granting programs on their sites and perhaps through social media.

You scratch my back, I'll scratch yours: Cause-related marketing

Cause-related marketing is a popular approach for corporations in which the business provides needed equipment or services for the nonprofit, and the nonprofit provides visibility in the community for the business by advertising the help it received. The business benefits from the "good guy" image it develops as a result of the positive publicity, and the organization benefits from the exposure and the share of the proceeds it receives from the business. For example, a computer company forms a link with an organization that works with kids with disabilities, or a local business may make itself a visible patron to a particular theater or musical organization.

If your mission has national or international appeal, you aren't limited to forming links with only corporations in your local area. As you look for corporations that may be interested in developing their cause-related marketing approaches with your organization, continue your research on a larger scale. Start with the top corporate givers featured in the most recent edition of the publication *Giving USA* (www.givingusa.org). Work through the list to find out which corporate-giving programs fund the type of programs you offer.

Additionally, keep on top of who's who at various corporations, and keep your thumb on the pulse of the giving market. The following publications can provide a resource for your corporate fact-finding initiative:

- ✔ *Corporate Giving Directory*, 31st Edition (Taft Group)
- ✔ *The Chronicle of Philanthropy* (www.philanthropy.com)
- ✔ *National Directory of Corporate Giving*, 15th Edition (The Foundation Center)
- ✔ *Fistful of Dollars: Fact and Fantasy about Corporate Charitable Giving*, by Linda M. Zukowski (EarthWrites)
- ✔ *Giving by Industry: A Reference Guide to the New Corporate Philanthropy*, edited by Michael Abshire (Aspen Pub)

Different ways that corporations give

A giant multifigure check may be the donation you'd be happiest to see, but, in fact, corporations give in a variety of ways, including the following:

✔ Giving the ever-popular donation

✔ Hosting days of giving in which the companies give their employees the whole day off to volunteer (The tendency now is to align the volunteer project with what the business does. For example, computer companies give computers to poor kids.)

✔ Offering matching gifts, in which the corporation matches a gift made by an employee

✔ Encouraging volunteerism

✔ Donating equipment

✔ Providing in-kind or pro bono services

✔ Donating space, such as office or warehouse space

✔ Creating partnerships in the form of cause-related marketing or sponsorships for programs

✔ Sponsoring foundation gifts

Note that some of these publications carry a big price tag, sometimes $600 or more. To keep your costs down, consider buying a used copy, but don't skimp and buy an older edition. Always buy the most current edition: the up-to-date information is well worth the price.

Most big corporations publish a brochure about their corporate-giving programs. Sometimes the programs are specialized and very focused, and sometimes the programs are general and support a wide range of causes. After you identify a corporation that may be aligned with your cause, call the company and ask whether they have a brochure that can provide you with more details about their giving strategies.

Finding the Right Corporations for Your Organization

Finding the right corporation is like finding the right mate. Not every corporation fits with your organization and its cause. You have to find a corporation that matches your organization in interests, priorities, and self-interest.

Finding the right corporation with a heart for philanthropy takes a little legwork, but with enough effort, you can find the perfect company for your organization. For this matchmaking effort, put on your business hat. Remember that with a corporation (as with every donor, but even more so with a corporation), giving is an exchange — something for something. Corporations want to get something out of the relationship, so consider what you have to offer and who may want to "buy" what you have.

Using the local community hook

Which corporations give in your community? When you start looking for their names, you'll see them everywhere: on theater programs, in the local newspaper, at the park, and in the schools. Keep a notebook with you so you can jot down names of local businesses that support nonprofits with missions in your area of service. You'll be glad you did when you begin building the part of your fundraising program that targets corporate giving.

Here are a few questions you can ask yourself and your corporate-giving team as you think about how and whom to approach for corporate giving:

- ✔ Which corporations give to your organization now?
- ✔ Which corporations in your location may have a link to your mission?
- ✔ Which corporations give to organizations that are similar to yours?
- ✔ Which of your board members, if any, have direct links to corporations?
- ✔ Whom do you know at any of the potential donor corporations?
- ✔ Which local corporations can you invite to participate on your board?
- ✔ Which corporations may benefit from the positive publicity of being involved with your mission?

If you don't have any strong, peer-to-peer links to people at local corporations, subscribe to your local business journal or get a copy of the member lists published by your local chamber of commerce. These member lists include all kinds of companies, including major electrical contractors, banks, real estate companies, and insurance businesses, that you can approach as you try to develop corporate-donor relationships.

If you have corporations represented on your board, you may already be receiving corporate gifts. As you start your planning for a corporate fundraising strategy, put together a focus group of these corporate representatives, and ask them what they'd most like to see in a presentation about your organization. Don't forget to ask each member of your focus group for the names of three people you can contact as you begin your corporate fundraising campaign.

Local corporations can be the best source for in-kind donations. For example, a national supermarket chain with a branch in your town may be willing to donate food for a fundraising event. Your best contact for such local in-kind donations is probably the manager of the local branch store or office, who has some latitude to donate to local groups.

Discovering where the CEO's heart lies

Often a company gives because the person in charge has a certain interest. For example, if the head of the local bank is an opera nut, you may find a sympathetic ear for your community operetta group. If you can connect with the CEO and have him or her turn you over to the person at the company who heads up corporate giving, you have a good shot at getting some kind of gift. After all, it's a brave corporate-giving manager who disregards the CEO's recommendation.

Because identifying with the head of a company is often the key to getting donations from that company, make sure you do your research before you set up a meeting with a particular CEO so you know what the CEO is interested in and what he or she may be interested in funding.

Suppose you've managed to get a meeting with the new CEO of Acme Paper Company — Mrs. Anderson. You go to the company's main office nervous about meeting with such a powerful person but confident about your cause. You've done your homework and know that the company Mrs. Anderson used to head up was a big giver in the healthcare sector, but now that she's with Acme Paper, you hope she'll follow its tradition of supporting animal rights causes.

As you're ushered into Mrs. Anderson's office, you're relieved to see pictures of dogs everywhere . . . until you find out that those pictures belonged to the outgoing CEO and that Mrs. Anderson is allergic to dogs. Don't worry — you can still recover. Keep your sense of humor intact, and use your assumption to find out what Mrs. Anderson really *does* care about; then use that information to show her why your organization's mission fits the causes she cares about.

Watch the social pages of your local newspaper to see whether the CEOs of any local companies are showing up at theater openings, hospital fundraisers, or local horse shows. If you're an arts group, an organization that helps pregnant women get healthcare, or an animal rights activist, you may just find the hook that will get your foot in the CEO's door. (After all, just because Mrs. Anderson is allergic to dogs doesn't mean she doesn't have half a dozen cats at home!)

Finding out what serves the company's interests

With a little strategizing, you can fairly easily figure out the types of connections between businesses and causes that make sense for corporate giving. Here are just a few examples of such logical connections:

✔ A pharmaceutical company gives money to fund a new community clinic.

✔ A software company donates free computers to schools, loaded, of course, with their own software products.

✔ The local car dealership gives to a program to put a stop to drunk driving.

✔ The large smelting plant that used to have issues with polluting the air gives money to fund an environmental study.

Ironically, even if corporations seem to be part of the overall problem — for example, a liquor company donating to a campaign against drinking and driving — they can claim that they're the good guys if their products are used responsibly.

After you identify companies with which your cause may have a logical connection, remember to listen to your own intuition. Does the connection feel right? Is this match a logical, natural connection? If so, you may have found a likely corporate donor.

Approaching a Corporate Donor

Every corporation and every industry has different concerns, but they're all in the business of making money. So why do corporations give money away? The answer is simple — because they see some kind of profit in doing so.

In many aspects, approaching a corporate donor isn't that different from approaching any donor. You determine

✔ What the corporation's interest is

✔ What its giving track record is

✔ How you can help the corporation participate in an area it wants to make a difference in, for whatever reason

But the corporate world does have a few unique differences, which we discuss in the sections that follow.

Researching the corporation ahead of time

The first step to finding the right corporations for your organization's corporate campaign is knowing which kind of entities you're approaching. Corporate giving usually comes from one of the following two sources (take note of the differences between them):

✔ **Company-sponsored foundations:** These foundations are separate entities under the law from the corporation they're linked to. Their giving typically is allied with the corporation's interests. The parent company contributes to the foundation on a regular basis. Their endowments may grow when the corporation is profitable and shrink when it isn't so profitable. Federal and state regulations for private foundations govern company-sponsored foundations. Just like other foundations you work with, company-sponsored foundations award funds in the form of grants.

✔ **Corporate direct-giving programs:** These programs are part of the corporation itself and, as such, don't have to meet regulations for private foundations. In this setup, the company typically can use up to 10 percent of its pretax money to make contributions to charity, though most companies give more like 1 percent on average. These programs have no endowment per se but work off company profits. Often companies have direct-giving programs in which the corporation matches gifts to nonprofits made by employees and directors, and the matches may be a variety of multiples, for example, 1:1, 2:1, or 3:1. Many corporations also set up in-kind gift programs in which they donate time and materials to nonprofits.

If you set up a matching-gift program with a corporate donor, be sure to get your thank-yous right. In some cases, development directors overlook matching gifts because they fail to recognize the original gifts that made the larger amount possible. For best practices — and the happiest donors — send thank-you notes that appropriately reflect the good that came from the gift as a whole to everyone who contributed to the matching gift.

To find out if a corporation has a foundation, go to a foundation directory, such as the Foundation Directory Online (`www.fconline.foundation center.org`) or the Foundation Finder at The Foundation Center's Web site (`www.foundationcenter.org`), and search for the corporation's name. To determine whether a corporation has a direct-giving program, go to the company Web site and search for direct-giving programs.

The Foundation Center offers a subscription-based corporate-giving directory that includes current information on corporate philanthropy programs. Go to `foundationcenter.org/findfunders/fundingsources/cgo.html` to find out more information.

The next piece of the corporate-giving puzzle is figuring out the types of programs corporations support. This step is very similar to what you do to find the right foundation to support your cause. All corporations or corporate-affiliated foundations publish information about the types of programs they fund. Look on their Web sites or contact them for a copy of their guidelines. The guidelines tell you whether the foundation leans toward the arts, health-related causes, education, community-focused issues, or whatever. Then direct your efforts toward the ones that seem like a good match for your cause.

Chapter 7 is all about researching donors, and Chapters 9 and 10 are all about approaching folks for major gifts. If you're serious about looking for corporate donors, read those chapters along with this chapter for more about researching.

Knowing your value to the donor

Don't ever forget that your organization has something to bring to the table in the corporate-giving exchange. For example:

- ✔ You lend an image of goodwill and credibility to the corporation.
- ✔ You offer tax advantages for corporations that donate pretax dollars.
- ✔ You provide a way for corporations to attract good employees who share their charitable interests.
- ✔ You help to improve the community in which the corporation exists and its employees live.

When you approach a member of a corporation for a major gift, you're working with somebody who understands the value of this give-and-take relationship better than most. Keep this fact in mind, and you may just feel confident approaching corporate givers in a businesslike way.

If you're having trouble finding the right initial contact at a company, try searching the company's Web site for the corporate affairs or community relations department. If, as far as you can tell, the company doesn't have such departments, start with public relations or marketing. Consider asking your board members or major donors who have existing corporate relationships to make introductions for your organization.

Putting together your presentation

When you approach a corporation or company-sponsored foundation for funding, you have to jump through all the hoops that other kinds of donors put you through. As you prepare to jump through these hoops, you need to

- ✔ Research the specific guidelines the corporation publishes for submitting applications.
- ✔ Meet all deadlines and include everything the guidelines require.
- ✔ Build a compelling case for your organization by including your up-to-date case statement, your accomplishments, and your ability to govern your activities professionally.

Don't forget the financials. Businesspeople are used to seeing balance sheets and budgets, and they expect to see that you're a viable business with some business-savvy leaders in your operations. If you have strong corporate types on your board, stress that fact. Include their résumés, or at least a short biographical paragraph on each of them, with your application. Try to set up one-on-one personal meetings with your key board members and the corporation representatives if possible.

Following up in a businesslike way

Any good businessperson will tell you that good follow-up is respected in the corporate world. Of course, you need to be aware of the likely time frames in the corporate or corporate foundation's grant application guidelines (or the time frames you get from the corporation's corporate-giving manager at your meeting), but if the estimated time of response has come and gone, follow up with a letter or phone call. You can inquire as to whether the corporation needs any additional information from you. This follow-up contact can lead to the unearthing of your application from a pile of applications and get you some attention ahead of less proactive applicants.

After you get one corporate gift, don't stop pursuing your corporate-giving campaign. Continue to notice the corporations in your area that are giving to organizations in your particular field, be it the arts, education, health, human services, or civic affairs. Look for new sponsorships, and be sure to feed your observations back into your ever-expanding research file. One day in the not-too-distant future, the file may lead to an exceptional major gift.

The difference between promoting and giving

True, corporations give, but some people argue that they do it in the name of promotion. Give a million, and you make the front pages of the papers. (Unless someone else just happened to give a billion that day, in which case your corporate gift may be buried on page three.) Give a million, and your company name is aligned with a cause. Give a million, and you become the national spokesperson and corporate sponsor of a program to combat the societal ill you're helping to fight. In this way, giving makes sense for corporations; not to mention, it also makes them money and friends.

But is it wrong?

Throughout this book, we point out that you can't and shouldn't second-guess the motives of your donors, assuming their intent isn't illegal. If you do, you spend all your time and energy qualifying the reasons behind the gift and not acting responsibly to steward the gift. Corporations give, and their gifts benefit your organization. If their promotions are in alignment with your mission and you can work out an equitable exchange, everybody wins — most of all, the people you serve.

Chapter 23

Building and Growing Endowments

In This Chapter

▶ Understanding the nuts and bolts of endowments and choosing the right one for you

▶ Finding ways to get people excited about funding an endowment

▶ Managing an endowment after you build it

*H*ave you ever read an old Victorian novel in which the hero lives off his trust fund or inheritance? Have you ever wondered how to create such a viable source of funding for your organization? An endowment is actually quite similar to a trust fund or inheritance: It provides a nest egg of funds, which, in addition to providing for the long-term needs of your organization, may provide some extra support for your annual fund or be used to start a new program.

In times of economic upheaval, however, endowments can take a big hit. The recession of 2007 through 2009 had its impact, and, as a result, the enthusiasm for endowments may be suffering a little. In the short term, the energy you spend building endowments may seem like an ill-advised investment, but over the long term, endowments rebound and provide ongoing support for your organization.

Endowments come in many types, and setting up and managing any of them require a specific set of resources. In this chapter, we help you discover what an endowment is, whether setting one up is right for you, and what's involved in getting and keeping one.

Endowing the Future

Although one-time major gifts are important for the ongoing work of your organization, an endowment differs from major gifts in an important way. The whole idea behind an endowment is to take advantage of the profits a substantial amount of money can generate, without ever emptying the treasure chest itself. With a major gift, the substantial amount of money is applied to the program it was donated to fund. The endowment process involves lawyers, paperwork, and administration. But if you're the right kind of organization, endowments can set you up for a more secure future. Keep reading to find out more about how endowments work and whether they can become another means of funding for your organization.

Understanding what an endowment is

An *endowment* is simply a donation of funds that brings with it a stipulation that it be invested. The principal stays intact, and the organization benefits from the proceeds of the investments. Each year your organization draws down a fixed percentage of the endowment, drawing part from the earnings and part from the appreciation. Your board sets these percentages and over-sees the management of the endowment.

Best practices suggest that you have a committee or board separate from your organization's board of directors run the endowment; you may also have one board member who serves on both boards. See the later section "Managing an Endowment" for more details.

Note that an endowment can consist of other assets besides money, such as property or securities. Trust funds, memorial trusts, and asset bases are other terms you may hear used for endowments.

Typically, you can have two types of endowments — restricted and unre-stricted. Here's how the two types differ:

- ✔ The payout from an *unrestricted endowment,* which comes from interest and appreciation, can be used in any way the organization's board sees fit.

- ✔ *Restricted endowment funds* are earmarked for a particular type of spend-ing, meaning that either the major donor stipulated how the money would be spent when giving the gift (this kind of gift is called *donor des-ignated*) or the organization specified that the fund would be focused in one area when setting it up.

Note: When your organization sets up funds to function as an endowment (whether it's restricted or unrestricted) instead of using donor funds to set it up, you have a *quasi endowment.*

The length of an endowment can also vary. An endowment may exist into per-petuity or have a fixed term. Here's how these lengths differ:

> ✔ A *permanent endowment* is intended to exist in perpetuity, which is a fancy way of saying it's meant to last forever. In other words, the endowment funds themselves aren't meant to be used up or spent. You can draw down only income dollars and appreciation for your purpose.
>
> ✔ A *term endowment* is set up with an expiration date. When you reach that date, some or all of the principal must be spent.

Keep in mind that many endowments are at least started with one huge gift from one source. But you can add to the endowment over the years.

Deciding whether you can (and should) build an endowment

Endowments aren't for every organization. Universities and community foundations are the prototypical endowment candidates (though not the only ones — today churches are beginning to add endowments, as well) because they share the following characteristics that normally make an organization a good fit for an endowment:

✔ They've been around for a while and are expected to be around for many more years to come.

✔ They have a reasonably guaranteed constituency. Whereas your community arts project may fade away if the founding members lose interest or move away, people are likely to want to provide a college education for kids for a long, long time.

✔ Their mission is broad enough. A community foundation that serves the community's needs, no matter what they may be, can adapt its mission as times change.

How do you know your organization has what it takes to build one? Here are a few key elements to look for:

✔ You have a completely committed board and staff that will stick with you through a lengthy process of endowment building.

✔ You have a very clear mission and a strong fundraising program already in place.

✔ You have someone who can serve as an endowment figurehead — someone who's visible in your community and who inspires trust and attracts money and support.

✔ You have the resources to provide donors with sound investment advice and management and a demonstrable investment strategy to attract donors.

✔ You have access to the level of givers needed to seed an endowment with substantial gifts upfront.

✔ You're part of an organization in which the long term is important.

When you build an endowment, you're talking to people about the idea of your group's longevity. Many donors want to see that the money they give results in a program or visible change today. If you can help people see the future and encourage them to get excited about the people you will serve and the programs you will offer down the road, you can get them to give. But remember: If you want donors to be excited about what you will do tomorrow, show them the great things you're doing today.

Building an Endowment

In an ideal world, you pick up the phone one morning, and Mr. Gray, a local billionaire, tells you he's giving $2 million to your group for an endowment, no strings attached. You thank Mr. Gray profusely, hang up, and shout, "Yes!!"

Although it isn't impossible that your organization will receive a gift large enough to form the basis of an endowment right out of the blue, it is more likely that you'll have to build an endowment in a methodical way. The following sections show you how to do just that.

Getting your board to buy in

The first step in building an endowment is to get everybody on your board to agree that an endowment is the right way to go. Everyone needs to commit to the long haul, and everyone has to feel confident that you can continue your other forms of fundraising and keep all your core programs and functions running, while also building an endowment.

While you discuss possibilities for your endowment, think through the messaging you can use to explain the endowment to potential donors. Why is an endowment a natural fit for your organization? What tangible benefits will donors be able to see after they've contributed? Having strong answers to these questions can also help you convince resistant members of your own group that building an endowment is a good idea.

After all the key members of your organization are on board, set a goal of getting a handful of significant donations as the start of your endowment. People give money to endowments when they see that the endowment already has a solid financial base. To that end, find out whether your board members themselves have contacts who are able to give such large gifts. And don't forget foundations and corporations as potential major gift givers. See Chapter 9 for more about how to cultivate major givers and Chapter 22 for how to approach foundations and corporations.

After you have a few large gifts that make up the centerpiece of your endowment, plan and run a long-term campaign to solicit additional gifts.

Explaining the value to donors

Some people aren't crazy about endowments because they think an organization that has some financial security may be less responsive to its constituency. If your mission addresses one specific issue, donors may wonder whether you're more interested in providing for the security of your organization or solving the problem you're supposed to address.

Although an endowment can offer some protection from the giving whims of the public, your mission guarantees your commitment to your service, whether you're struggling to fund your livelihood or not. And because many social problems are interrelated, if the one your mission addresses is resolved completely, you can likely find a related cause to turn your efforts toward. For example, if a cure is found for a disease, you still have to address the issue of fair distribution of that cure to populations that need it most. If you lower the number of homeless people in your town, you still need to be sure that the population trains for and maintains jobs to keep them off the street.

The financial independence provided by an endowment lets your organization focus on solving problems and raising money for special programs. With very few exceptions, an endowment isn't a blank check. It's a cushion that allows you to focus most of your attention on the important issues like feeding the hungry or building homes for the homeless.

Making an endowment part of your overall fundraising effort

Getting an endowment in place may take many years, so don't count your endowment eggs before they hatch. In the meantime, you have to keep your other fundraising efforts, such as your annual fund drive and special program fundraising, going strong. Be sure that you have enough staff or volunteers to handle all your fundraising activities. Also, be sure that donors understand the different types of funding you're now seeking. If possible, encourage them to support both the ongoing costs of your organization and its long-term sustainability.

For more details on endowment building, check out *Nonprofit Essentials: Endowment Building* by Diana S. Newman (Wiley).

Managing an Endowment

As you think through your plan for building an endowment, put considerable thought into what it'll take to manage the endowment effectively. The people who donate to your endowment demonstrate their trust in your organization, and you need to have good administrative processes, strong investment strategies, and responsible stewardship practices in place to honor that trust.

Providing oversight and establishing policies

Establishing the infrastructure of people and processes for your endowment is an important part of providing for its long-term success. Many organizations today set up a separate committee or a separate board to oversee the endowment (that is, a group separate from your board of directors); doing so ensures that both the best interests of the organization and the best interests of the endowment are considered in decisions related to endowment issues. Depending on the way you set up your endowment-oversight committee, you may choose to have directors serving on both boards so that each board is aware of the activities of the other. You may also choose to work with a lawyer to set up a formal trust or foundation with a trustee to administer it.

After you set up your oversight committee, you need to create an endowment policy document that lays out policies regarding the following:

- Governance structure
- Gift acceptance policy
- Gift restrictions
- Donor recognition
- Investment strategy
- Spending policy

Strong policies and management structure give your board, staff, and constituents confidence in the stability of your endowment. To find out more about policies and procedures for your endowment, check out Board Source (www.boardsource.org), a nonprofit organization specializing in board effectiveness.

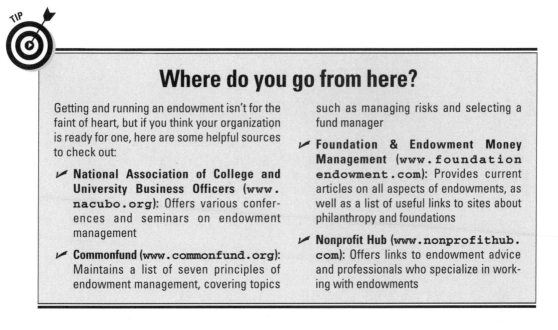

Where do you go from here?

Getting and running an endowment isn't for the faint of heart, but if you think your organization is ready for one, here are some helpful sources to check out:

✔ **National Association of College and University Business Officers** (www. nacubo.org): Offers various conferences and seminars on endowment management

✔ **Commonfund** (www.commonfund.org): Maintains a list of seven principles of endowment management, covering topics

such as managing risks and selecting a fund manager

✔ **Foundation & Endowment Money Management** (www.foundation endowment.com): Provides current articles on all aspects of endowments, as well as a list of useful links to sites about philanthropy and foundations

✔ **Nonprofit Hub** (www.nonprofithub. com): Offers links to endowment advice and professionals who specialize in working with endowments

If you have restricted endowment funds, don't forget that someone has to ensure that any income from the endowment is used in strict accordance with that restriction. Spending the funds any other way is illegal. (See the following section for more details.)

Seeking professional help to manage endowment dollars

Most endowed organizations have an investment manager on staff to deal with daily investment issues, but even those with staff typically rely on outside resources for help. Investment companies can offer a lot of help with your investment program, but you don't want to let the investment company control the endowment. It's important to stay actively involved in and informed about your endowment. Have an independent accountant keep close tabs on the endowment funds — how they're earning and how they're used.

You can use several different software programs to help manage your endowment fund. MIP Endowment Management (www.mip.com) and Fundriver Online (www.fundriver.com) are two software products currently available. In general, however, only very large endowments use this type of software because these types of services may be very expensive.

As you set up your investment strategy, keep in mind that many organizations are now looking at alternative investments that support their organizations' missions. For example, you may invest in environmentally responsible companies or funds if your own mission is to clean up the environment. For help with finding alternative investments, explore options with your board members and talk with your investment manager to find out what other organizations serving your industry's area are currently doing.

Check the laws and regulations regarding endowments and trust laws in your state to be sure of your obligations. When you're dealing with such a large sum of money, having solid professional help and advice from both legal and financial perspectives are musts. Setting up and administering an endowment is like running a good-sized business — professionalism is a must. But the return on your investment of time, energy, and resources can be the long-term financial security of your organization and its work.

Part V
The Part of Tens

The 5th Wave   By Rich Tennant

"The next time we get an additional round of funding, don't say anything. You're lucky I convinced them that 'Ka-Ching, Ka-Ching!' was Swahili for thank you, thank you!"

In this part . . .

In typical *For Dummies* fashion, this part of the book lists a collection of ten items, grouped around a particular subject. Each chapter presents information that's useful to any fundraiser, including a few great opening lines and some predictions for the future of fundraising. Read whichever ones suit you best.

Chapter 24

Ten Predictions about Fundraising

*O*ne of the lasting effects of going through a tough economic time is a diminished feeling of security. Givers become more cautious; organizations become more selective; individuals evaluate donation opportunities more carefully before deciding where to give. As the economy improves and the fundraising landscape changes, growth will come again, bringing with it changes, unique ideas, and new approaches. This chapter offers predictions about how fundraising will change in the years to come.

Huge Amounts of Wealth Will Be Transferred

Before the great economic meltdown of 2007 to 2009, experts happily estimated that older generations would transfer from $40 to $106 trillion to future generations over the next 45 years — making it the greatest generational transfer of wealth in history.

Scholars based this estimate on assumptions about the huge baby boomer population that's focusing on estate planning, the drafting of wills, and the passing on of wealth. This estimate also took into effect the U.S. stock market and the dramatic appreciation on investments in the last 20 years. Enhancing the estimate even further was modern technology which made stock ownership more common. More than 40 percent of the U.S. population currently owns stock, a statistic that's up from 29 percent just 12 years ago.

Unfortunately, the world has changed. Between 2007 and 2009, stock portfolios took a hit that may have reduced their investment values by up to 40 percent. Nevertheless, the generational wealth transfer will be sizeable in the next few decades, which is an important issue for planned-giving campaigns. The estimated amount to be transferred may be only $20 to $50 trillion, but it's still serious money. Lots of folks will be in a position to leave a major legacy in the near future.

Givers Will Become More Savvy

People have gained access to a wealth of advice and information thanks to the Internet. Legal sites provide articles and kits for writing wills, creating trusts, and planning estates. Books abound with suggestions on how to handle your money, many of which give advice about the tax advantages of giving or structuring your estate to leave bequests to charities or other causes. In short, givers are becoming more savvy about when, why, and how to give, so you need to know how to keep up with them. (Check out Chapter 7.)

Even with all this self-help, however, people aren't handling their financial planning alone. Lawyers, accountants, investment advisors, and estate planners are cultivating a vast new market of potential givers. These professionals provide the expert advice that creates new contributions to the nonprofit sector. The various giving mechanisms we cover in this book are the tools that they use, and the personal relationships they build with clients will have a major impact on philanthropic giving.

Early indications suggest that the following means for giving will flourish:

- ✔ Using private foundations to fund issues that people care about
- ✔ Setting up trust accounts with community foundations
- ✔ Adding bequests to philanthropic organizations to wills
- ✔ Creating major gifts, planned gifts, and challenge grants (see Chapter 21)

In short, givers will become more tactical and strategic. They'll want to know their gifts will make a difference. Planned giving will become more important, and donors will want to be sure their gifts' recipients follow their intentions. In some cases they will ensure that happens by specifying that the money is to be distributed within a given period after their deaths.

People's preference will still be to give to a cause they care about instead of forcing their heirs to pay high inheritance and estate taxes. As a result, as increasingly informed donors make plans for their accumulated wealth, their choices may result in increased giving. If it does, the historic rate of personal giving as a percent of personal income may grow.

Attorneys General Will Become Major Regulators of Nonprofits

Although the Internal Revenue Service (IRS) has been the major overseer of the nonprofit world (through the tax code that differentiates for-profits from nonprofits), as a fundraiser, you must now consider a new force in each state. In past centuries, attorneys general were the public's representatives in the charitable world. However, these office holders seldom became involved in that world, and few constituents asked them to intercede.

With the proliferation of state nonprofit statutes that grant attorneys general specific nonprofit-related responsibilities, the relationship between nonprofits and their attorneys general and the office holders themselves are now in the limelight. For instance, most states require all nonprofits to send a copy of Form 990, which they prepare for the IRS, to their own state's attorney general for review. In addition, as attorneys general have become more politically ambitious, they've found that getting involved in the allegedly suspect nonprofit world is one way to gain favorable publicity that may lead to higher office.

In some states, attorneys general have responded to questionable fundraising activities, alleged improper administration, and possible violations of trust in the nonprofit world. Attorneys general can contest the actions of nonprofit leaders. In short, they represent the public viewpoint.

Most responsible attorneys general realize how important the nonprofit sector is to society and are reluctant to sully its reputation. Rather than create public confrontations, attorneys general often work with nonprofits to ensure that they execute their fiduciary responsibilities properly. In the future, nonprofits will seek the counsel of their state's attorney general more and more.

As a case in point, Earlham College and the Conner Prairie Interactive History Park were involved in a controversy over which of the two organizations would be the beneficiary of a major grant worth millions of dollars. The donor had given the money to Earlham College provided that it first benefited Conner Prairie. The remainder of the gift was to benefit Earlham. Questions about expenditures and stewardship inevitably arose. The Indiana attorney general, Steve Carter, didn't want either organization to have its reputation publicly sullied by the situation because he recognized that both organizations were important elements in the community. He was able to negotiate a settlement that was court supported, and, as a result, both organizations were able to move forward without harm to their public reputations.

Women Will Play a Bigger Role in Giving

Today women own more than half of all investments in America. As they age, their salaries will increase, and they will inherit wealth from parents and spouses. In fact, 85 percent of women will control their family's wealth at some point according to the Woman's Philanthropy Institute.

Because women continue to gain influence in the financial world, you need to spend some time and effort understanding how to find and cultivate female donors. You can begin by asking yourself these questions:

- ✔ What types of causes do they tend to support?
- ✔ What kind of financial concerns do they have that may differ from their husband's, father's, or brother's?
- ✔ What will they want to leave as a legacy when they pass on?

Women's giving programs are proliferating throughout the United States. United Way, for example, offers special giving groups that design their fundraising activities around women's issues. Community foundations also often have special donor-designated funds that support women's causes. In short, women are having a big impact on giving — and that impact is expected to increase.

More than half of all volunteers are women, and more women are becoming important fundraisers. We believe that, in general, women make great fundraisers for the same reason they make good salespeople — because they're good listeners. For that reason, we expect the fundraising profession to be increasingly populated with women in the future.

E-Giving Will Grow

The emergence of online commerce as a major factor in retailing is a relatively recent phenomenon. However, in the second quarter of 2009 alone, U.S. retailers enjoyed online sales of $32.4 billion. For a variety of reasons, online fundraising approaches represent a similar opportunity for nonprofits of all types.

E-mail is rapidly taking the place of many direct mail communications because it's less expensive, more flexible, and can be used to target specific audiences. In other areas of fundraising, electronic communication is replacing paper-and-postage methods as well. As a result, click-and-mortar approaches (as opposed to *brick and mortar*) will be the winning combination for successfully marketing nonprofit causes. In other words, it's important to have a convenient location where your nonprofit actually does its work, but you need to have a reaching presence online, too, because a click on the Internet is likely to be the simplest and easiest way to get contributions in the future.

Adding an online element to your fundraising efforts offers many benefits that will become more prevalent in the future. For one, the development of secure online payment systems like PayPal now makes donating online safe for donors, which means you can expect your number of online contributions to grow. Online fundraising also enables you to mobilize support quickly for time-sensitive issues. For example, when a food pantry is running short on donations, you can contact donors right away via e-mail or through your Web site or social network site to secure additional contributions. When you take your fundraising online, you communicate in the realm in which many of your younger donors are most comfortable. As a result, social marketing can bring many new — and more closely engaged — donors to your site and cause.

Nonprofits Will Go Commercial

Burton A. Weisbrod, a Northwestern University professor who published the book *To Profit or Not to Profit: The Commercial Transformation of the Nonprofit Sector* (Cambridge University Press), believes that the commercialization of many parts of the nonprofit world is inevitable. He cites decreases in governmental and contributed funding that force nonprofits to sell something — often in competition with for-profit organizations. Weisbrod points out that the nonprofit sector has been both criticized and acclaimed for its trend toward commercialization. He writes, "The rationale for its special tax treatment and subsidies rests on the belief that it provides services that are materially different from, and preferred to, the services that private enterprise provides." When the demand for nonprofit services goes up and the necessary financing isn't available, commercialization occurs.

Thus, scholars predict that nonprofits will dramatically increase their use of revenues other than voluntary contributions. As they do, the interactions and relationships between nonprofits and the rest of the economy become more common. In some cases — especially with hospitals, universities, and some social service providers — the drive for revenue brings nonprofits into headlong competition with private enterprise. For example, the nonprofit YMCA and YWCA sometimes find themselves in direct competition with for-profit recreational organizations.

In addition to seeing competition between nonprofit and for-profit ventures, you likely will see increased cooperation and a blurring of the lines between the two entities. For example, the government may rely on nonprofits to implement certain government programs rather than attempt to do the work itself. Nonprofit universities conduct scientific research for the benefit of private firms. Universities also enter into major deals with private companies that sell athletic equipment and other products that often benefit from alliances with the universities' reputations. In other words, the private sector has already found a way to profit from the aura and reputation of the nonprofit sector.

Nowhere in the economy is the competition and cooperation between non-profits and for-profits more obvious than in the healthcare industry, where nonprofit hospitals advertise for business, cooperate with for-profit ventures when advantageous, and ardently compete when necessary.

The ultimate extension of commercialism is the voluntary conversion of non-profits into commercial ventures. Although the IRS, through its regular auditing procedure, may suspend the tax status of a nonprofit and thus convert it to a for-profit venture, the more likely conversion takes place voluntarily by the nonprofit that finds that the nonprofit structure and the rules and regulations that go with it make competition difficult. For example, in today's society, conversion of mutual insurance companies and healthcare providers to for-profit status has become commonplace. Conversions of this kind are usually the result of decisions by management that the mission of the organization can best be met in the for-profit world. For example, conversion makes it possible for the company to seek different kinds of financing from the for-profit marketplace.

In addition to voluntary conversions, some states have attempted to define nonprofits by requiring that a certain percentage of revenue be contributed income or that a certain percent of revenues received should be used for philanthropic purposes. Although no consensus exists on what percentages are reasonable, some nonprofits will no doubt have to convert to for-profit status to survive.

Even though a nonprofit may become more commercial or competitive, the nonprofit doesn't necessarily break faith with the core values or primary reasons why it was created in the first place. Both objectives — becoming more commercial and fulfilling the organization's mission — can coexist.

Nonprofits Will Increase Their Role in Community Leadership

As many U.S. cities and towns lose local and national corporate headquarters, the local community will become more dependent on philanthropic leadership. Except in the largest metropolitan areas, community foundations, large nonprofits (including hospitals), and large individual givers will become more important leaders. Where wealth accumulates, the people who control it gain power. Government and the business sector have always been important leaders in local communities, but with the help of community foundations, nonprofits can become almost coequal partners.

Community foundations and large private foundations have become important conveners around community problems and are often the initiators for funding community needs. They're often the funders of major community plans and visions for the future. Ultimately, community foundations and nonprofits like them will have a say in virtually every aspect of community life.

Inheritance Tax Law Changes Will Change the Giving Game

The federal inheritance tax law, as it exists in 2009, calls for the tax to be completely eliminated in 2010. Nonprofit experts have debated for decades the effect this tax has on individual giving. Some say it substantially affects large gifts, while others say most of those large gifts would take place with or without the tax incentive. Although economic studies differ, some evidence supports the idea that potential inheritance liability for heirs affects giving decisions. The familiar refrain is, "Why not give your money to something you care about instead of letting the government take it?"

Although the inheritance tax isn't one of the larger revenue producers for the federal government, Congress is particularly sensitive to revenue decreases during the recent period of record deficits. As currently administered, the tax allows deductions of $3.5 million per estate and then taxes the remainder at accelerating rates, depending on the size of the estate. Chances are that Congress will allow only a $1 million exemption in 2011 and beyond. Regardless of the outcome, planned-giving programs will need to react to the changes.

Corporations Will Jump on the Cause-Related Marketing Bandwagon

Corporations have begun to realize that aligning themselves with a worthy cause not only improves their image with the buying public but also offers lucrative benefits in marketing punch. When you approach corporations in the future, consider the marketing angle of your proposal. For example:

- ✔ Can you think of a company-sponsored event that would get the corporation's name and logo out there in a positive way?

- ✔ Can you interest the corporation in a promotion in which a portion of what it gets for its products goes into your coffers? The corporation gets new customers and higher sales that far outweigh the amount of money it hands over to you from its sales.

✔ Would the company like to place your logo on its promotional materials, attracting the buyer who has sympathy for your cause, and pay you a royalty for the use of your name?

✔ Would the company like to create an employee workday built around your cause?

These types of co-marketing ventures will grow more and more popular as corporations look for the *quid pro quo* for their charitable efforts. (Check out Chapter 22 for more about corporation-related fundraising strategies.)

Fundraising Costs Will Be Scrutinized

The relationship between the amount of money given to an organization and the percent that the organization puts toward the cause for which the money was solicited has received growing scrutiny. In recent years, the U.S. Congress has focused on nonprofit governance and charitable integrity. In addition, attorneys general have used state nonprofit statutes to review the actions of nonprofits in their states. Public opinion polls continue to reflect skepticism about how nonprofits spend the money they collect. In some states, audits may be conducted for public review.

For these reasons, the importance of communicating clearly and honestly how much money you raise as a nonprofit, how much it costs to raise the money, and how much you actually spend on your organization's mission will become critical for you and all nonprofits. Equally important is your organization's ability to demonstrate effectiveness in your mission. The public's trust is at stake with these issues, and they are at the heart of maintaining your donor relationships.

Many nonprofit organizations are adopting a version of the Public Trust Initiative started by the Donor's Forum of Chicago as part of their efforts to show the public that they can and should be trusted to fulfill their missions. You can get a copy of this list of fundraising best practices at www.donors forum.org/publictrust/principles.html.

Chapter 25

Ten (Plus One) Great Opening Lines

*P*ersonal visits to donors are important for a couple of reasons. First, nothing beats good, old-fashioned, face-to-face contact for building relationships. And second, people find it very hard to turn down someone who's looking them in the eyes. So try out some of the lines in this chapter (or your own versions of them) the next time you meet your donor face to face.

"How about a little good news?"

Especially in turbulent economic times, people may feel saturated with bad news. When you show up on the doorstep with your organization's materials, start with the good news. Describe all the great things your organization is doing. And don't forget to mention specifically how the donor's gifts have contributed to major successes since your last meeting.

"Would you like to watch the birth of a baby elephant?"

Get the donor hooked right away. What does he care about? What interests him? Capture his imagination as soon as you can, and he'll be eager to hear your next word.

"Hi, Mrs. Jones, I just left a meeting where we were discussing . . ."

This natural comment can lead right into whatever you want to address with Mrs. Jones — a new program, a building, a campaign, and so on. You don't want to flounder around here — or leave the impression that you're making it up just to create a graceful transition into what you really want to talk about — so use this statement only when it's true. You may, of course, change it to "I was just thinking about . . ." or "We were just talking about planning. . . ."

"I recently visited the program you sponsored. Very inspiring! I'd love to show it to you sometime."

Not only does this line get the donor's imagination going as she wonders about the effects of her gift, but it also recognizes her for her past donations and invites her to come with you to see the results.

"Now, how can I help you?"

This kind of question may get a baffled look and the comment, "I thought you wanted something from me!" But it does open the door to the idea that fundraisers really do help donors find positive and proven ways to facilitate good in the world and meet their financial planning goals, as well.

"Research shows that giving is good for your health."

Said to the right people (like a group of doctors), this opening line gets donors listening right off the bat. Why? First of all, we want it to be true. Second, it tells donors upfront that their philanthropic endeavors will benefit them. If for no other reason, donors will continue listening just so they can look for an opportunity to disprove you.

"You have no idea how much good your last gift did for our organization!"

Recognition is a good thing — especially when you can say something substantial about the results of the donor's past contributions.

Misrepresentation is never the best policy. Don't get in to see a donor under false pretenses. Acting like you're conducting a survey at a festival when you're really looking for an opportunity to promote your organization only creates distance between you and the prospective donor. Sure, use your opportunities, but do so in a forthright manner.

"More people go to zoos today than go to all sports activities combined."

This "Gee whiz!" statement really gets people interested. What kind of "Gee whiz!" statements can you come up with about your own organization and its causes? Take an afternoon and research trivia or statistics related to your area. The Internet offers great tools for this kind of research. The interest you gain — and the conversations that take place — will be more than worth the expense of your research time.

"Seven out of ten of our city's families use United Way services in their lifetime."

This "Gee whiz!" statement is based on fact and may appeal to both logical and emotional types. Know the good your organization has done and be ready and willing to talk about it. Distill the facts down to three or four good opening lines that may interest a prospective donor and leave him wanting to find out more about what you do.

"Hey, I just received this great picture! The new wing of the library is finished!"

Especially for people who have already given to your organization, seeing evidence of the great things you're doing is very heady stuff. Show donors a picture of the newly renovated monkey exhibit at your zoo, display your newly purchased property, or make known the turnout at the recent fundraising event you sponsored.

The Web isn't the same direct-contact medium as face-to-face visiting, but you can put images on your Web site that show happy people doing good work and suggest that your prospective donor visit the site. Images are a great idea on Facebook, too, because when you post images, they appear in the news feeds of all your fans.

"Cute dog!"

Hey, what's the best way to a pet lover's heart? Liking her dog! This approach may seem like an old salesman's gimmick, but there's an important idea at the center here: Connection is key. When your donor realizes that you share some common interests, she starts listening.

Index